Requiem for a German Past

Life In the Third Reich

Richard Bessell

Requiem
for a
German Past

A Boyhood among the Nazis

Jurgen Herbst

THE UNIVERSITY OF WISCONSIN PRESS

February, 2004

The University of Wisconsin Press
1930 Monroe Street
Madison, Wisconsin 53711

www.wisc.edu/wisconsinpress/

3 Henrietta Street
London WC2E 8LU, England

Library of Congress Cataloging-in-Publication Data
Herbst, Jurgen.
Requiem for a German past: a boyhood among the nazis / Jurgen Herbst.
250 pp.   cm.
ISBN 0-299-16410-1 (cloth: alk. paper)
ISBN 0-299-12184-4 (pbk.: alk. paper)
1. Herbst, Jurgen—Childhood and youth.   2. Youth—Germany—
Biography.   3. World War, 1939–1945—Personal narratives, German.
4. Germany—Social conditions—1933–1945.   5. National socialism.
I. Title.
DD247.H365A3   1999
940.54'8243—dc21   99-18490

The German poem, by Christian Morgenstern, and the English translation,
by Max Knight, which appear on page 119, are taken from *Christian Morgenstern's
Galgenlieder (Gallows Songs)*. Translated by Max Knight (Berkeley: University of
California Press, 1963). Copyright © 1963 by Max Knight. The German poem and the
English translation are used by permission of Insel Verlag, Frankfurt, Germany,
and the University of California Press, respectively.

To the memory of

Felix Pollak

poet extraordinaire

dearest of friends

requiem: a solemn chant (as a dirge) for the repose of the dead

Webster's New Collegiate Dictionary, 1973

Contents

Illustrations

Preface

YEARS AGO in Gino's restaurant on Madison's State Street, Felix Pollak, that incomparable Vienna-born master of poetry and prose in two languages,[1] made me promise to write this book. Felix had read a German-language manuscript that I had composed in 1953. In it I had sought in novelistic form to come to terms with my past as a boy in the Germany of the 1930s and '40s and thereby to free myself from the trauma and pain of those years. Felix insisted that one day I return to that manuscript. Now, after an interval of two score and some years, I have done so. I have kept my promise.

Requiem for a German Past gathers my recollections, the recollections of a boy who grew to manhood during what can be called only the darkest, most hideous, time of his country. It is the story of my life among ordinary, decent people, among brave and fearful men and women, and among villains, cowards, and criminals. It is the story of my life in a home full of loving care within a world that more and more began to order its affairs by a rigid, perverted concept of national honor. It is a story of a friendship that drew its inspiration from the love of boys and their dedication to a military code of personal honor and loyalty, a friendship that was ready to endure scorn and deprivation and to risk personal well-being and life in the face of a brutal evil that demanded unquestioning allegiance. It is a soldier's story of testing his courage and facing terror and death in battle.

It is also a story of a father's life of scholarship and of sacrifice to his country, and of a mother's life of love that was destined to fade away in sadness, suffering, and death. It is a requiem for ideals that once promised personal fulfillment in devotion to people and country. And it is a requiem for loved ones and friends whose lives were extinguished in the disaster that ensued.

1. For Pollak's bilingual poetry, see his *Benefits of Doubt* (1988) and *Vom Nutzen des Zweifels* (1989); for his prose, *Lebenszeichen: Aphorismen und Marginalien* (1992).

As they appear here, these recollections incorporate excerpts from contemporary letters, diary entries, and passages from and adaptations of the original German manuscript. In these pages I neither attempt to analyze and explain, nor do I answer directly the questions that I know many readers will have. I never meant to prepare an *apologia pro vita mea*. Instead, I have tried to set forth, as best as I could, descriptions of the events, circumstances, ideas, and feelings that once shaped and were part of my life and, whenever I thought it was necessary or appropriate, to add reflections of a later day. I wrote this book primarily for my children who grew up in a different world and who have a right to know where their father came from. I wanted to help them, if they desired to do so, to reconstruct and understand for themselves the world I lived in.

If I have succeeded in this, they and the readers of this book will enter into a boy's life that was propelled throughout by idealism and commitment to a tradition consisting of love of scholarship and poetry, loyalty to a Prussian conception of military leadership, and adherence to a Lutheran Protestant Christianity. They will experience for themselves how that tradition, inexorably and step by painful step, came into conflict with the demands of a brutal and evil ideology.

This was a conflict we boys experienced in our own existence. For me it began on the day following *Kristallnacht* when I was ten years old, and it never disappeared, not even when the world I had lived in had collapsed in ruin and death around me. Though we boys were not often able to articulate it clearly, it was a conflict that we well knew and dreaded, and one that we intermittently, though unsuccessfully, tried to deny or escape. It was a conflict that assaulted us with questions and doubts until, in the final days of my life in Germany, it left me with nothing but despair and loathing.

I do not want to overdramatize my story. As we boys lived our lives, day by day and week by week, they moved along in all the ordinariness of daily existence as ordinary lives unfold everywhere. Dramatic and traumatic events did not occur every day. When they did, they broke into and interrupted the ordinariness of everyday life, but then they were absorbed in the rhythm of our daily doings and became themselves ordinary parts of it.

My story, therefore, is for much of the time a story of boys as they can be found everywhere, at any time; a story of boys who wanted to live life to the fullest and who, more often than not, succeeded in that desire. Despite all the terror and pain, ours was a rich life, a life of friendship and love, a life in which adults played only a minor role, and where our own adulthood began when we received our first commissions as youth leaders at age twelve or thirteen. It was then that we left childhood behind and became boy soldiers.

Our elders, parents and teachers, were worried and feared they would lose their children and pupils. Fathers were called to arms, left home, suffered and died or came home crippled; mothers spent hours each day searching for food and clothing or were assigned to war industries and canning factories; they grew sickly and worried, worried, worried.

So we, the boy soldiers, carried on by and for ourselves. We took responsibility for "our" boys, and we did not take that responsibility lightly. We understood it to be our duty, a duty that was part of the ordinariness of life and in which we found purpose and fulfillment, a duty out of which grew our loves and friendships.

Did we leaders of boys leave our parents and teachers, or did our parents and teachers leave us? We could not have said. We would not have known. We never asked such questions. All we knew was that we had a task to perform. In a world governed by war and danger we had our boys to lead. In the midst of all the pain, the worry, and the fear around us, we were creating and upholding a world of boys, of honor, of pride, of loyalty, and, yes, of love. This boys' world was what carried us through. It was, as we assumed, the "new time" that, as the Nazi song had it, would "march with us into the future."

Of course, there was no march into a new, shining future. The Nazi world the song had celebrated came crashing down on us, and we had simultaneously known and not known that it would happen.

Those of us who still lived found out that it had been the teachings and the influence of parents and teachers, not the loudly proclaimed Nazi slogans of a better future, that had allowed us to survive and had kept us out of the hands of the masters of evil. Our parents and teachers had been present all along, though we did not always see or hear them. They had implanted their seeds in our souls while we were still children; had taught us of love, decency, and commitment, honor and loyalty, less so by words than by deeds.

Our fathers and teachers, veterans all of the First World War, had talked and read to us of the soldierly life. They and our mothers had made sure we attended religious classes in church and school. As a result, no words impressed themselves more deeply on my memory than the Prussian *"mehr sein als scheinen"* ("substance over appearance") and the Biblical "be thou faithful unto death, and I will give thee a crown of life."[2] In my case, the traditions of the German army and of Lutheran

2. Revelation 2: 10.

Christianity remained my guide to nearly the end. The faithful soldier who cannot sacrifice to a criminal imposter the loyalty he had sworn to his people and God provided the model for the boy soldier who fought to the last day of the war. The intrepid Protestant whose conscience demands Luther's "here I stand, I can do no other" was the redoubt I had prepared for myself should I be confronted with the final choice.

When the end finally came I could stay with neither the loyal soldier nor the conscience-bound Luther. Even these models of probity seemed to me fatally affected by the general collapse of all things German. I had arrived at my personal "zero hour": the loss of my loved ones and the collapse of the ideals I had lived by.

If there were to be a new beginning for me, I would have to learn again how to draw strength from that which had been precious and noble in my past. If I were to take with me into another world my commitment to *"mehr sein als scheinen"* and my promise to remain "faithful unto death" then I should have to cherish and cling to the loves, friendships, and memories of a lost youth beyond the ruins and graves of my German past.

It was my mother who gently led me to that recognition. Her last gift and testament came to me through the pages of a thin, small book in which she had marked for me the words of a requiem:

> Mourning your dead, dear boy, is no good service for them. . . . Don't turn us into ghosts. . . . Allow us entrance that we may dwell and stay among you in dark and in joyful hours . . .[3]

It was the requiem for all I had loved and the requiem for everything that had been noble and precious to me. It carried me into a new life in another world.

3. Walter Flex, *Der Wanderer zwischen beiden Welten: Ein Kriegserlebnis* (München: C. H. Beck, n.d.), 94–95. For the full text of the requiem, see chapter 17.

Requiem for a German Past

1

In My Father's House

WHEN I THINK BACK to my childhood I see myself as an only child, accustomed from the beginning to play by myself in my room with my toy soldiers. My mother usually was busy in the kitchen or was reading a book in her sitting room. My father was away at work in the famous Duke August Library in Wolfenbüttel, my home town. On weekends he stayed home studying and writing in what we called the *Herrenzimmer*, the gentleman's study, which, in our apartment on the Harztorwall, served as our living room as well. I was used to my mother and my father working or reading by themselves alone. I thought everybody did that. So I never felt lonely or forsaken when I played by myself in my room. That was the natural way to spend one's time.

When my father was home on weekends he sat in our living room at his desk with books piled all around him. Sheets of white paper were everywhere, between pages and underneath the books. A shiny Continental portable typewriter stood in the middle. Every now and then, after much shuffling of papers and moving of books, he rattled on that machine for three to five minutes, slid its carriage back everytime it pinged a signal, and pulled sheets of paper out at the top whenever he had filled them with rows of letters. The typewriter intrigued me. Though I was forbidden to touch it, I did take it out of its carrying case sometimes when my father was in the library and my mother had gone shopping. I rolled a sheet of paper into it from the top, and pecked at some keys to type my name or some other short word. I kept an ear out for the creaking of the garden gate to close up the typewriter the minute I heard my mother come home. But I was proud of myself that I had been a writer, even if for only a few minutes.

My mother, though, warned me that my father's work as a scholar was important. I was not to disturb him and ask him to play with me or tell stories about the war. If I wanted to talk to my father, she said, I had to wait until he was ready. So I often sat on the floor, underneath the big living room table, surrounded by some of my toy soldiers and railroad cars, which I had brought from my room in the hope that I might entice my father to play with me. Most of the time he paid no attention to me. Sometimes, however, he would turn around in his chair and look down at me, and I, hoping to snare him, would ask him a question. He usually shook his head, said, "No, no, not now," but then, a few minutes later, he would almost always look again, and I was ready.

I pretended there had been an accident on my railroad, a car had tipped over and spilled all the soldiers on the carpet. My father would get up from his desk, walk over, bend and sit down next to me on the rug. Then we fought battles, bombarded my toy soldiers with the pencil stubs my father used to carry in his vest pocket. We had trains collide and used a crane to set the cars back on the rails. That was great fun. I became very excited, so my father said that now the railroad workers had to take their lunch break and the soldiers had to pull back to rest, and we had to pause as well and wait for a while. When my mother then entered the room and saw us sitting on the floor, she smiled and shook her finger at my father. That was the signal for me to load my soldiers on the railroad cars and drive them across the hall into my playroom. I felt very happy.

Sometimes, instead of playing with my toy soldiers, my father would sit on the carpet with me and tell me of his life as a soldier during the Great War. He had joined up as a volunteer on the war's first day when he was nineteen years old, and had come back home on its last day as a lieutenant. He had been wounded and had a big hole in his upper back which I could see when I watched him shave in the morning. The hole was big enough for me to place my hand in it, though I never did that. And every now and then he would leave us for a weekend to serve with the reserves. When he sat on the carpet with me and spoke of the war he told of being hungry and thirsty and dirty and lonely, and of the enemy shooting at him. I asked him whether he had not been afraid. He said no, a soldier was not afraid. A soldier had his comrades who stood by him and comforted him. He had his sweetheart to think of at night and songs to sing to her:

> Not I alone, did sing my song,
> Annemarie,

T'was all of us who sang your song,
We of the company.[1]

And my father would hum the refrain. It sounded very sad. It made me think of my mother, because her name was Annemarie too. It never occurred to me then that my father could not have known her during the war. But I imagined her in another song my father sang:

In the rose garden
I shall wait for you.
When the clover is green,
or the snow lies white.[2]

To me as a six- or seven-year-old, this was my father, the soldier, the brave man who suffered and fought for his country and who loved his sweetheart whom he missed. I took in his words of comradeship, of loyalty, of bravery, and of love for people and country. It seemed to me if I, later in life, only could be like him, both a scholar and a soldier, I could not ask for more. I was very proud of him, the scholar and the soldier, the *Gelehrte* and the *Soldat* or, perhaps more exactly, the scholar–soldier. To me as a boy there was no contradiction between the two. I thought my father perfectly illustrated the combination. I was determined to follow in his footsteps. And so, early in my life, I began to think of a career among books and arms, scholars and warriors, among men who were quiet and studious, but also strong and brave. I thought of my future self as a man who took, combined, and preserved the best of his home, his family, and his country; a man who was, for his students and his soldiers, an inspiring model to follow.

Today, three scores and some years later, I still think of my father as the scholar and the soldier, though I wonder whether he had chosen the life of the scholar–soldier or whether he was the scholar whose lot it was to serve as a soldier in two wars, and lose his life in the second. I look at his portrait that hangs on the wall above my desk. It is drawn with colored pencils and shows the left side of my father's face

1. As I remember them, these were the German words:
   Nicht ich allein, hab's so gemacht,
   Annemarie;
   Nein, alle haben Dein gedacht,
   die ganze Kompanie.
2.   *Im Rosengarten*
   will ich Dein erwarten
   Im grünen Klee,
   im weißen Schnee.

The author and his mother, Christmas 1929

as he gazes pensively through his glasses into a distance that cannot be seen. I do not know what he is looking at. I doubt that he is looking at anything. His eyes, rather than focusing on an object, invite me to join him in contemplating a problem, a riddle, a mystery. It is a look I well remember when I, as a little boy, asked him a question and he would take his time to search for words that I could understand. However, in the picture, it is answers for himself for which he seems to search. The father I remember as the scholar, the *Gelehrte*, had dedicated his life to the search for answers.

The picture, however, in its realism of time and place, portrays him as a soldier in his officer's tunic with his rank insignia and the number "17" of the Braunschweig infantry regiment on his shoulder. The soldier who drew the sketch added the initials "HB," the date "29. 4. 1943," and as identification of my father, "scholar of peasant ancestry." A year later he added a few more words, as an afterthought, perhaps, or, more likely, as a mourner's lament: "My good captain and friend, Dr. Herbst, ✠ 17. 8. 44 in Nisch/Serbia."

When the picture reached my mother and me in the waning days of 1944 I was about to begin my own career as a soldier. I then asked myself, was I really to follow in my father's footsteps? Was that his bequest to me, the life of a scholar and a soldier? Was that what he wanted me to do? There was little time to weigh such questions. The war pressed in on us from all sides and I did not know for certain how to answer, though I told myself, perhaps to drown out my own doubts, that that was indeed my father's legacy for me. I asked my mother what she thought about my father's life as a scholar and a soldier. Did he endorse that double role? Would he have chosen it if wars had not determined his steps? Through her tears she said only: "He was a scholar and he served his country; he had no choice."

Perhaps, I thought, I shall have no choice either.

But when I was still a little boy I thought that as a grown-up I would want to work just like my father, sitting behind a big desk, surrounded by books, and read and write. I knew that what my father did was called research, and I knew also that both he and my mother were never without books. In our living room, my father's room, just to the right of his desk stood the big *Bücherschrank*, its glassed-in midsection showing off leather-bound novels of World War I, books by Edwin Dwinger and Werner Beumelburg that later, when I was in my teens and had learned about the war from Bodo Wacker, my German teacher in the *Große Schule*, I hungrily devoured. There were many smaller volumes of church history and philosophy and others that dealt with books and their bindings, some of them written by my father. I did not find those titles very interesting, though I felt I should at least

7

The author's father at his desk at home

leaf through them to find out what my father's work was all about.
To the right and left of the center glass door, wooden doors could be
opened behind which stood row on row of cardboard file boxes, some
of them crammed full with envelopes holding little paper slips with
names and numbers scribbled in my father's handwriting, and others

stuffed with blank postalcards that, too, bore strange notations. Some of the shelves were full of clippings from newspapers and magazines and what my father called *Sonderdrucke,* special reprints of articles and essays he or one of his colleagues had written. But that was not all. There were three more bookcases in the *Herrenzimmer.* One was black and reached to the ceiling. It loomed between the two windows that looked out on the park in front of the apartment. It was filled with history and art books and editions of the collected works of authors like Goethe, Schiller, Uhland, Hauff, and others. Another shelf, brown and half as high and placed next to the entrance door, was crammed with paperbacks. Finally, in front of the tall, white tile stove in the room's corner, stood a small brown shelf with the many volumes of *Meyer's Konservations Lexikon,* a treasure trove for me once I had mastered the art of reading and could find answers there to questions like What is a vagina? and What does it look like?, questions that I did not want to ask my mother or my father.

We had moved to the apartment on the Harztorwall when I was six years old and became a pupil in the primary school on the Karlstraße. Books, those that I needed for school and those that encircled my parents' living room, became very much part of my own little world. They surrounded me and followed me everywhere, at home and in school. They were favored presents at birthdays and at Christmas time, and, once I had learned how to read, they also began to crowd every available space in my playroom. I literally disappeared among books when, as I sometimes did, I visited my father in the Duke August Library. He was usually too busy to pay me much attention but he did not mind if I wandered off into what was called "the magazine." That was fine with me, and I was never happier than when I could vanish in the stacks among the miles of metal shelves with their books neatly lined up. I followed the spiraling iron stairs up and down, from under the roof of the huge building to the basement with its dark and dusty storerooms. I soon selected my favorite hiding places where I would sit on some empty shelf space and leaf through dusty parchments, fascinated by their sometimes brightly colored and sometimes somberly darkened and musty pages, mystified by their gothic letters and Latin text, but always prompted to keep on looking for something new, something unexpected, something that would make me famous as discoverer— famous as I had heard people say my father was, because he had there found manuscripts previously thought lost or nonexistent.

My admiration for the soldierly life, actually, had begun even before I listened to my father telling me about the Great War and to Bodo Wacker's narratives in my high school classroom. It had been stimulated even before I read the novels by Edwin Dwinger and Werner

9

Beumelburg. It began when I was three years old and we still lived in the last house at the edge of town where the Kleine Breite (the Little Broad Road) ended as it met the Jahnstraße. The Jahnstraße was named after *Turnvater* Jahn, the father of the German "Turners" who, a hundred years before I was born, had taught that gymnastics and clean, healthy living would lead to a strong and vigorous Germany. The Jahnstraße ran along the training grounds of the Reichswehr, the German army of the 1920s and early '30s. The grounds stretched for miles up to and beyond the horizon. I could look across them from the window of my room in the house on the Kleine Breite. That is how I came to know something about the soldiers of the Reichswehr. I saw the troops often, right out of my window. The soldiers clad in their field gray uniforms rode in their cars and trucks across the expanse to the east of our house, pulling their cannons behind them and, sometimes, fighting mock battles, with lots of smoke blowing around the hilltop that overlooked the training ground. I was fascinated by what I saw and I tried to recreate these scenes in my playroom. In a wooden toy truck and metal toy staff car I carted my companies and battalions of plastic soldiers to their positions and led them to victorious combat. I spent hours, mornings and afternoons, in my solitary war games and rarely ran out of ideas about how to arrange and vary the scenes of battle. I lived and dreamt soldiering.

My father often took me out on the training ground for a walk at supper time, and then we marched across the grassy plain and hills. My parents had discovered that I, who was a notoriously bad eater, would munch almost anything as long as I could trot along, beat my drum, and pretend to be a soldier. It was then, too, that I learned from my father how to estimate distances, take cover, and deploy my troops who, we pretended, followed us in company strength. My father acted as my military advisor. Often, on days when the sun was shining, I used to ride on my tricycle on the Jahnstraße at noon time, peering down the asphalt ribbon anxiously, looking for the little black dot in the distance that, as it came nearer, slowly grew in size until it was big enough for me to know it was my father who came home for lunch on his bicycle. I could hardly wait to tell him what I had seen on the training ground through my window or what battle scenes I had arranged with my toy soldiers in my room, and I wanted his advice as a company commander. After all, he had been a soldier in the Great War. What better advice could I get? I wanted to be a soldier like him. Soldiering was something I thought I would do all my life.

It was Gerhard, my mother's brother, who lived with my grandparents in far-off Chemnitz, and who often visited us on the Kleine Breite, who introduced me to another kind of soldier than the one I knew from my father and from the Reichswehr I had observed out of my window. Uncle Gerhard usually came at Christmas time when my father and I had unpacked my windup railroad that ran on tracks that were so big they took up the whole floor of my room. I was three years old then, and I know that for sure, because my mother told me later that my uncle had come in 1931, the thirteenth year of the Weimar Republic of whose existence I was then blissfully unaware. Uncle Gerhard did not like the Weimar Republic. He said so several times, because, he said, thirteen horrible years were enough, what with inflation after the Great War when there was never enough money to buy food and clothing, the moral filth in the big cities, and the incompetence of the politicians. Young people like myself, he said, had to be ready to lead our fatherland out of its miserable state.

I wasn't quite sure what moral filth was and why and how politicians were incompetent—or, for that matter, what incompetent meant. But I had heard enough about inflation from my mother to know that it made our money worthless. My mother had told me more than once, how, as a student, she had rushed out early in the morning when the shops opened to buy a head of cabbage for one million marks, afraid that if she was late or had to stand in line for an hour or so, the price would have gone up to a million and a half.

I could only guess what my uncle meant when he spoke about moral filth in the big cities and about incompetent politicians. I was going to look for that filth when we went to Braunschweig, the big city near Wolfenbüttel, right after Christmas day. My mother wanted to shop there at the year-end sales. She, Uncle Gerhard, and I boarded the streetcar and rumbled along in the old creaky wagons through the Lechlum Woods, which stretched to the north of Wolfenbüttel, and then continued through the villages and open fields. In Braunschweig we walked past the store windows and looked at the mannequins who showed off pretty dresses for women and green loden coats for men. I didn't see any filth there. But then we heard music, fifes and drums, and singing. There were men marching in brown uniforms, carrying a red flag with white and black markings. People on the sidewalk next to us stopped. Some waved and applauded, others whistled and booed.

"These men in their smart uniforms," Uncle Gerhard said, "are our hope. They will do away with the filth, decay, and incompetence."

"How will they do that?" I asked, and my uncle replied: "They are soldiers for a new Germany. They'll bring us better days."

"But they don't wear a soldier's uniform," I said. "Their shirts are brown," and I looked at my mother because she had remained silent and shook her head.

"Well, Jurgen," she said, "these are a different kind of soldiers than

11

your father was. Besides," she added, "your Uncle Gerhard and your father and I don't always agree. But it is true, we don't like filth and incompetence either."

I still didn't know what filth and incompetence meant but I sensed that, whatever they were, when both my parents and uncle disliked them so, they must be bad. And soldiers, even though they wore brown and not gray uniforms like the Reichswehr, were supposed to fight everything evil and harmful. So, perhaps my uncle was right also in his approval of the marching men.

Still, one thing puzzled me. Wherever I had seen soldiers, real soldiers in field gray uniforms, and wherever I had heard people talk about soldiers—my father and, later, after I had entered the *Große Schule,* my teacher, Bodo Wacker—people applauded and said good things about them. But here in Braunschweig, where the soldiers wore brown uniforms, some people hissed and booed. How could they do that, I wondered, if the men they booed were soldiers? They were a different kind of soldiers, my mother had said. Just how different were they?

I trusted my mother and what she said. She, too, knew about soldiering, and she, too, like my father, was, in a manner of speaking, a veteran of the Great War. Five years younger than my father, she had lived through the terrible winters of 1917 and 1918 in Chemnitz with her family, my grandfather Felix and grandmother Alma, her sister Mausi and my uncle Gerhard. She was a teenager then, and had been cold and hungry. She had subsisted on a diet of boiled turnips and cabbage with frozen potatoes and no meat or fat to speak of. I heard her remark once that instead of monuments with soldiers on horseback brandishing drawn swords we should just have a big turnip, cast in stone, erected in our marketplaces. That would be a more fitting memorial to the suffering of the children and women during the war. Her health suffered permanent damage; an anemic condition and stomach upsets remained with her for the rest of her life. In 1919 she entered the University of Rostock on the Baltic Sea as a student of German literature. In the following year, she decided to transfer to the University of Leipzig in Saxony. It was there that she met my father.

My father was the first member of his family who attended a university, and only the second who entered a white-collar career. His family roots went back to the agricultural lands of the Ruhr valley. From the late 1700s on, his ancestors had been weavers and tailors, carpenters and blacksmiths, teamsters and foundry workers. The first white-collar worker among them was my father's father, born in 1865, of whom I remember nothing. He made his living as a postmaster, moving from the Rhineland, where my father was born in Düsseldorf, to Delitzsch, a small town in rural Saxony near Leipzig. From there my father came to the university.

My mother's family, just as my father's, were rural folks. They traced their ancestry back to Lutheran ministers and soldiers to the generation of my mother's grandparents. From what little we know of earlier times, a judge, a local official, a shoemaker, and their wives and children were among them and had resided in rural areas of Saxony and Thuringia. During or shortly before the Great War my grandparents with their two daughters and one son moved to Chemnitz, the city that was thirty years later to become Karl Marx Stadt in the communist German Democratic Republic.

In Leipzig my parents met for the first time. My father studied history and, in the center of the German book publishing trade, immersed himself in the bibliophile's specialties of bibliography, the craft of bookbinding and its literature, and what we today would call library science. My mother, working for a doctorate in German literature and, like my father, stimulated by the Leipzig environment, planned to enter the publishing industry. I never found out what it was that made her give up, just short of reaching her goal, her plans to obtain a degree. Whether it was the financial difficulties created by the inflation, the urgings of my father—a possibility that, knowing his unconventional attitude as a person who believed strongly in the equality of the sexes, I have always discarded—or the possibility that my mother simply decided that she would find an outlet for her literary interests at my father's side and did not need the doctorate, I cannot say. But when, in 1924, just after the worst of the inflation had passed, my father submitted his dissertation and received an invitation to start work at the Duke August Library in Wolfenbüttel, my parents decided to leave Leipzig, set their wedding day, and prepared their move to the little North German town.

In Wolfenbüttel, the former residence of the Dukes of Braunschweig-Lüneburg, the library's famed collections of Bibles, maps, and incunabula, unmatched anywhere in Europe, promised a fertile field of research for my father. The city's literary reputation proved to be of special attraction to my mother. Wolfenbüttel had been the one-time home of the philosopher and mathematician Gottfried Wilhelm Leibniz, and of the playwright Gotthold Ephraim Lessing. When Lessing during the last decade of his life presided over the Wolfenbüttel library he wrote there two of his most memorable dramas, *Emilia Galotti* and *Nathan the Wise*, the latter one of the German language's most powerful pleas for toleration and humanity. Wolfenbüttel, too, had been home to the young Wilhelm Raabe from whose pen flowed a series of short stories and novels that I would read with fascination

The author's parents at home, 1937

during my high school days. And it was to Wolfenbüttel where the humorist Wilhelm Busch, the creator of the Max and Moritz stories, which later were to provide the model for the Katzenjammer Kids, came on frequent visits and spent many of his vacations. Given all these incentives and attractions, the additional fact that Wolfenbüttel promoted itself as a city of gardens and schools made it ever more persuasive to my parents to accept the invitation. No doubt, too, they were thinking of the children they might have and of the schools these children would attend. I, of course, not having been conceived, never mind born as yet, was not consulted how I might feel about Wolfenbüttel's schools. In retrospect, though, I could only be grateful to my parents for the town and the schools they had picked for me.

So, having made their decision, my parents were married by my grandfather Felix on May 30, 1925, in the Church of the Cross in Chemnitz, Saxony. Everyone present there, I was told later in a cherished family tale, knew what had happened when my mother came home to Chemnitz from Leipzig to ask her father for permission to break off her studies and marry my father. Grandfather Felix looked at her disbelievingly and then exclaimed: "You fool, all that work for nothing!" and gave her his blessing.

From my third year to my sixth the memories of my home on

the Kleine Breite in Wolfenbüttel and of my grandparents' apartment in Chemnitz provided the two geographical poles of my existence. I looked forward each year to summer vacation when my parents and I embarked on the long train ride from Wolfenbüttel to Chemnitz. We used to stop over between trains in Leipzig where my Uncle Paul, my father's brother, and his wife, Tante Mieze, with their two daughters, Bärbel and Ursel, would await us on the platform and accompany us as we switched trains in that huge station. It seems that no one in that group ever forgot how my teddy bear rode in my backpack and made people laugh and wave at us as we marched from one platform to another. I heard that story from my Leipzig relatives decades later again and again.

Chemnitz itself struck me, even as a little boy, as a rather unappealing city, the soot from its factories filling the air and covering every inch of space outside. While in Chemnitz I had to wash my hair every night and carefully wipe the black dust away from my eyes and out of my ears. I did not like that. But there were nice woods at the outskirts of the city where we went whenever we could to escape the dirt, feed the squirrels, and follow the many walking paths that inevitably ended up at a restaurant where we sat down for coffee, cake, and whipped cream, a ritual that, after the worst of the depression had passed and, as my Uncle Gerhard said, Adolf Hitler had made us human beings again, we never omitted. It was something I liked very much, though Uncle Gerhard, who had his bachelor apartment in Chemnitz, always warned me that, while the cake and whipped cream were all right, I should watch the peanuts. If I continued to munch them as I did instead of feeding them to the squirrels, I would turn into a squirrel myself.

One of the great attractions for me in Chemnitz was Grandmother Alma's cooking. She had a wonderful knack of serving Saxon specialties, such as a soup made of blood sausage with egg whites floating in the broth or a pancake-like concoction called *Quarkkeulchen*. These were made of fried eggs and a curdy cream cheese and then smothered with cooked prunes. Even though I was not a hearty eater, I had my favorites. I loved dumplings made of yeast and served with stewed cherries and, even more, dumplings made of potatoes and served with any kind of roast and some vegetable like cauliflower, brussel sprouts, or kale. Meal times in Chemnitz were something to look forward to, and I always was on my best behavior. I would never have risked angering Grandfather Felix or Grandmother Alma and being sent away from the table. The food was just too good.

By the time I was six and arrived for the vacation, my first cousin had just been born to Aunt Mausi and her husband, Uncle Heini, who

The "protector" of the little girl, 1935

also lived in Chemnitz. It became my task to push the baby carriage, and I took great pride in playing "protector" of the little girl. Uncle Gerhard, however, would have none of that. I was a boy, he said, not a baby's maid, and I was growing up to be a soldier. So he gave me a red flag on a black pole, with a swastika in the middle of a white field, put his old steel helmet of the Great War on my head, and urged me to march ahead of the rest of the family on our wanderings through the woods. I wasn't sure I really liked that because I was fond of pushing the baby carriage. That was a real task, I thought, whereas marching ahead with flag and helmet was just make-believe. Besides, the helmet really was too big and heavy and it made my head hurt. So I was very glad when Grandmother Alma and my mother intervened. Aunt Mausi rolled up the flag and placed it and the helmet at the foot of the baby carriage, and asked me to push the carriage again. Thereafter, we left helmet and flag at home.

At my grandparents' apartment I played railroad or streetcar. The carpet in the living room had all sorts of intricately snaking lines that made for a great network of pretend rails on which I moved the wooden blocks from a construction set. Uncle Gerhard approved of that. In fact, at one Christmas after my sixth birthday, he gave me a beautiful silvery train to add to my railroad at home. It was the "Flying Zeppelin," with a rotating propeller at its end. From then on, Uncle Gerhard could do no wrong. By that time, too, the Weimar Republic was no more, and the soldiers in their brown uniforms had become a familiar sight on the streets. Uncle Gerhard, who himself wore such a shirt at times, no longer spoke about filth and incompetence, but he also didn't seem to be very happy when he wore his brown uniform. "The damn thing," he said, "takes too much of my time." He didn't exactly explain what the "damn thing" was. Grandfather Felix said he should watch his mouth when he spoke in his house.

I thought all of that a bit strange. When I asked my uncle whether he didn't like to be a soldier, he replied only that the men in the brown shirts were not "real" soldiers, after all. I felt vaguely reassured because I hadn't forgotten my mother's remark in Braunschweig that the brown-shirted soldiers were different from my father's kind of soldiers. "Real" soldiers, I was now all the more convinced, wore field gray, not brown, uniforms. That was why, a few years later in Wolfenbüttel, I was bitterly disappointed when an anti-aircraft regiment moved into the city's army barracks. In their blue air force uniforms I could not quite accept these soldiers as "real" either.

Without clearly realizing it at the time, in my childhood years I had been steeped in the traditions of German *Wissenschaft*, of the Prussian–

The author wearing Uncle Gerhard's steel helmet

German army, and, through my grandparents in Chemnitz, of Lutheran Protestant Christianity. Loyalty, courage, steadfastness, faith-
fulness, righteousness, and love of God, country, family, and friends
— these were the virtues I had been taught to live by. They made up an
inheritance that in my childhood and early manhood years appeared
immensely attractive to me and that, despite the growing intensity of
the war that would engulf me in my teens and despite the revelations
of its horrors, still proved, until very nearly the end of my life in Germany, the rock on which I believed I could stand and survive.

Above all, it was the picture that I, as a child, had built up of
my father that embodied for me that inheritance and that sustained
my determination to create a life in his image for myself. He was to
be my model. I could not tolerate the slightest doubt in his right and
righteousness. Any such doubt would have undermined my sense of
selfhood and destiny.

Thus it was that, later in life, as my childhood lay in the past and
I lived in another country, a sense of unreality overcame me when I
listened to others talk about their fathers. I heard friends speak of an
ambivalence they harbored toward their fathers, an ambivalence that
had arisen out of conflicting emotions of love and anger and that had
persisted into their adult lives. My friends remembered their fathers
as protectors whose love they had not earned and as disciplinarians
whose anger they had not deserved. They remembered their own inability to understand what they took to be the contrariness in their
fathers' manifestations of love and anger and their own confused reactions. They felt resentful because they could not see how they had
earned such treatment from their fathers, and they felt guilty because
they also seemed to think that they somehow deserved it. As a result
their memories of their fathers were tinged with ambivalence, an ambivalence that shifted uneasily between expressions of love and outbursts of anger.

I did not understand what my friends were talking about. I thought
I knew of no ambivalence in my feelings toward my father, had never
felt that I could not understand his behavior, and did not share my
friends' resentment and guilt. My father had never left me in doubt
about his love. When I had disappointed him and he had disciplined
me, I had accepted his sorrow as justified and his punishment as just.
It was another token of his love. I had been disturbed only that I had
given him occasion to be sad and angry and that I had failed to live
up to his expectations. My father, I used to tell my friends and myself, could have done no wrong. For me he had always been a tower
of strength and righteousness: the quiet, serious scholar, loved by my-

self and my mother, and the loyal, incorruptible officer, revered by his comrades and soldiers.

As time went on, however, my sense of unreality led me to question whether I was so different from my other friends after all and whether I did not secretly harbor ambivalent feelings toward my father. Had his path through life been as straight and uncomplicated as I thought it had been? Had I never been puzzled and unsatisfied when he responded to my questions and I listened to his explanations? When I pondered what my friends and acquaintances had said and when I tried to place what I knew about my father into the circumstances of his life, there were parts that did not seem to fit so easily and smoothly as I had thought.

I remember asking him early on, when he was still at home and working in the library, why, when we visited in Chemnitz, Uncle Gerhard sometimes wore the brown shirt of the SA, the storm troopers of the Nazi party. My father said only that Uncle Gerhard had his reasons, and each one of us would have to decide for himself what was best.

I was all the more puzzled about his answer when some time later my mother and my grandfather told me that my father steadfastly refused to join the SA and the Nazi party and thus had excluded himself from any chance of becoming the director of the Duke August Library. To become a party member and thereby to declare his loyalty to the Hitler government was a step the party expected everyone to take who aspired to any elevated position in the civil service. So why would my father refuse to join and yet not appear to mind that Uncle Gerhard wore the brown shirt? By the time I heard of this I could no longer ask my father because the war had begun and he had left home to be a soldier again. When I asked my mother about it, she, too, said only my father could explain that, but, she added, he had done the right thing.

When I was twelve and my father came home on his first leave from the war I had other, more pressing, questions to ask him. I wanted to know why the Führer, two years ago, had himself assumed control of the army and had dismissed several generals. My father said only that good soldiers do not question their superiors. I, seeing myself as the son of an officer and a future soldier, accepted that answer and did not think it right to ask further questions. But I still felt uncomfortable with the idea that the Führer, who had not been trained as an officer and had not risen through the ranks, could dismiss soldiers, even generals, from their posts. That did not seem right to me, and I really wanted to know how that was possible.

But then I asked my father to go out with me wearing his uniform and the service medal he had been awarded. I wanted to show him off to my friends. But my father refused. He was glad, he said, being home, to wear his civilian clothes. Besides, he said, we were going to church together on Sunday to listen to Propst Rosenkranz preach at St. Mary's. We could meet my friends there. But that wasn't the same, I thought, as an afternoon stroll down the Lange Herzogstraße, Wolfenbüttel's main business street. Few of my friends came to church, and my father would not be in his uniform. I just could not understand him. What better clothes could there be than an officer's army uniform? I was quite disappointed. My father's refusal did not fit my image of him as a proud soldier.

The next year, when I was thirteen and Germany had been at war for two years, my father came home on leave again and remarked that the time might come that I would have to enlist in the armed forces. What branch did I have in mind? he asked. Though I had always thought of volunteering for an army officer's career I was not ready to say so. Perhaps it was my lingering unhappiness with my father's refusal to go out with me in his uniform or with his unwillingness to answer my question about the dismissal of the generals that made me hesitate. At any rate, I responded somewhat truculently that, wanting to belong to the very best unit there was, I was considering joining the Armed SS, the party's military fighting units.

Among us boys, soldiers of the Armed SS, portrayed by the Nazis as combining the most desirable qualities of army and party, represented an ideal that both fascinated and awed us. We had very few personal acquaintances who actually belonged, and most of us boys seemed to feel more comfortable with soldiers of the regular army, air force, or navy. But when my father asked me I blurted out my answer as though to spite him and myself.

I was not prepared for my father's reaction. There was nothing of the quiet earnest scholar or the resolved conscientious soldier about him when, his face turning a purplish red, his veins standing out in his throat and neck, he shouted at me so that it seemed it could be heard miles away: "Never, never will you ever join the Armed SS. You can do anything you like with your life, but you will not, never, under any circumstances, join the SS. Do I make myself clear? Do you understand that?"

I was far too taken aback to give any coherent response or to ask why not. I had never before seen my father in such a state of furious anger. I could only mumble, "Yes, yes," and withdraw into my room. I was not disposed to ever raise that issue again, and I could only wonder what it was that had provoked such an outburst.

When my father had departed again for his unit I asked my mother why he had been so angry. She only shook her head and said that she thought she knew, but that it was best not to talk about it and that he had been right in his telling me never to even think of joining the SS.

When, in later years, I thought about these instances and tried to reconstruct for myself the probable causes of my father's outburst and of his refusal to explain why he had not answered my questions, I wondered whether there had not been more than one reason. After all, he was serving in Poland and, as a railroad transport officer, he must have seen the trains carrying their human cargo to the concentration camps at Auschwitz and elsewhere. Did he want to protect me from the knowledge of evil? Was he afraid that he might disillusion my faith in my country? Did he realize that, had he told me what he knew and feared, there was the very real risk that an incautious word of mine would expose me, my mother, and himself to arrest, deportation, and incarceration? These, I thought, were reasons enough to have sealed his lips.

And yet, I could not rid myself of the thought that, notwithstanding the probable reasons for his silence, I would have wanted him to share the doubts and ambivalences in his life. It would have helped me to better deal with the questions that were to come and disturb me. But, thinking of how difficult it had always been for me to face ambivalence, I could not help wonder whether, had he even wanted to share and explain, he would have been able to do so.

But even more so I wondered why for so long I had fervently resisted questioning the belief in my father's righteousness and infallibility. At first I surmised that I had done so simply because, for all practical purposes, my memories of him extended only to the first eleven years of my life. Then he had left at the beginning of the war, and I had seen him thereafter only for at most two weeks a year. I could not bear, I told myself, to destroy my happy childhood recollections of him. They were uncomplicated and comforting, and I wanted to keep them thus. At the same time, I dimly realized that by holding fast to an unblemished picture of my father, I, who strove so much to be like him, could escape ambivalence and doubts in my own life. But the more I thought about it, the more I began to suspect that, while partly true, that surmise could not fully explain my reluctance to probe into the ambiguities of his life and into my relationship with him.

After all, my memories of him did not end in 1939. After that year until his death in 1944 I not only saw him every year when he was on leave, I also received many letters from him. It was during these leaves and through the letters that I learned to my dismay that, far from leading the life I thought my father wanted me to live, I had often disappointed him. He let me know, not always justly, I thought, of his disapproval and censure. When I finally admitted these instances to myself, I realized that my relationship to him had not been as unperturbed and free of conflict as I had persuaded myself to believe. I had known resentment and guilt.

During my fifteenth year, when my father had been away from home for four years, his letters from the front admonished me not to neglect my duties toward my mother, who had become sickly and despairing. My father seemed to think that I could do more to help her. I could do more of her shopping and more of her house and garden work. His remarks made me feel unjustly reprimanded, especially so because they appeared to undercut the praise he had had for my past efforts. I felt particularly aggrieved because I had dug up the strawberry and flower beds in our garden, had picked raspberries, currants, and gooseberries, and had pulled our wooden handcart through town filled with bushel baskets of apples, pears, and cherries that I had harvested. While I recognized what the garden meant to my parents during this time of war-conditioned food shortages, how it relieved my mother's mind of her great worry to keep me fed and healthy, I nonetheless resented being chained to it and made its slave. My father's strictures only aggravated my distress. To this day I feel a distinct dislike of any kind of garden work, except for mowing the lawn—a duty I did not then have to perform because we had signed over the use of the grass to the custodian of the Library, who cut and fed it to his rabbits.

My father also expressed great disappointment over my steadily deteriorating grades in school, and he admonished me that I should devote more time and attention to my homework. He criticized the many afternoons I spent with my friends in the *Jungvolk*, the Nazi youth organization for ten- to thirteen-year-olds in which I, as a fifteen-year-old, had become a leader. When he wrote that academic work was particularly important for me because I had by then filed my application as a volunteer aspirant to an army officer's career, I faced an unsolvable dilemma. Though I admitted to myself that success in school was requisite to my admission as an officer's candidate, I had—as I shall recount in more detail below—poured all my energies into my career in the *Jungvolk*. This, I thought, was the perfect introduction to an officer's life, far more pertinent to the skills and experiences required in the army than anything the school could give me. Thus my commitment to an officer's career confronted me every day with the choice of doing my homework for school or of planning and carrying out meetings with the boys of the *Jungvolk*. Most of the time I opted for the latter.

My relationship with my father reached its lowest point in the summer of 1944. As I thought about it later, the incident I am about to narrate became even more disturbing to me because it was only one

23

month later that he was killed. He had come on leave in early July. I had by then turned sixteen and had been admitted to our local *Jungvolk*'s elite leadership training platoon, the *Führerzug*. It so happened that for weeks we had been preparing ourselves for what was to be our supreme test of courage and ability to survive in the wild. Our *Führerzug* was to hike at night through the Lechlum Woods at the northern edge of town and to engage in a mock battle with another *Jungvolk* unit assigned to ambush us somewhere in the darkness of the forest. There was to be a fistfight in which the object of each group was to tear off the colored strings we and the boys of the opposing group had tied around their wrists. For us this was a supremely exciting adventure and we looked forward to this event with high expectations.

As it happened, this maneuver was to take place during my father's last night on leave. My mother begged me to stay home, and my father said he would like to have me with him for that night but that it was up to me to decide. I felt torn as I never had experienced before. I did not want to refuse my mother's request, and I did not want to disappoint my father and tell him, through my actions, that I valued him less than the excitement that awaited me in the woods. But the motives pulling me toward the night-time adventure proved stronger than my mother's tears and my father's wish. I decided to join my comrades in the woods.

While my father's letters and his resigned sadness at my departure for the *Jungvolk* war games had made it clear to me that I had disappointed and hurt him, I still suppressed the recognition that, in persuading myself that my *Jungvolk* activities were helpful for my future career as army officer, I had been less than honest with myself. I came to recognize that more persuasive in my reactions than the supposed career benefits were the emotional rewards and immediate gratification I reaped from being acclaimed and followed as a leader of boys. In the case of the nocturnal war games an even stronger motivation— and this realization I repressed with heightened vehemence—was my fear that, had I not joined my comrades that night, they would have accused me of cowardice. I was afraid that I would never thereafter be able to join them in the boasting and mutual backslapping of adventurers who had proved their mettle in dangerous situations. I was afraid that they would exclude me in the future from sharing in their most treasured memories.

So I left home that night, feeling terrible and hardly daring to look my father in the eyes, sensing, deep down, though not admitting it openly, that I went out ostensibly to "prove" my courage as a future soldier while I slinked away as a coward who could not admit to himself and those he loved most the real motivation for his actions.

It has taken me many years to admit to myself the role played by ambivalence, doubt, resentment, and guilt in my relations with my father. In committing myself to the career of soldier I could not but protect his image as a German officer of irreproachable honesty and righteousness and thus preserve my self-image as one who wanted to follow in his footsteps. But this identification with my father also made it increasingly difficult for me to come to understand him and myself. Had he not refused to answer my questions about the dismissal of the German generals? Had he not objected strenuously to my remark that I had considered joining the Armed SS? What did he really think? Where did his sympathies lie? I could guess, but I did not know.

My questions became even more pressing and disturbing when, later in the same month the war game had taken place, the news came of the unsuccessful assassination attempt on Hitler's life, and we learned of the army's involvement in the conspiracy. What would my father say? Where did he stand? Did he know of the plot? Had he supported it? His death made it impossible for me to ever explore these questions. In the closing weeks of 1944, when I served as an instructor in a *Hitler Jugend* training camp, the conflict between the duties I thought I owed to the Nazi regime and the loyalties to what I held to be my father's bequest—and which now more and more appeared to be in conflict with each other—reached its climax. In my own mind I opted for what I hoped and believed to have been my father's commitment to his God, his country, and the traditions of its army. I contemplated my resignation as a *Jungvolk* leader and my rejection of anything the Nazis stood for. But how could I be sure that I was indeed following in the footsteps of my father? I could only hope that I was right.

The painful memories of this wrestling with uncertainties in the midst of chaos and conflicting impulses led me in the months immediately following the end of the war to reject all attempts and appeals to find out more about my father. I was afraid of what I might learn. I could not tolerate the possibility that the idealized picture of my father's straightforward probity, sense of justice, belief in God, and love for his family and country might not stand the test of truth. I could not tolerate the thought of ambiguities, ambivalences, doubts, resentments, and guilt darkening the memory of my father. I felt dimly that my own probity, my sense of justice, and my love were intimately bound up in his. Questioning him was to question myself, and I was far too vulnerable and defenseless to allow that to happen.

After the war's end I was not alone in this refusal to face reality and probe the past. Many of my former countrymen of the war generation clung to their picture of an uncomplicated past. We refused to disturb our comforting views of our relationships with our families, our traditions, and our collective past. It was for us the only comfort we had left amidst the chaos of defeat, death, disillusionment, hunger, and homelessness.

But this upholding of a simplified past and this refusal to face the reality with all its ambiguities and incongruities did not and could not last. We came to understand that such an unproblematical view of the past and of human relationships was false. My own sense of unreality of which I spoke compelled me, step by step, to finally face the ambiguities that I had dodged all along and to accept and to begin to unravel the ambivalences and complexities of the past I had lived through. My friends and I then embarked on a spiritual pilgrimage that led each one of us on separate and convoluted paths to different goals. It was a voyage of self-discovery that helped us, little by little, to come to terms with our past and thus to start thinking about our future. It enabled me to accept and affirm the ambiguities in my father's life and to see him as I think he would have wanted to be seen: neither as hero nor as villain, but as a man who under terrifying circumstances sought to live his life as honestly and lovingly as he could.

2

Discovering Social Class

I WAS SIX YEARS OLD WHEN, following the long-established German custom, my parents escorted me right after the Easter holidays to my first morning in the *Volksschule*, the public primary school on Wolfenbüttel's Karlstraße. The *Volksschule* was the common school for all youngsters between the ages of six and ten. In the province of Braunschweig, where the Evangelical-Lutheran Church was the established denomination, the *Volksschule* offered religious instruction in the Protestant faith. Catholic children went to a parochial school associated with St. Peter's Catholic Church. But since my parents were Protestants the *Volksschule* was the school for me.

As we marched along the street I carried in my arms a two-foot-long *Zuckertüte*, a gayly colored cone made of molded cardboard. It was called sugar cone not because it was made of sugar, but because inside were Easter eggs, chocolate candy, sugar canes, and licorice, my favorite. I was not supposed to eat any of these sweets until I got home again. But I was to show them off to the other little boys and girls on their first day of school, and I was to admire their *Tüten* and what goodies they contained. I was mortified when I discovered lollipops in most of them—lollipops which I never was allowed to suck because, my mother claimed, they would make my teeth grow crooked. I also carried a brand-new backpack that smelled of fresh leather and held my books, paper, and a wooden box with a lid that slid back and forth in grooves. Inside the box were my pencils, one with a hard and sharply pointed lead tip for writing and another one soft for drawing. There also was a metal pencil sharpener and a piece of rubber for erasing. Over my shoulder hung a sandwich case that matched my backpack. In it were *Butterbrote*, dark brown rye bread slices with sa-

Beginning school, with class cap and *Zuckertüte*, 1934

lami, liver sausage, or cheese between them. I would eat those during the mid-morning break.

On my head I wore the *Schülermütze*, a bright red cap with a white and black ribbon around it, telling everyone that I was a pupil in the *Volksschule*'s first grade. I was very proud of it because now I was somebody, no longer just a little kid, but a pupil who belonged somewhere other than just at home. Everybody had a home, I told my mother, but not everybody went to the first grade of the *Karlschule*. The next year I would exchange the red cap for a dark blue one with a yellow and green ribbon that signified the second grade. But I never wore the orange third-grade cap because the Nazis banned it.

My father said the Nazis did that because they believed that colored caps accentuated class divisions. I wasn't quite sure who these Nazis actually were—except, of course, for Uncle Gerhard in Chemnitz, who sometimes wore a brown Nazi shirt but, I assured myself, had never said anything against wearing school caps—but I disliked them anyway because I wanted to wear that orange third-grade cap. Now, my father explained, the Nazis didn't mean the differences between first and second and third class in the *Volksschule*. They meant, he said, the difference between those boys and girls who, like myself, after the fourth grade would transfer to a secondary school and those who would continue to go to the *Volksschule*. The caps would make it easy and obvious to tell whose parents could pay to send their children to the *Gymnasium* or the *Lyceum*, the Latin secondary schools for boys and for girls, and whose parents belonged to the working classes and sent their children to the tuition-free *Bürgerschule*, as the upper four grades of the *Volksschule* were called. Secondary schools prepared their students for middle-class careers and if, on graduation, the students passed the final leaving examination called the *Abitur*, they could then go to a university. Obviously, they were better off than the children in the *Bürgerschule*.

So the Nazis didn't want us to wear our *Schülermütze*. When I entered the third grade I wore nothing on my head, and when it snowed in the winter my mother gave me a green knit cap. By the time I turned ten and joined the *Jungvolk*, I, like everybody else, had to buy a navy blue, almost black, ski cap as part of my uniform. It no longer indicated the distinctions in our schooling. I had to wait seven years, until I was fifteen, when I could once again savor the thrill of having a cap to show off to everyone how far I had come. By then I had been promoted to the position of a *Jungzugführer*, a leader of a platoon of thirty *Jungvolk* boys, and I could put a silver eagle on my cap instead of the red and white Hitler Youth diamond that all the lower ranks wore. But, of course, I did not know that when I had to give up my school cap, and I resented its loss very much.

My entrance into the *Volksschule* in 1934 was the reason why my parents decided to give up our home on the Kleine Breite and to move to an apartment on the Harztorwall. But while we still lived on the Kleine Breite I attended a private kindergarten. The children I met there came from homes much like my own. The sons and daughters of middle-class families, we were well scrubbed and well dressed and spoke a refined high German with only a faint trace of the adulterated "a" that sounded more like an "ö," and that, to the knowledgeable, identified the born Braunschweiger. But we never used—though we could understand—"plattdütsch," the low German dialect that was common in the surrounding villages and among the working people of Wolfenbüttel. Somehow—I couldn't have said just why—it didn't seem right for us to speak "plattdütsch." I suspect it was because we knew instinctively that, had we used "plattdütsch," those who spoke it regularly would have recognized us as fakes. It just wasn't our language.

We four- and five-year-olds walked everyday to kindergarten, a little more than a mile away. We took shortcuts through potato and bean fields, skipping along the footpath used by the farmers to reach their land. We ran through plum and apple orchards and skirted the fruit and vegetable gardens that grew strawberries, onions, and carrots until we reached the sidewalk of the major highway that led past the school building to Braunschweig. We were, as I have said, well scrubbed and well dressed, though our behavior, to judge by the scolding we received from our teachers, did not quite match our looks. Neighbors complained that on our way home we raided fruit trees and strawberry beds and pulled carrots out of the soil. They were right in their accusations because we were hungry when we left the kindergarten but generally had little appetite by the time we arrived home. My parents were upset more than once when it took me an hour or more to show up for lunch.

On the Harztorwall I entered a different world. The Harztorwall, the dam at the city's gate to the Harz Mountains, was a parkway without sidewalks—a middle-class residential area, my parents called it—and only cars of people who lived there or trucks that made deliveries were allowed to enter. But there was only one person on the Harztorwall who owned a car, and he was the director of a bank. He walked to work every morning and took his car out only every other Sunday for an afternoon drive at four o'clock. That was his routine—at least until the rationing of gasoline became more stringent as the war continued. Had we wanted to, we could have set our calendar and clock by the appearance of his car. The other vehicle that appeared regularly was the milkman's motorized three-wheeler that showed up every morning before I went to school. I hardly ever encountered traffic on the Harztorwall.

The street was part of the green belt that separated Wolfenbüttel's Old Town and center from the river Oker and the earthen dam that surrounded the city. The belt, a large expanse of grass, paralleled the dam and was interrupted at points by trunk roads that led to other towns. Huge beech and oak trees stretched their branches toward the sky. Some of the beeches had leaves of blood-red color that made them stand out starkly against the green of the oaks and the other beech trees. The red ones were the favorite homes of black crows which built their nests in them and from above surveyed and, with their caw-caws, commented on what they observed in the park. Later, by the third or fourth year of the war, when shortages of fuel had made us more aware of the cold wintry blasts that swept over us from the East, and when enemy planes had begun to drop an occasional bomb on our homes, the cawing crows on the bare branches of the beech trees that stretched starkly against the leaden clouds, made me think of Nietzsche's poem,

> Cawing crows,
> their wings awhir, are moving towards town.
> Soon it will snow—
> Cursed he who does not have a home.[1]

In my memory the Harztorwall remains a street for all seasons: The springtime of anticipation and promise as I began my daily walks to school, the summer of the greens of the oaks and the reds of the beeches that shone through our windows in the sun's brightness, the fall of the fogs which enshrouded what had seemed clear and distinct and dampened our hopes and spirits, and the winter that was to come with its crows and curses to bring us tears and death.

In the spring of 1934 my daily walk to the *Karlschule* introduced me to a different social world. It was not a very long walk. It took ten minutes at the most. It led from our apartment down the Harztorwall, past the city's Lessing Theatre, a few feet into the Lange Straße, and then to the huge red brick school building on the Karlstraße. The boys and girls I met there and who became my new classmates represented a cross-section of the city's population. Many of their fathers were craftsmen

---

1.   *Die Krähen schrein*
        und ziehen schwirren Flugs zur Stadt.
        Bald wird es schnein—
        Weh dem, der keine Heimat hat.

such as carpenters, bricklayers, and cobblers. They had jobs as city trash collectors and mail carriers. They worked in, and some owned, the shops on the Lange Herzogstraße, Wolfenbüttel's main business area. They drove the streetcars that ran its length and thence past our friends' the Finks' house and the kindergarten and on through the Lechlum Woods and fields to Braunschweig. They delivered milk and butter and eggs to our doorstep in the morning before we had even gotten up. They built houses in the *Siedlung,* the new settlement near the army barracks to the south of town. My schoolmates' mothers washed other people's laundry and cleaned their houses or hired themselves out to farmers in the surrounding villages and helped with the harvest. None of them lived on the Harztorwall. Their homes were either in Wolfenbüttel's Old Town or at the edges of the city on the other side of the greenbelt, the station, and the railroad tracks. It was the children of the latter who passed by our house on the Harztorwall and who soon became my friends.

Among them there was no uniformity of dress, appearance, or language. They wore hand-me-down clothes of their older brothers or sisters. Their shirts and trousers, blouses and skirts were often faded and did not always fit well. The boys kept their hair long, and, as soon as we were out of the classroom, both the boys and girls spoke "plattdütsch." They used words I had not heard before, and sometimes I could not even guess what they meant. But I knew enough not to repeat them at home.

Still, around the dinner table at noon, when I had come home from school, I experimented with grammatical constructions and slang expressions I had heard my new friends use. Every now and then I threw in a few words of "plattdütsch," though I didn't always quite know what they meant. I wanted to see my parents' reactions. My mother looked at me disapprovingly and said, "Jürgen, here we speak high German, not 'plattdütsch.' High German is our language."

But my father, who always came home from the library for our midday meal, only grinned and said something about me trying out my wings. He even inquired with obvious sympathetic interest about my new friends, some of whom were known as the town's little ruffians. He encouraged me to invite them in for lunch as they walked past our house on the way home. I never followed up on that suggestion. I liked those boys outside. In fact, I liked them so much that in school I shared their lollipops—one lick for me, one lick for you—but somehow I could not quite get myself to have them at my mother's table or in my playroom. Perhaps that was because I remembered my mother's horrified face when I told her about the lollipops.

On our way home my friends and I often lingered and prepared for ourselves secret lairs in the clumps of the lilac bushes, whose blossoms were white, blue, and violet of different hues and which grew in great profusion on the greenbelt. We stocked our hideouts with beechnuts for food and with acorns and water pistols for our weapons. During school vacations we spent entire mornings and afternoons crouching behind the dense foliage, spying on the people who went by, unaware of our hidden presence, and pelting them with showers of acorns for which they held responsible the squirrels in the trees above.

The earthen dam, part of the greenbelt that dated back to Wolfen-büttel's days as a fortified city in the twelfth and succeeding centuries, had become a pleasure walk. Mothers with baby carriages and couples in love promenaded up and down; an occasional bicyclist slowly ped-aled past. Songbirds twittered in the trees and bushes that shaded the path. On the benches facing the Oker young men and women sat and smooched. We boys, creeping out stealthily from our lilac bushes, would suddenly rush at them and scare them with war whoops, bar-rages of acorns, and squirts from our water pistols. We knew that we caught our victims off-guard. Before they even recognized what had happened, we had disappeared again in the over-hanging leaves at the Oker's edge or in one of the many dense growths further along the park.

I really liked my new friends, and I wanted to be like them. I wanted to wear my hair long as they did, tear holes in my pants and speak "plattdütsch." I followed them on the way home as they climbed over the fence behind the school yard to skip stones on the Stadt-graben, the little lake that was home to ducks and swans, and I rolled with them on the grass in the park. My mother wanted to know why my pants were torn (they had gotten caught on the fence) and why my shirt was green (it had been stained on the grass). I said it had hap-pened during the mid-morning break at school.

Once, when my mother gave me money on a Saturday to go to Mr. Gottschalk, the barber, for a haircut, I said I didn't want to go be-cause I wanted to let my hair grow like my friends. But my mother would not listen and said I had to get it cut. If I didn't, it would get too dirty. So I went to the barber and asked him to cut it only a little in the back. That was a mistake, because when he was finished I had all that hair on the top of my head and nothing in the back. When I came home my mother looked at me, shook her head, and wondered out loud whether Mr. Gottschalk needed new glasses. But it was far worse on Monday when I went back to school. My friends kept on rub-bing the back of my head and shouted gleefully, "Baldy, baldy, with a garden on top."[2] It took about three weeks until the damage corrected itself. I never again told the barber how to cut my hair.

My entrance into the *Volksschule* had brought me in touch not only with my new friends in class but also with people like Mr. Heine and Mrs. Frobart. Mr. Heine was my first-grade teacher, and I liked him very much. He was a young man, of medium build, with a perpetual smile on his face. He taught us to read from a book with nursery rhymes and other little poems, and we sang those rhymes as often as we read them. Mr. Heine accompanied us on his violin. Music and reading went together, and I then always assumed that every poem was at the same time a song, and every song a poem. So it seemed when Mr. Heine taught us. Singing was fun, and so was reading. But best of all, I thought, was reading aloud, when Mr. Heine asked me or one of my classmates to read a passage from a book. We did much more of that as we advanced from first to third grade, Mr. Heine moving with us year after year.

Mrs. Frobart joined us when we moved to the Harztorwall. She came to us twice or three times a week and did our laundry and cleaned our apartment. As far as I can remember, Mrs. Frobart always had been an old woman. Her hair was white and her voice much louder than that of my mother. She spoke "plattdütsch" most of the time, and called my mother 'Madam Doctor,' though it was my father's title, not my mother's, which she used. Mrs. Frobart was with us throughout most of the year but she did not come along when we went to Chemnitz or to Kellenhusen, a beach resort on the Baltic Sea. Only my father, my mother, and I would go there. Mrs. Frobart stayed in Wolfenbüttel. She went to the country, she said, to help a farmer.

But even at home, Mrs. Frobart was not always with us. She would eat with us only when my mother and I ate in the kitchen. My mother would set the kitchen table and serve the food. She had prepared it while Mrs. Frobart was working somewhere else in the apartment. When we ate in the kitchen, Mrs. Frobart was our guest, my mother said, and she shouldn't serve us. She did that only in the dining room, and then only when we had guests. When my father was home at noon, he, my mother, and I would eat in the dining room without Mrs. Frobart. She stayed in the kitchen and ate by herself. Once I left our dinner table and went into the kitchen and asked Mrs. Frobart why she ate alone. She said that my father and mother had things to tell each other, and it wouldn't be right for her to be present. While I thought about that and wanted to ask her why it wouldn't be right for her to hear what my parents discussed, my mother came in the kitchen and asked

2. "*Glatze mit Vorgarten.*"

me to go back into the dining room. So I never heard the answer to my question. I wondered about it a lot because I didn't think that my parents had ever discussed secrets at the dinner table.

Mrs. Frobart had time and answers for all my questions. My mother was too often in a hurry and would tell me to ask my father. But Mrs. Frobart always had time. I liked it when she came to clean up my room. While my mother wanted me to go out and play when that happened, I tried to stay. I wanted to ask Mrs. Frobart all sorts of questions. One day she stood on the wide windowsill in my room and washed the windows. I leaned against the white wardrobe that held my clothes and toys and asked her why it was that the sparrows never flew into my room. There were so many outside in the yard that came flying over from the Krumme Straße—the Crooked Street—in the Old Town. Mrs. Frobart said that sparrows needed plenty of fresh air and that my room was too small for them. That did not make sense to me. My room was large enough for me, and I was bigger than a sparrow. So I asked her, "Why is the room too small, Mrs. Frobart?"

"Because, Jürgen, a sparrow has to fly," she replied.

That answer I could understand. Later, at lunch in the kitchen, I asked my mother: "Why does a sparrow have to fly?"

"Because it has wings, silly," she said and shook her head. Mrs. Frobart, who sat with us, only smiled.

Once my mother and I visited Mrs. Frobart at her home. It was very strange, I thought, because Mrs. Frobart lived in a farm house in the middle of the city, right next to the Lange Herzogstraße. Hers was the only farm house around, and it didn't quite seem to belong there among the city dwellings. From her house I could hear the streetcar rattle and ring its bell. A great big hall was her kitchen and living room. On one side there was a black stone oven over which yawned a huge and sooty chimney. There were thick, white curtains in front of the windows, and many flowers stood on benches all over the place. There was a sofa in front of one of the windows. On it lay Mr. Frobart. He was dressed in blue working overalls and had a cold pipe stuck in his mouth. He hardly ever moved; he did not say anything, did not even read the newspaper. He just looked at me with his light blue eyes through his black-framed glasses. In the corner, between the windows, high up on the ceiling, hung a dusty, black funnel. When I looked up at it, "It's the gramophone," said Mrs. Frobart. She opened a square wooden box that stood on a wallshelf above the sofa.

"The happy Wanderer" and "This Must Be a Piece of Heaven"— the sound poured out of the funnel. I had not heard these tunes before because we did not have a radio. My mother bought one only after the war had started and she wanted to hear the news bulletins from the front. I did have a small "His Master's Voice" windup gramophone in my playroom but the only records I had were children's songs like "Fuchs Du Hast die Gans gestohlen" and "Hänschen Klein."[3] So I liked to listen to Mrs. Frobart's music and felt very grown-up when I did.

On the cobblestoned yard outside chicken, geese, ducks, pigeons, and a few goats scurried around. I had to be careful to walk across it because of the droppings, which made the stones very slippery. There were two pigs in a pen in a stable, but it was so dark behind the dirty window panes I never could really see them. I just heard them grunt the way pigs do every now and then.

There were other adults I knew in Wolfenbüttel besides Mr. Heine and Mrs. Frobart. They were people much like my father and my mother who lived in apartments much like our own, apartments that did not look like the Frobart's farm. These were people like the Finks, who lived in a big house in the middle of a huge, parklike garden with a big red beech tree; people like the Fuchtels, who lived in the house right next to the *Große Schule,* the *Gymnasium* I would attend after my ninth birthday; and people like Dr. Duesberg, our family physician who lived in a house surrounded by chestnut trees. All of them were good friends of my parents. The Finks were a large family with five children, three girls and two boys. Mr. Fink, who was the Director of the Anton Ulrich Art Museum in Braunschweig, the two older girls, and the older son all joined the Air Force when the war began. The boy, Ajax, who became a night fighter pilot, was killed in action. His funeral was the first military burial I witnessed. I often played with the youngest girl, Nucki, and the younger boy, Helmut, under the huge red beech tree and the chestnut trees that overshadowed the big, park-like garden surrounding the Finks' house. Mrs. Fink was my mother's best friend, and when both my father and Mr. Fink had gone to war, Mrs. Fink became our frequent guest. My mother and I spent many an afternoon at her house. The Fuchtels I knew less well. Mr. Fuchtel was a teacher in the *Große Schule,* one of the few enthusiastic party mem-bers who always wore the party emblem on his lapel. I would even-tually become one of his students. The Fuchtel's son, Konrad, often came to play with me. Of him I remember only a searching conversa-tion we had when we were eight or nine years old. First doubts had entered our minds about the existence of Santa Claus, but we were not quite ready to declare our disbelief. So we compromised. Yes, we said, there was a Santa Claus; but the Easter Bunny just was not cred-ible. We wouldn't believe in it any more. As for Dr. Duesberg, I tried to keep my distance. I knew that he was a family friend, but he was

---

3. "Fox, you have stolen the goose" and "Little Jack."

a physician, and that meant he was a person who often hurt me. He pierced my ear drums more than once with a sharp, funnel-like instrument, and, when I had a fever, he prescribed two-hour-long whole body wraps in hot, wet sheets. I feared his treatment for middle-ear infection and I hated the hot, wet wraps with a passion. When I lay between these sheets and the sweat poured all over my face, I tried not to move the slightest bit for the full two hours because every time I did my skin made new contact with the wet sheets and my misery grew. I counted and counted the seconds and minutes, and for many years the concept of two hours was in my mind inextricably bound up with my memories of the sweating cure.

There were other adults whose homes I had never visited and of whom I knew only what I could observe when I watched them on the street. There was, for example, Mr. Ebert, the mailman. I saw him every day. I watched him out of our living room window when he came in the morning and opened the garden gate, his heavy leather bag full of letters and packages slung over his shoulder. I heard him come up the steps, open the big, heavy housedoor and slide mail through the slot in our apartment door, climb upstairs to the Hoffmanns, who lived above us, come down the stairs again, and leave the house. I also saw him often in the late afternoon when he returned from his route. He walked along the earthen dam on the other side of the park, next to the Oker, on his way back to the post office, which was just a few hundred yards away from where we lived. I knew his name because he was the father of an older boy I knew. Both Mr. Ebert and his son had white hair. That's why we called the boy *"Schimmel,"* the German word for white horse. But Schimmel Ebert was three or four years older than I, and I never really talked with him. That was an unspoken rule among us boys that the younger ones would not address the older ones, and the older ones thought it below their dignity to speak to a younger one. So I really never had any good reason to talk to either Mr. Ebert or his son. All I knew about them came from a remark I had overheard my father make to my mother, how he admired Mr. Ebert because he had managed, on his small salary, to build himself a house in the *Siedlung* near the army barracks.

Another person I had seen often but never spoken to was the caretaker of the park. I had met him several times together with my father when we left the house in the morning, I accompanying my father on his way to work at the library. The caretaker was an old man, a hunchback. He wore a torn, dark brown work jacket, a light blue workingmen's cap, and, in summer as well as in winter, heavy, awkward boots. They were gray, rather than black, because the caretaker did not ever seem to polish them. A pipe stuck between his yellow teeth. His nose was red, and the pipe was rarely lit. He carried a long broom of brush-wood. He swept the street, heaping up dust, leaves, and paper in little piles. He pushed a small, two-wheeled iron cart along the gutter, and at each pile, with a penetrating metallic sound, put it down on its V-shaped leg. With his left hand he placed his shovel before the pile of leaves, and with his broom in his right hand pushed the litter onto the shovel. Then he leaned the broom against the cart and seized his shovel with both hands to empty it over the cart. Thereafter, he placed broom and shovel side by side on his cart, and with the iron wheels clanging along the pavement, made his way to the next pile.

I liked the caretaker, and watched him carefully at his work. He was very systematic, and never once varied in the sequence of his move-ments. I never had spoken with him. As he paid attention to his work, he rarely seemed to notice other people. Sometimes I saw him around noon when he sat on the grass somewhere in the park, his cart by his side, munching a sandwich, a beer bottle in his hand. But I never knew whether there was beer or cold coffee in his bottle. I never looked the caretaker in the eyes, but I assumed they had to be dark brown, just like his jacket.

One morning, when my father and I left the house, the caretaker was sweeping before our garden gate. My father approached him, lifted his hat, and said, "Good Morning, Mr. Heims."

"Good Morning, Doctor Herbst," said the caretaker, "we shall have a beautiful day."

"You think so?" said my father. "It's still pretty warm, though it is fall, you know."

"Won't stay warm long," replied the caretaker and removed his pipe from between his teeth. "It will be a cold winter, because the summer's been too hot."

"How's your rheumatism?" asked my father.

"Not good, not good," said the caretaker. "Am afraid of the winter. When the east wind blows and we have to shovel the snow, bad times are coming for people like us. Winter is never good for us poor. Hope to heaven, it won't last too long this year."

And we walked on. I was very confused. I never before had heard my father speak with the caretaker. I asked him: "Why did you speak with the caretaker?"

"Why should I not?" my father responded. "I have known him for a long time. He has given me good advice about my roses in the gar-den. He is an excellent gardener and knows his flowers. You can learn a lot from him."

That remark of my father's perplexed me. He, the doctor, learned from the street sweeper? I couldn't get rid of that thought for quite some time. Eventually, of course, it faded from memory. It never, however, gave me courage enough to speak to the caretaker on my own, even though I saw him many times thereafter. I didn't know why. I would have found it hard to do, though it did not seem hard for my father.

My father never used many words. When, that fall day, he talked to the caretaker and saw my astonishment he waited until I asked why he spoke with him. He knew I would not understand his answer, not then, anyway. He also knew that I would find it hard to believe. It would not have made a difference if he had said more and spoken at greater length. My father knew that for a boy of six, social class was a mysterious, vaguely threatening, though very real presence. It created a gulf, a gulf that I found hard to cross. It kept people at a distance from each other, made them eye each other with suspicion. In the presence of people I did not know it made me cautious and more than usually quiet and silent. I doubt that any further words of my father would have changed that.

It was different with my father. He talked with everybody. He was an exception in many ways. He was different from our neighbors and friends, different even from me. He was a better person. Everything seemed simple when he saw and described it. Everything seemed natural when he dealt with it.

I remember years later, when the war was in its fourth or fifth year, I visited the Frobarts, who by then had moved out of the farm house in the city and now lived, as we once did, on the Jahnstraße in an apartment at the edge of town. Again, Mr. Frobart lay on the couch and listened and did not say a word. But Mrs. Frobart anxiously inquired about my father. "That wonderful man, that dear man," she said. "Oh, I hope nothing will happen to him and he will come back safe and unhurt when this dreadful war is over. Your mother misses him so much. I am sure, you do too, and I do.

"There are so few like him," she added after a little pause, and tears glistened in her eyes. Wherever I went and met people who knew my father, I found they spoke of him much like Mrs. Frobart did.

As I became older and my father was no longer present to guide or advise me, I encountered social class in different ways. When, at age nine, I left the school on the Karlstraße to attend the *Große Schule,* a state-run fee-demanding Latin high school or *Gymnasium,* social class met me on my way to and from school. When, on weekends, my mother sent me on errands, I found myself beset by threats of ambush from the working-class rough-necks of Wolfenbüttel's Old Town. When, having turned ten and become a *Pimpf,* a member of the *Jungvolk,* I learned that, far from overcoming and eradicating class differences—a goal the Nazis claimed to pursue—the Nazi youth organization nurtured and sharpened them. I learned, too, that class differences were present when I became interested in girls. I found out that it was risky to explore boy–girl relationships that crossed class lines.

In 1937, the year I left the *Karlschule*, the *Große Schule* selected about one in ten of all the boys in the common schools of Wolfenbüttel and surrounding villages. Those of us whose parents had applied for our admission to the *Große Schule* had to sit for a written examination to see whether we would meet the entrance criteria. There were no girls among us because the *Große Schule* was an all-boys school. Girls whose parents desired a secondary education for them had to apply to the *Lyceum*, the girls' secondary school that, together with a municipal high school for boys, was quartered in the *Schloß*, the palatial former residence of the dukes of Wolfenbüttel–Lüneburg.

My classmates in the *Große Schule* were the sons of middle-class professional, merchant, and farming families. I no longer saw my little long-haired ruffian friends from grade school whose lollipops I had shared and with whom I had rolled in the grass. But on my daily walks to and from the *Große Schule* I ran into other boys of the city's working classes who had already entered upon their apprenticeships and attended a part-time vocational continuation school. They took special delight in ambushing secondary school boys like myself with barrages of rotten apples and tomatoes and in chasing us out of what they considered "their" neighborhoods. In their eyes boys like myself were conceited, pampered "sissies" whose lives they had sworn to make as miserable as they could.

I fought a daily battle with myself whether to try to evade or to meet their challenge. It was a matter of which route to take to school. I could avoid most of the unpleasantness by walking through the center of town across the marketplace and along the Lange Herzogstraße. But I hated myself for thus cowardly evading my antagonists and leaving to them uncontested "their streets"—the *Krambuden* (dry goods stalls) and the *Große* and the *Kleine Zimmerhof* (Great and Little Carpenters' Yard). Such an easy way out did not square with my boy's sense of honor. I finally decided on an irregular schedule, going across the marketplace one day and through the *Krambuden* the next. This, I tried to persuade myself, was a clever way of throwing my pursuers off my track.

It did not always work, however. I vividly remember one warm, sunny May morning when I was caught by one of my opponents just a few steps away from my doorstep. As it would happen, that encounter also turned into one of my few great triumphs in that battle. I had just stepped out of the garden gate and was walking along the Harztorwall, which lacked sidewalks but was bordered by a row of lilac bushes on the left whose first light purple flowers had just begun to peek through the fresh green leaves. I noticed the bakery delivery boy approaching on his bicycle. He carried a huge basket strapped to his back full of *Brötchen*, the hard rolls, baked fresh every morning, that we used to eat for breakfast with jam, sausage, or cheese. The boy, too, was caught up by the beauty of the spring morning, whistling as he pedaled along. When he saw me he broke into a broad grin, stepped full force on his pedals and aimed straight at me, shouting gleefully: "Step aside, high-school sissy!"

Here was my chance, I thought. The boy must have forgotten the encumbering basket on his back, and I was determined to make the most of the opportunity. I held my hands out ready to grab his handlebars and shouted back at him: "Come on, come on, if you dare."

He came on, and then stepped sharply on his coaster brake. But it was too late. I had already grabbed the bars, twisted them around, gotten a whiff of that heavenly smell of freshly baked bread, and with all my might pushed the bike and the boy with the basket into the lilacs. Hard rolls flew all over the bushes, and the boy could not get back on his feet with the cycle and the basket weighing him down. I laughed and shouted at him: "Try it again, next time, if you will," and continued jauntily on my way to school, the sweet smell of lilac and fresh *Brötchen* wafting after me.

During vacations when I did not have to worry about going to school but had to run errands for my mother into my persecutors' part of town, the battle with the working-class boys took other forms. Our butcher, grocer, baker, and cobbler all had their stores in the low-ceilinged and dark houses on the crooked and narrow streets of Wolfenbüttel's Old Town. The butcher shop on the Kleine Kirchstraße, which passed in front of St. Mary's, was an exception. Through its great plate-glass windows the sunshine would pour onto the clean scrubbed wooden tables inside. Dozens of sausages hung on hooks from a bar fastened to the ceiling, and behind the counter stood metal tubs of hamburger meat and later, after the war shortages had begun, of undefinable and strange-smelling meat substitutes. I liked it in that shop, and especially so when Mrs. Goewecke, the butcher's wife, would cut me a slice of spicy sausage. "Just to try it once," she would say and smile, "and you'll come for more." But, of course, that also stopped as the war went on.

The grocery store on the *Harzstraße* was less attractive with its round, dirty, splintery wooden baskets of potatoes, cabbages, brussel sprouts, turnips, and other vegetables, some of which were half-rotten and all of which had clumps of mud clinging to them. In good weather the baskets were piled in no particular order outside on the sidewalk. When winter came or when it rained, they were arranged inside the plate-glass window in which, as the years went by and the occasional bombing raids increased in frequency, larger and larger sections were replaced by chunks of plywood. Fresh supplies would be brought in at any time of day and promptly sold out. If there weren't any carrots available at noon time, they might well be back by three o'clock, and I would have to rush over there for a second time.

The bakery was a most intriguing place because it had two entrances. One, the front door, opened to the Krumme Straße, which wound its way through the Old Town; the other led in the opposite direction through a long, dark, and narrow passage past the baking ovens to a glass door that connected to a garden path that, in turn, permitted access to the Harztorwall. I found the bakery intriguing because, by giving me a choice of exits, it more than once allowed me to escape being waylaid by the boys of the Krumme Straße.

But the place I liked best was the shoe repair shop on the Mauren Straße, the Bricklayers' Street. It was quite small, low, and dingy with a cast-iron, pot-bellied stove in the corner, a gas flame always burning on the work table in front of Mr. Reinhardt, the master, who would heat and melt his wax there to polish the shoes he cobbled. There were always scores of boots, shoes, galoshes, and leather satchels lying around in great profusion on the floor, and I could never figure out how Master Reinhardt could unerringly pull the right pair of shoes out of the pile when asked to do so.

Master Reinhardt was a talkative fellow who, to me, had always looked to be nearly seventy years old, although I am sure now he was no more than forty. In his back room, which I never saw, he raised canaries. When I turned ten, my parents presented me with "Strolch" as my very own bird to care for. "Strolch" lived to be six years old, and, as my mother told me when I came home from the war, had been evacuated back to Master Reinhardt's rookery the day American troops entered Wolfenbüttel. Master Reinhardt found him there the day after, lying dead on the floor of his cage. He was a very patriotic bird, Master Reinhardt had said to my mother.

I felt no particular antipathy toward or strangeness in dealing with the adult merchants and people of the working-class districts of the town. Quite the contrary, once I had gotten to know them, except for the grocer and his wife, who struck me as perpetually gloomy and frowning, I liked to talk with all of them, and I enjoyed the homey atmosphere of their surroundings. Perhaps it was the smells—the enticing aroma of fresh liver sausage in the butcher shop; the appetizing fragance of *Zuckerkuchen*, a local speciality sugar cake, in the bakery;

and the scent of leather and hot wax at Master Reinhardt's—that attracted me. But above all it was the people's friendliness and their fond respect and interest with which they always asked about my father and inquired about my mother's health that made me willing to face the gauntlet of the neighborhood boys. They all gave me a sense of being welcome because of the warm feelings they held toward my parents.

But there always remained my awareness of the gulf that separated the boys of the Old Town from me and my friends in the *Große Schule*. When I appeared in the Old Town, doing errands for my mother, I had to think of ways of outfoxing my adversaries, the two entries to the bakery being only one of them. There were other houses with hidden passages, and there were secret gardens that connected several buildings and could not be seen from the street. I always had the choice of sneaking through one of these labyrinths or of taking my bicycle on the streets and using speed as my means of escape. Yet to rely on my bike brought its own problems. More than once, when coming back to where I had parked and locked it, I would find the air let out of the tires or, even worse, the tires slit or punctured. Though I experienced nothing but kindness and support from the working class and small merchant adults of the city, social class antagonism and animosities were a reality for me and ever present in my dealings with working-class youths.

What in retrospect might seem an astonishing paradox, but what was in fact no more than a reflection of the town's social structure and the natural outgrowth of ingrained class-consciousness, was the fact that in Wolfenbüttel the Nazi youth organizations, despite their official commitment to a classless and racially homogeneous society, came to serve as perhaps the strongest factor in confirming and strengthening social class divisions among youth. They did this by paralleling, and thus reinforcing, the city's school structure.

Beginning in 1937, all the city's ten- to thirteen-year-old boys and girls were required to join the *Jungvolk* or the *Jungmädel* where they would meet every Wednesday and Saturday afternoon for their activities. In like fashion, the fourteen- to eighteen-year-olds had to enlist in the *Hitler Jugend* and the *Bund Deutscher Mädchen* whose units usually met at night after working hours. When youngsters approached the age of fourteen, they had the option to move up into the *Hitler Jugend* or *Bund Deutscher Mädchen* or to stay with the *Jungvolk* or *Jungmädel* as leaders of the younger ones. This was particularly attractive for high school students who were loath to be ordered to night-time activities and who were free of school duties in the afternoon and thus could meet with the *Jungvolk or Jungmädel*.

When my classmates and I approached the age of transition from

Jungvolk to *Hitler Jugend* our teachers and parents encouraged us to volunteer for leadership positions in the *Jungvolk* in order to have a better chance of being exempted from promotion to the *Hitler Jugend*. They preferred, as they put it, to have "responsible youngsters," that is, *Gymnasium* boys and *Lyceum* girls, as leaders of the young ones. Good middle-class teachers and parents that they were, they looked with fear and horror on the prospect of having their children led and supervised by male or female working-class apprentices and journeymen. But if we high school students were leaders of the *Jungvolk*, they believed their children were in safe hands.

And thus it happened that I and many of my high school friends stayed with the *Jungvolk* instead of moving up to the *Hitler Jugend*. I felt rather ambivalent about the whole matter. During my first two or three years in the *Jungvolk* I found little that I liked about it. I hated the hours we spent in the municipal gymnasium on rainy days and in the winter. We were made to climb ropes and ladders, swing from rings under the ceiling, struggle over double and single bars, jump and tumble along an obstacle course, and line up for boxing and wrestling matches. On winter days when it fell dark outside early and we finally emerged from the cavernous gym, I was tired, often bloodied, exhausted, and reeking of sweat.

It was better during warm and sunny weather when we marched to the city athletic fields where we played soccer and competed with each other in the sixty-meter dash and broad and high jump. We learned to throw wooden clubs that bore a resemblance to hand grenades and we marched into the countryside where we were taught how to camouflage ourselves with bunches of grass and twigs, to estimate distances, to read maps, use the compass, follow animal and human tracks, build fires, erect and safeguard tents against windstorms and water, and in every way possible to prepare ourselves for military service.

When we weren't exhorted to show our athletic prowess or learn how to act as soldiers we gathered in one of the city's school buildings for what was called a *Heimabend*, an evening at home. Despite the name these meetings took place neither in the evening nor in any one's home. We listened to our leaders telling us over and over again of the history of the Nazi party, of the exploits of its heroes, young men like Horst Wessel and Baldur von Schirach, and asking us to memorize the life of Adolf Hitler. There were readings from *Mein Kampf*, and we viewed rows of pictures showing the heads and bodies of men and women who were supposedly representatives of various racial groups. We soon learned that the blond, tall, slender, and straight figures were the Nordic, Aryan types that we all were supposed to be. The dark, small, thick, and bent bodies, on the other hand, belonged to undesirable and *minderwertige,* that is, less worthy, races. We should look down on them as inferior beings.

I never was a good athlete. I hated the sessions in the gym and liked only slightly better the exercises on the sports field. I also thought that my father had shown me already how to behave as a soldier out in the open country, and he had taught me better than the *Jungvolk* leaders could. Except for the group singing we practiced, the *Heimabende* were dreadfully boring affairs. So I begged my mother to write excuse slips for me to stay away from the twice weekly meetings as often as she possibly could without calling undue attention to my delinquency.

When the question arose of whether I would move on to the *Hitler Jugend* or stay with the *Jungvolk* I was faced with what I thought were rather unpleasant alternatives either way. But I received unexpected help from some of my classmates in the *Große Schule.* They, being a year older than I, had already made their decision and had stayed with the *Jungvolk.* They now persuaded me to do likewise. They also helped to make my decision easier by seeing to it that, right after my thirteenth birthday, I received, much to my surprise, a promotion to the rank of *Jungenschaftsführer,* a position as leader of a group of ten newly admitted ten-year-olds. My main duty was to visit them and their parents in their homes during the week to make sure they would appear at the next Wednesday or Saturday meeting. But it also included an assignment to drill them in the fundamentals of marching in step and moving in formation and of learning to stand at attention, turn right, turn left, and about-face. I discovered that I actually liked that. It made me feel like the officer I wanted to be, standing in front of the boys and shouting commands at them. When I told my mother how I felt about that, she pointed out that if I were to move up to the Hitler Youth, instead of commanding my *Jungvolk* boys, I would stand in the ranks and be ordered about. Besides, I knew, it would be the older boys from the Krumme Straße and the Zimmerhof who would do the ordering.

Thus I decided to stay with the *Jungvolk,* and in the following years I became an enthusiastic leader and soon advanced to higher ranks. I counted myself lucky to have escaped what I expected would have become an unending series of hazings and persecutions at the hands of the *Hitler Jugend* working-class leaders. In the *Jungvolk* I was among my own. I enjoyed the approbation of my teachers and parents, and I felt myself becoming a soldier and an officer. My *Jungvolk* leadership position did nothing to lessen my middle-class consciousness.

Boy–girl relationships, too, were conditioned and limited by my awareness of social class. It affected my feelings toward and relations with girls. Here my earliest recollections go back to my days in the kindergarten when, as I already described, we well-scrubbed and neatly dressed four- and five-year-olds took an hour or more for our walk home from school. My best friend on these long and often circuitous rambles through fields, orchards, and vegetable gardens was Ursel. Ursel lived around the corner from our house on the Kleine Breite, and it was she whom I tried to impress with my raids on the plum and apple trees. And as she was determined not to be outdone by me, our combined yield of juicy plums and tart apples was more than we could possibly eat. No wonder that our neighbors complained and my parents all too quickly discovered why I had hardly any appetite when I showed up for our midday meal.

When this happened for the third or fourth time my father decided to act. I received my first thrashing at his hand. As much as I felt hurt in my dignity, that pain was nothing compared to the sense of injustice that overcame me when I heard subsequently that my punishment had become public knowledge. It being summer time and all the windows were open, Ursel had witnessed my wailing and crying. To add insult to injury, she told me the next day, with a very superior look in her eyes, that, as a girl, she of course had not been paddled. Girls were a nuisance, I concluded from that, and best to be ignored. I was going to continue walking home with Ursel, but I wasn't going to pay her much attention. She was a girl, after all, only a girl.

When my interest in girls was reawakened in my early teens, I saw them fall into two distinct categories corresponding to the divisions I was familiar with from the world of boys. There were the *Lyceum* girls, who also were the leaders of the *Jungmädel,* and there were the working-class girls who held jobs, went to continuation school, and attended the meetings of the *Bund Deutscher Mädchen.* We waited for the *Lyceum* girls after school and after the Wednesday and Saturday afternoon meetings of the *Jungvolk.* We boys would line up on one side of the Lange Herzogstraße—the Lange as we called it—and the girls would come walking along on the other. We would comment among ourselves about the qualities, both physical and mental, of the ones passing by. In our remarks we implied with more or less directness how intimately we knew all these girls from personal experience, though, as I compared what I heard against my own knowledge or, rather, ignorance, I either felt envious or suspected that all I heard was wishful thinking on the part of my comrades. At times I would screw up my courage—especially when my friends had goaded me and said I would never do it—to go across the street and ask one of the girls whether she would mind if I walked home with her. Sometimes the answer was no; but more often it was yes. It wasn't until I reached fifteen that I began a longer lasting, "steady" relationship with Ulla, one of the *Lyceum* girls.

I never got to know any of the working-class girls, and in the stories that we boys told about them they were made to appear as willing and available sex partners. They could be "had," my older classmates assured me, and they told lurid stories about fondling them after dark on a street corner or taking them to a park bench or a grassy clearing in the Lechlum Woods. I never knew whether these stories were true or made-up, but they did encourage me once to try to fondle a girl I had encountered in a side street off the Lange. She appeared willing to talk to me and walk with me, but when I grabbed for her she called me a pig and a pervert and said she would have her boy friends come and let me have it. That made me forget all about the working-class girls and their supposed availability. From then on I decided to stick to my own kind. I was, after all, a proper middle-class boy.

3

Wolfenbüttel's *Große Schule*

IN THE SPRING OF 1937 my parents removed me from the *Karlschule* and placed me as a "three-year boy" into the *Sexta* of the *Große Schule*.[1] There were three of us "three-year boys" in this beginning class of some thirty or so regular pupils who had spent four, instead of only three years, in one of the primary schools in Wolfenbüttel or one of the surrounding villages. After much advice-seeking and soul-searching my parents had concluded that, despite the excellent efforts of Mr. Heine, my time in the *Volksschule* was wasted. I now knew how to read and write, had a good grasp of elementary arithmetic, and was ready for more challenging material like beginning mathematics and English. Latin would be added two years later in the *Quarta*, physics a year thereafter in the *Tertia*, chemistry in the *Untersekunda*, the Lower Second, and French in the *Obersekunda*, the Upper Second. In the *Volksschule*, my parents said, I had begun to lose interest and incentive to do well in my studies. Thus, despite their misgivings that my young age might not find me socially and emotionally prepared to keep up with the ten-year-olds, they decided that it was best for me to continue my education among the boys of the *Staatliche Große Schule, Oberschule für Jungen*. I was to remain in that school until its war-conditioned closure at the end of my seventh year abruptly terminated my high school education in the summer of 1944.

My parents' initial misgivings were justified to the extent that throughout my first few years in that school I was never allowed to forget that I was a "three-year boy." My predicament, however, had little

---

1. The *Gymnasium* called its lowest grade the sixth, the *Sexta*, and then counted upwards to finish with the *Prima*, the first grade. As both *Sekunda* and *Prima* were again divided into a lower and an upper *Sekunda* and *Prima*, the *Gymnasium* of the Third Reich had eight grades altogether.

to do with my own shortcomings and malfeasances that, my teachers testified, consisted of my "inclination to be talkative and of classroom behavior that left something to be desired." My predicament instead derived from the quite apparent expectation of Mr. Berger, my English teacher, that we "three-year boys" could not possibly be as capable as the "four-year boys," an expectation gleefully underscored at every possible occasion by my older classmates.

In German schools it was the practice that, except for attending instruction in music, physics, chemistry, workshop, and physical education, each grade stayed in a classroom of its own for all its lessons. The teachers had their own lounge and conference room from which they would emerge every hour to be with us and to which they then would retreat for the intermission periods. When my lesson plan called for English instruction my stomach was all in knots as I looked toward the appearance of Mr. Berger with a mixture of fear and disdain. His English classes began with us having to transcribe sentences from the German *Sütterlin* script to Latin letters. What infuriated me was Mr. Berger's order that we "three-year boys" had to carry out this exercise three times for every one time required of the "four-year boys." In the absence of any failure on our part to produce the desired letters correctly and legibly I saw no justification for such an imposition. I did not know then what I do know now; that is, that at that time German *Gymnasium* teachers received little, if any, psychological and pedagogical training. They were subject specialists, very well prepared in their academic fields, but often inept as disciplinarians and instructors of little boys. Mr. Berger was a case in point. But there was little I could do to make him change his mind, and I suffered in silence.

This injustice toward us "three-year boys" was not the worst of Mr. Berger's failings. His reliance on flogging during our first three years marked him as a veritable tyrant, ever ready to vent his anger with his cane on our backs. Though we only dimly recognized it then, there was an element of sexual perversion to the beatings. Our classroom was arranged with two columns of desks, grouped into two- or three-seaters. As we soon noticed, Mr. Berger's anger was aroused most frequently by boys sitting on the three-seat benches. Invariably he would run, his cane held high above him, to the opposite outside seat of the three-seat bench, throw himself on the pupil next to him, his abdomen coming to rest on the boy's head, reaching with his right arm across the pupil in the middle, and beating down on the fellow at the other end. However ineffective and haphazard such long-distance application of the rod was compared with the normal way of caning the culprit in front of the class, Mr. Berger obviously preferred it. Fortunately for me, I was seated on one of the two-seat desks and thus escaped both the beating and the panting and thrusting of Mr. Berger's sweat-soaked, sour smelling body.

But I was terrified, nonetheless. In the lower grades caning and other forms of physical punishment were permitted parts of class-room procedures, though sparingly used. Mr. Berger kept a cane in a locked wooden wardrobe that stood in the corner of the classroom. We, of course, tried our best to sabotage the use of the wardrobe by sticking wads of paper or clay into the lock or by nailing shut its door. But it did not help us much. Mr. Berger would order the custodian to come and open the wardrobe so he could threaten us again with his stick. Once we "borrowed" from the custodian's office the key to the wardrobe and made a clay impression. In due time, we found a will-ing locksmith who created a duplicate key. We quickly "liberated" the caning stick and, with the help of a razor blade, saw to it that it would splinter and break when used next. And break it did in Mr. Berger's hands as he swung it above his head, even before it had gotten close to his next intended victim. Mr. Berger swore he would find and revenge himself on the perpetrators of this dastardly deed and promised he would be back next time with an even heavier stick. And so he was, and we could look forward to further beatings.

Most other teachers disdained the use of the cane and, if they relied on physical punishment at all, used a wooden ruler instead. But even then the ruler served more as a potential threat than as an actual in-strument of control. Mr. Warneke, our Latin teacher, sometimes asked us to stretch out our hands and, declaring that he was going to "help us memorize," struck one of my classmates on his upturned palms with his ruler. It was a playful whack, most of the time, to which the victim responded with exaggerated moans and cries for mercy. When it looked as though Mr. Warneke would repeat the blow, we all, as if on command, recited loudly and in unison the little verses we had learned from our grammar book:

> *Hic, haec, hoc,*
> *der Lehrer hat'n Stock,*
> *huius, huius, huius,*
> *so lernt's der kleine Julius.*[2]

We probably didn't realize it then, but Mr. Warneke managed to serve up a mixture of instruction and discipline diffused with humor that

2. *Hic, haec, hoc,*
the teacher carries a stick;
huius, huius, huius,
so learns the little Julius.

proved extremely effective. We were lucky that his style of teaching was far more representative for the *Große Schule* than Mr. Berger's.

Still, I can remember painful and humiliating experiences. Our geography teacher, Mr. Kühnhold, ordered me to sit in the first row of the class because I talked too much in my seat in the back. I followed his order whenever he was to appear for his lessons in our classroom. At all other times, however, I remained in my original seat in the back. I had not counted on our teachers talking about us in their lounge, but they did. As a result, when Mr. Kühnhold next appeared in our class, he went straight to me, sitting in my front row seat, and, without warning or saying a word, delivered a stinging slap to my face. He turned to the class and said, "That will teach him," and proceeded to begin his lesson.

I was deeply hurt in more than just a physical way, and felt helpless because I also believed I had only myself to blame for the humiliation I had suffered. It never then occurred to me to think such punishment unusual, unjust, harsh, or illegal. For all I knew it had been that way as long as there had been teachers and pupils. Those in authority would have their way and mete out their punishments as they saw fit. Besides, I had been disobedient. So I never told my parents about it either. I knew I would not have gained a sympathetic hearing. Do as you are told, they would have said, and you will not be punished. As for Mr. Berger's triple assignment, that was not a punishment, they would have said; that was a way of making sure I learned my lessons well.

Mr. Berger's caning and Mr. Kühnhold's slap were reserved strictly for us pupils in the lower grades. Once we moved up into the *Oberstufe*, the upper tier, leaving behind the first four grades, and at age fourteen entered the *Untersekunda*, we were expected to behave like young gentlemen and were treated as such. Disciplinary matters such as insubordination and student rebellions were handled in a much more formal manner with investigations and inquiries before the faculty. Minor disturbances, lack of attention in the classroom, and negligence with homework were dispensed with through teacher–student conferences, letters to parents, and the twice-annual grade reports. Reprimands were noted in the class book, a record of daily lessons, kept in the teacher's desk and compiled by each teacher before he left the classroom.

All through our early years we *Sextaner* and *Quintaner* were told by the upper classmen that Mr. Berger was a martinet only with us little boys; that he was far too much of a coward to behave like that among the upper grades; that he would give up his cane as early as the *Tertia*. His lecherousness, however, would remain and take other forms. By the time we reached the *Tertia* we found that out for ourselves, and

Mr. Berger became the object of our contempt and ridicule. He had to be afraid of our exposing him, and he thus became the most ineffectual teacher we had, easily manipulated by us for favors and coverups of scholastic misdeeds. That did not stop him, though, from pursuing his sexual desires in ways other than beating us, and we exploited his weakness to the fullest.

Mr. Berger used to bring to class copies of the English-language version of the German Air Force magazine, *Der Adler,* and have us orally translate its contents into German. He would sit before us at his desk, the *Adler* held high in front of him, and in five-minute intervals would call out one of our names: "Go on, Müller, translate." He did not know that we had long since discovered that inside his copy of *Der Adler* he had hidden the latest girlie magazines. These he perused with great delight, oblivious that we, supposedly translating from the *Adler,* now invented the most extravagant stories of dinosaurs and elephants fighting air battles over London and issued edicts of the Reichsluftfahrtministerium—the National Ministry of the Air Force—that declared never-ending vacations for schoolboys everywhere.

Mr. Berger, it should be said, was the only teacher of his kind among the original faculty that had greeted us at the beginning of my high school career. But when by the fall of 1939 the war began and many of our teachers were called to arms, more of Berger's kind appeared in our classes. Some of them were of questionable character and others academically and pedagogically incompetent.

One of the latter was the mathematician Mr. Schulz, whose only qualification for teaching, we could discern, was the high rank he held in the party's labor force auxiliary, a position that kept him out of the army and safely at home. I found it exceedingly ironic that in his algebra classes I consistently earned "1"s, the German equivalent of the American "A," but also knew that I had not the faintest idea of what I was doing. It was enough for Mr. Schulz that, with the help of an open-book collection of mathematical formulas, we replaced symbols with numbers and then figured out the results. I thought I had learned that already in the *Sexta.*

In physical education the story was similar. This was even more inexplicable because the *Große Schule* could look back on a century-old tradition of uniqueness and excellence in gymnastics, a tradition I shall describe further below. But our wartime physical education teacher was untrained to coach any sport or instruct in any athletic exercise. His fields of expertise were geography and history, and, as far as sports were concerned, his imagination was limited to four kinds of activities. When it rained he let us loose in the gymnasium to do as we pleased. In good weather he lined us up on the school yard, divided us into three groups, and barked: "The first half plays soccer, the second does the broad jump, and the third goes out on the sidewalk for the sixty-meter dash." He then retired to the corner of the yard, leaned against a tree, lit his pipe and daydreamed or read a book. "Sweet dreams, third half," we said to ourselves, and, after the first five minutes of pretending to pursue our various activities, we all wound up with the soccer players.

Still, nothing should obscure the fact that throughout my first two years, from Easter of 1937 to the summer of 1939, the *Große Schule* exerted a formidable shaping influence on us boys. This influence, mainly unbeknownst to us, counteracted the official Nazi doctrines with which we were increasingly bombarded in the newspapers, the movies, and the Nazi youth organizations. Founded as a Latin school during the Reformation and given its first curricular instructions by the Wittenberg theologian Johann Bugenhagen, a colleague of the famed *praeceptor Germaniae,* Martin Luther's collaborator Philipp Melanchthon, the *Große Schule* looked back on a four-hundred-year history as a *gymnasium illustre.*[3] The spirit of humanism and Protestant Christianity pervaded its classrooms and hallways and did so when I entered the school in 1937. Pictures, busts, and Bible verses adorned the hallways and the walls of the *Aula,* the school's auditorium. The words of our teachers in literature, history, and religion reminded us daily of the heritage of the Greco–Roman world, the German classics, and of the works and teachings of Wolfenbüttel's very own literary threesome: Gotthold Ephraim Lessing, Wilhelm Raabe, and Wilhelm Busch. We visited the Duke August Library and the *Lessing Haus* that stood in its shadow. We read most of Raabe's novels and short stories, and we did not need much encouragement to pore over Busch's drawings and poems of Max and Moritz. We were steeped in literary tradition.

But our legacy was athletic as well as intellectual. When I entered in 1937 the school was home to what was arguably Germany's oldest independent physical education society. Founded in 1828, the student-run *Gymnasial Turn Gemeinde* chose "God, Liberty, Fatherland, Honor" as its motto and adopted the republican colors of black, red, and gold for its flag. Supported in its autonomy by the faculty the society watched over the physical education and the behavioral discipline of the student body. The society's student-elected monitors carried supervisory powers over all students, shared the administration of the school's physical education curriculum with the faculty, and were re-

---

3. For a history of the school, see the exhibition catalogue by Johannes Tütken, *Glaubenslehre, Bildung, Qualifikation: 450 Jahre Große Schule in Wolfenbüttel—Ein Beitrag zur Geschichte des evangelischen Gymnasiums in Norddeutschland* (Berlin: Akademie Verlag, 1993).

sponsible for many of the school's social events. They made sure that the school's Latin motto, *mens sana in corpore sano*—a healthy mind in a healthy body—was observed in action as much as in words.

For us *Sextaner* and *Quintaner* the annual *Assefahrt* in 1937 and 1938 was the most exciting and memorable extracurricular event sponsored by the *Turngemeinde*. The entire student body, dressed in uniforms of white pants, blue jackets, and grade-specific colored caps, assembled in the school yard. Preceded by the school's fife and drum corps, we then marched out on the Rosenwall, part of the green belt that surrounded the city, turned through a few smaller streets onto the Lange Herzogstraße where people had lined up to see the parade, and continued over country roads to the Asse, a low mountain range ten miles away. There we participated in athletic contests and ate mounds of *Zuckerkuchen* and strawberries with whipped cream. To those of the *Sextaner* who declined the proferred bus ride back to town and instead volunteered to march back at night with the older boys, the school's principal, Oberstudiendirektor Hermann Lampe, presented a chocolate eclair the next morning in class.

While the faculty viewed the *Gymnasial Turn Gemeinde* as an excellent vehicle for fostering self-discipline and responsibility among the students and did its best to support and uphold its authority, the Nazi-directed school administration of the state of Braunschweig regarded it as a thorn in its side. The society's democratic traditions obviously did not sit well with either the party or the *Hitler Jugend*. The Braunschweig ministry pressured the student leaders to hand over the society to the *Hitler Jugend* and to subject it to supervision and direction by the party. The students, however, refused to comply. They delivered neither flag nor documents and membership lists and rather preferred that the society ceased to function. The *Turngemeinde* survived in this inactive status for another three years until it was formally dissolved in 1941 by Mr. Hogrebe, the school's then Nazi-appointed *Rektor* who had moved into Mr. Lampe's office.

The leadership of the Hitler Youth had achieved its goal: After 1938 there was no longer any *Assefahrt* and no longer did the student body of the *Große Schule* parade through town in its school uniforms. Our blue coats and white trousers were mothballed in the school's attic, and alumni saw to it that the society's papers and memorabilia were safely stored. Our physical education classes came nearly to a standstill and took the shape of the "third-half" soccer games I already described. When the *Turngemeinde* was officially laid to rest in 1941 we *Tertianer* never even heard about it.

The dissolution of the *Turngemeinde* and the abolition of the *Assefahrt*, however, were but two steps in the gradual subjection of the

Große Schule to the dictates of the Nazi education authorities. To me they were the most visible. The others had begun earlier before I even had been admitted to the school. Once I attended, I heard of them only in whispers and as rumors, never in their full details. They all centered around our director, Hermann Lampe.

Oberstudiendirektor Lampe, as he was officially called—and I do not know anybody who ever called him anything else—became for us the unforgettable model of a man who, in every fiber of his being, lived and stood by the ideals the school represented. He was a Latin school teacher of the old type. Thoroughly trained in the classics, a gentleman of incorruptible honesty and moral rectitude, he stayed in his post until he was forced to leave. I never had him as a classroom teacher, but I remember him as he walked through the foyer, stepping out of his office next to the school's entrance door, always in a dark gray suit with a gold watch chain across his vest, dark horn-rimmed glasses halfway down his nose, his black hair combed back and parted in the middle, and then disappearing in the teachers' lounge. His very rectitude compelled him as a civil servant, bound by his oath of office, to enforce the directives of the Braunschweig education ministry to limit the admission of Jewish pupils. But he sought and found ways to keep the boys attending the *Große Schule* until the last of them left when his parents emigrated to Palestine in the spring of 1934.

Lampe's final battle with the education ministry took place in 1938, my second year of attendance, and the year of the last *Assefahrt*. The little I learned of what went on I picked up from overheard bits of conversations at home and at school. At the center of the dispute stood my first-year religion teacher, Ernst August Wille. "Parson" Wille, as we called him, reminded me a bit of my grandfather Felix. He stood tall and straight as an arrow, sported closely cropped hair, and possessed a sonorous voice that, rolling down from a pulpit over his listeners, could easily have filled any church, no matter how big and how high. He presented to us a commanding figure. I used to think of him as one of the prophets of old as they must have looked in their youth.

Parson Wille taught us Protestant students—our few Catholic classmates were excused from attending his instruction—our catechism and hymnal and assured us that, even if we couldn't understand it now, we would soon find ourselves in times in which we would derive comfort and strength from the hymns he had us memorize. How right he turned out to be! In the years that followed when the bombs fell on Wolfenbüttel or the mortar shells exploded around me in the marshes and dugouts of the war's final battles, or when, after the shooting had ceased, the revelations of horror in the concentration camps shook our belief in ourselves and our nation, I would think back to Parson Wille's

55

class and our thunderous singing of words that were meant to assure us that, after all and despite it all, this was still God's world and we were still God's children:

> *Großer Gott, wir loben Dich;*
> *Herr, wir preisen Deine Stärke.*
> *Vor Dir neigt die Erde sich*
> *und bewundert Deine Werke.*
> *Wie Du warst vor aller Zeit,*
> *so bist Du in Ewigkeit.*[4]

Or, then in war and today in peace, when after nights of thunder and fire the sun rises again on a beautiful morning, and I walk along with a lift in my stride, I can hear Parson Wille's tenor lead us in

> *Die güldne Sonne, voll Freud und Wonne,*
> *bringt unseren Grenzen*
> *mit ihrem Glänzen*
> *ein herzerfrischendes, liebliches Licht.*
> *Mein Haupt und Glieder die lagen darnieder,*
> *aber nun steh ich,*
> *bin munter und fröhlich,*
> *schaue den Himmel mit meinem Gesicht.*[5]

Time has vindicated Parson Wille. His words and teaching proved their truth for us. But on one cold and rainy day in February of 1938, near the end of the school year, Parson Wille was gone; transferred, we were told, to a school in Braunschweig in exchange for another teacher who was said to be a loyal Nazi.

From rumors circulating through the school we learned the rea-

---

4.   Lord Almighty, we sing your praise
Lord Almighty, we praise your strength.
All the earth bends down her knees.
and admires your works.
As you have been before time began
So you shall be in eternity.

5.   The golden sun full of joy and gladness
brings to our limits
with its brilliance
a heart-warming, lovely light.
My head and my body were struck to the ground,
But now I stand upright,
am lively and happy,
Look at the sky with my eyes all aglow.

son for Wille's disappearance: in his teaching of the *Oberprima*, the graduating class, he had refused to present the doctrines of the Nazi-sponsored German Christians, and instead had taught Luther's catechism and scripture. In the eyes of the Braunschweig school ministry Wille had thus become a participant in religiously motivated insubordination against the regime. Thus he was removed and replaced with a Nazi. But when the new teacher appeared to take over religious instruction and turned it into presentations of *völkisch* ideology, about three-fourths of the graduating seniors left the lessons. Many in the lower grades followed their example. The school's classes in religion dwindled away.

The Nazis, who, soon after their seizure of power, had declared religion to be an elective, were hoisted on their own petard. To strike back, they ordered an investigation of the circumstances surrounding the developments in the graduating class, expelled a few students and barred them from attending any high school in the state of Braunschweig, and declared others to have been instigators and, when they were to take their final school leaving examination, subjected them to a special ideological test. In January of 1939 the Braunschweig education ministry then relieved Hermann Lampe from his post as director because he "had failed to prevent a church-instigated conspiracy." Lampe later said that it had been the mission of the school to shape character in its students that they might pass any and every test. "Such a test," he said, "our students have passed with high honors. The school can be proud of them."[6]

There were other teachers in those early years who remain unforgettable in my memory. One of them was my first homeroom teacher, Bodo Wacker. We called him "Mickey Mouse," because he was a little fellow with quick and darting movements and an ever present twinkle in his eyes. His most notable feature was a forehead that rose above his eyelids far up to the crown of his head with nary a hair on it. Way on top, a bush of black hair, combed to the rear and the right, appeared to just hang on, looking as though in perpetual danger of losing its hold and disappearing behind.

Wacker was a splendid raconteur. His fields were German and history. His lessons consisted of narrations of literary lives and plots, of historical events and dramas, all of them superbly told. We listened with rapt attention and fascination. There never was a student who fell asleep in his classes. He loved to regale us also with his stories of

6. For the passages dealing with the school's history I have relied heavily on Tütken, *Glaubenslehre, Bildung, Qualification,* and Kurt Selle, ed., *Festschrift 450 Jahre Große Schule Wolfenbüttel* (Wolfenbüttel: Heckners Verlag, 1993).

trench warfare in the Great War in which he, like my father, had been a soldier from the first to the last day.

I responded to his accounts with special interest and admiration because both he and my father then served as reserve officers in the Braunschweig infantry regiment. Wacker, like so many veterans of his generation, was a patriot, a Christian, and a believer in the German army and its traditions. He was willing to give the Nazis their chance, though he remained a skeptic when asked about their promises. At times, his skepticism would verge on cynicism, and he would not hesitate to let us know, not in so many quotable words, to be sure. Words were dangerous; they could be repeated and reach ears for which they were not meant. Wacker made his point through his gestures, his facial expressions, his hamming up his stories. Parody was his favorite means.

The prescribed way of beginning a class session in all schools of the Third Reich was for us students to rise from our seats when the teacher entered the classroom. The teacher then would walk to the front, face us, raise his right arm in the Nazi salute, and say, "Heil Hitler, boys," and we would reply, "Heil Hitler, Herr Studienrat," before we would sit down again.

Not so when Mickey Mouse Wacker was the teacher. All through his time with us during the first grade, he entered our classroom, walked to the wooden mapholder that stood in the front corner by the window, raised one of its arms until it pointed toward the ceiling, saluted it silently with his own raised arm, then turned to us, smiled and said: "Good Morning, boys, sit down." There was no German salute for us, no "Heil Hitler," in his classroom, and we knew exactly what risks he took. When I told my father about this, he just looked at me and said: "You will never tell this story to anybody." He did not have to tell me why not.

Then there was Mr. Pfaff, our mathematics teacher during my first two years. It was he who, when called to arms in 1939 like Bodo Wacker and my father, was then replaced by the high-ranking and thoroughly incompetent labor leader. Mr. Pfaff had a knack for making algebra and geometry comprehensible to ten- and eleven-year-olds. He split us up into competing teams and, as he would say, lubricated our little brains until they ran on over-drive, manipulating numbers and symbols. We did compete fiercely and spurred each other on to win the contest by solving the most problems in the shortest time. We worked with compass and circle and with the help of razor blades, construction paper, and glue sticks fabricated all sorts of more or less complicated cubes and spheres.

Mr. Pfaff had once been in America, and, when we had especially pleased him with our class work, would in the last five minutes tell us stories of that visit. He spoke of skyscrapers and elevators, movie palaces and subways that to us seemed inconceivable and, we thought, in all likelihood products of his fabulous imagination. We were most intrigued with his description of automats in the walls of buildings, machines that, he said, when prompted with a coin, would squirt Coca-Cola into a cup or place a frankfurter on a paper plate and then ask you whether or not you wanted mustard on top. We didn't really believe him but we loved his stories and always begged for more.

There were Nazi teachers, too, among the faculty of the *Große Schule,* members of the party and the SA, the brown-shirted "soldiers" of the party. One of our German teachers and our music teacher belonged among them. We knew that because they wore the party emblem on their coats, and we had seen them at rallies or May Day parades in their brown uniforms. They were good teachers, no better or worse than their non-party colleagues, and we liked their lessons. From Mr. Fuchtel, the German teacher, we heard a great deal of why the Nazi party was good for Germany, and we had little reason to doubt what he said. It was Mr. Fuchtel who gave me my first introduction to research when he asked me in the *Untersekunda* to write a report on what the acquisition of western Poland meant to the German Reich. He invited me to his study in his home and supplied me with mountains of *Schulungsbriefe*—Nazi Party Instruction Bulletins— in which I could find discussed every aspect of the question I was to investigate. I remember that I dutifully compiled all the information contained in these bulletins and that I received a "1" for my work. But I can no longer remember what it was that I had learned of the subject. I only recall that it seemed a trifle boring to me.

Mr. Adenstedt was our music teacher. He was best at teaching us harmony and rhythm. These were to me then rather abstract notions, but he managed to make them meaningful and interesting. He divided our class into four or five groups and put us through our paces humming "do," "re," and "mi" and singing rounds until the sound echoed back to us from the high-ceilinged *Aula* in which we met for his lessons. He would knock rhythms with his fingers on the top of the concert grand piano, and we were to identify the songs they represented. His favorite music, however, was hymns and songs of Nazi composers that celebrated Germany and exhorted us to be ever on guard and mindful of the country's many enemies. I liked the tunes, the words appealed to me as one of the fatherland's youthful defenders, and we all sang with great enthusiasm:

Deutschland, heiliges Wort, Du voll Unendlichleit,
über die Zeiten fort, seist Du gebenedeit,

and

Volk der Wälder, Volk der Berge, halte Wacht auf Deinen Höhn,
Völker gibt's und Feinde viele, die nach Deinem Reichtum sehn.[7]

I don't think it ever struck me as rather incongruous that while we sang these secular hymns, above us, high on the walls of the *Aula*, were emblazoned Biblical verses that recalled the school's past as a Protestant *Gymnasium:*

Die Furcht des Herrn ist der Weisheit Anfang,

and

Ihr Seid Christi—Christus aber ist Gottes.[8]

All I remember is that I liked the melodies, and that I thought Mr. Adenstedt's classes more interesting and pleasant than those of Mr. Berger or Mr. Schulz.

Not all of my memories of the *Große Schule* revolve around my teachers and lessons. We boys, after all, also created a world of our own in which teachers and adults generally appeared only as intruders. Our taste for fun and inclination to mischieviousness, no matter what the circumstances, were ever present and irrepressible. We played tricks on our teachers, placed imitation dog poop in their desk drawers, smeared glue on their chairs, paid an organ grinder to play outside our classroom window, and indulged in endlessly telling stories of our teachers' foibles and weaknesses.

There was our physics teacher, Mr. Wienbreyer, nicknamed "Uncle Ömme." Uncle Ömme, who in 1945 was to serve as the first postwar Rektor, was no admirer of the Nazis. We knew this because we watched him at every opening ceremony at the beginning of the school year. We all, students and teachers alike, had to line up in front of the school building. When Mr. Manselmann, our custodian, raised the flag

7. Germany, sacred word, you of infinity,
    throughout all times, thou shalt be blessed, and
    People of Woods, People of Mountains, stand guard on your heights;
    there are people and many enemies who long for your treasures.
8. The Fear of the Lord is the Beginning of Wisdom
    You are of Christ, and Christ is of God

on the mast, we sang the "Deutschland Lied" and the "Horst Wessel" song, all the while saluting with our right arms stretched into the air. Not so Mr. Wienbreyer. His face distorted in a grimace as though he suffered agonizing pain, he slowly raised his left arm, which he then, all throughout the ceremony, seemed barely able to keep up in the air. Someone once mentioned something about an old wound from the Great War. But nothing more was said about it. We boys never spoke about it either, not even amongst ourselves. I thought of what my father had said to me about Bodo Wacker's morning greeting. I assumed he would say the same about Mr. Wienbreyer's arm, if I had asked him. But I didn't. There was no need for that.

We called Mr. Wienbreyer Uncle Ömme because of his habit to open nearly every sentence with a rasp in his throat. So, when one day in the physics laboratory he had set up an arc lamp on his desk, aglow at full strength, he warned us: *"Ömme, this is a very dangerous instrument. Don't ever touch this carbon stick with your hand . . ."* While he talked he demonstrated just how, if one were careless, one might do that, and, as he continued to hold on with his right hand to the carbon, he said, *"and then, ömme, grasp this stick with your other . . ."* The rest of the demonstration got lost in his shout of pain and the roar of laughter that rose from our side of the room. Uncle Ömme dismissed the class.

Our Latin teacher was a particular favorite of mine. He was the perfect example of the old-fashioned high school professor, superb in his knowledge of antiquity and remorseless when drilling us in the intricacies of grammar and translations. His personal authority was so overwhelming that it never occurred to us to exploit or poke fun in his presence at his legendary absentmindedness. But we never could resist retelling over and over again the stories of his antics. I shall always remember the quizzical look in his eyes when, one day, open grammar book in hand and ready to pin me into my seat with a question both he and I were sure I could not answer, he approached me, hesitated, looked at me as though he had never seen me before, and asked: *"Herbst, excuse me, just what is your name?"*

When, by 1943 I had reached the *Unterprima*, the seventh high school grade, nightly air raid alarms began seriously to interfere with our work in school. Sirens would wake us up at night, and my mother and I would get up, huddle around our radio in the living room, and listen to the announcements about the course of advancing enemy bombers. Often we heard the deep-throated roar of airplane engines passing overhead, the occasional sharp bursts of anti-aircraft artillery, and watched the play of searchlights on the night sky. If these alarms lasted for more than an hour, school would begin at a later time the next morning unless, as began to happen ever more frequently, the sirens would sound during daytime as well. Then we would be sent back home again or assembled in the school's air-raid shelter.

But whether there were alarms or not, we boys of the *Große Schule* took turns every few weeks sleeping in the school's basement air-raid shelter to be on hand should incendiary bombs be dropped on the building. Fortunately that never happened. Instead, throughout the fall and winter of 1943, our fire watch assignments in the totally blacked-out building provided us with ample opportunities to raid the apple and plum orchards along the Oker behind the school and to have our fun with the school's Nazi-appointed Director Hogrebe, who lived in the house next door and whom none of us respected or thought of any importance. We set off fireworks underneath his bedroom window, fed catnip to his and other neighborhood cats, and watched his fruitless efforts to stop the cats' meowing. We thought all of that hilarious.

We especially enjoyed it when Director Hogrebe felt it incumbent on him to inspect us in our sleeping quarters in the air-raid shelter. The shelter's door was made of steel and closed with bars on the outside and on the inside, the bars being joined to each other so that they could be moved from either side. When we, who usually left the shelter through the windows, saw or heard Mr. Hogrebe coming, we blocked the bar on our side of the door with a heavy piece of lumber and then listened to him pull with all his might on the outside and shout and plead with us to open the door. Of course, the door would not budge, and we pretended to be fast asleep. When called to explain the next morning, we had heard and knew nothing, of course.

On other nights we explored, flashlight in hand, the blacked-out building's every secret recess, broke into Mr. Hogrebe's office, read his confidential files, and enjoyed many a tryst with the girls from the vocational school—never our own girl friends from the *Lyceum* who steadfastly refused to visit us at night. When, on a cloudless night, the moon shone through the tall windows of the *Aula* and bathed its interior in its white light, we often sneaked in to perform our shows and impromptu operas. One such night, as we stood grouped around the grand piano and sang *La Traviata's* drinking song at the top of our lungs, the large *Aula* doors slowly opened and the custodian, Mr. Manselmann, appeared, flashlight in hand and clad in his bathrobe, quietly said: "Please, boys, it's enough for tonight. The neighbors would like to sleep."

It is hard for me to say what precisely or primarily it was that tied us classmates together and shielded each one of us in a silent understanding against denunciation and betrayal. It did not seem to matter whether this protection pertained to such juvenile pranks as stealing apples or to such more serious matters as rifling through the director's desk. Without us ever speaking about it, it included such potentially job- or even life-threatening matters as Parson Wille's religious instruction and Bodo Wacker's and Ömme Wienbreyer's ridicule of the Nazi salute. I cannot tell whether it was our schoolboys' sense of solidarity existing in all such similar schools, whether it was our consciousness of belonging to a specially educated elite of students and teachers that instinctively coalesced to guard its own, whether it was because most of us boys felt bound together by our positions as *Jungvolk* leaders that, again, made us distance ourselves from the working-class-dominated *Hitler Jugend*—whatever it was, it was inextricably intertwined with the atmosphere and spirit that pervaded the *Große Schule* and that drew into itself everyone who took part in its life.

To me the strongest proof of its all-embracing power came with the appearance that night in the *Aula* of our custodian. Mr. Manselmann, by no means a member of the middle-class but an *Angestellter*, that is, working-class employee, refused to chastise or report us to Director Hogrebe, as he was expected to do. His sympathy for us in our situation was obvious. He knew we were there if need be to face the bombs and extinguish the fires. His soft-spoken plea to us to let him sleep told me that he, for one, had freed himself of the stereotypes of class and office. He cared for us as students of the school he served. He was very much an integral part of us.

And yet, the poison of fear and suspicion that pervades every totalitarian society was not entirely absent either, not even in our class. I knew, when I was nine years old, that I could not say whatever came into my mind. My father had made it very clear that I was not to speak of Mr. Wacker's morning greetings. I also could not help but wonder a few years later why my father would not answer all my questions about the generals who had been sacked. I could not be sure I knew the reasons for his silence, but I did begin to search for them. And there had been his outburst about my wanting to join the SS.

On another occasion, when I was thirteen and was sick with the flu, I overheard my mother and Dr. Duesberg, our family physician, standing at the foot of my bed, talk about criminal deeds that were being perpetrated by the Nazis in Poland. They spoke so softly that I could not hear every word. When Dr. Duesberg turned to leave he smiled at my mother and hummed a then popular tune,

> *Es geht alles vorüber, es geht alles vorbei;*
> *Auf jeden Dezember folgt wieder ein Mai.*

Only he substituted different words for the second line:

Auch mit Adolf Hitler und seiner Partei.[9]

I was outraged. That was treason, was it not? I asked my mother afterward whether I shouldn't have to report Dr. Duesberg to the police. That's what I had been told to do in the *Jungvolk,* and was it not my duty? My mother only looked at me and asked whether I wanted to send her and Dr. Duesberg to a concentration camp.

I had realized by then that there were reasons why people were afraid to speak, although these reasons were not entirely clear to me in all their details. I was afraid myself, afraid what I might do to my mother, to Dr. Duesberg, to Bodo Wacker, to Ömme Wienbreyer if I spoke to anyone about the things I knew about them. I recognized this fear as real and that I had caught it myself, little by little, though I had hardly noticed it as it grew at each small step. I wondered whether it was the same with my friends, but it was exactly that fear that kept me from asking them. I simply assumed they shared it, yet I didn't know for sure.

But I never did forget the instance when, on a summer morning in 1944, not long before our school was closed and most of my classmates sent to man the anti-aircraft batteries in the surrounding countryside, that fear gripped me with jolting intensity. The air-raid sirens had interrupted our lesson, we had descended into the basement, and after the all-clear had sounded we were waiting in our classroom for our teacher to reappear.

As we sat idly on top of our benches, one of us started it: "Hermann Göring said that no British bomber will ever fly over our country."

Another added: "Der Führer said German soldiers do not know the word retreat."

And soon there was no stopping: "Our U-boats will totally isolate England." "Our Africa-Korps will soon join the Arabs in Jerusalem." "The *Hakenkreuz* will forever wave over the Caucasus."

So it went, until the words escaped out of my mouth and I shouted: "This is how they lie!"

There was abrupt, absolute stillness. My eyes fell on one of my classmates, who happened to be the son of our local SS chief. As I stared in his face, an ice-cold hand seemed to brush down my back. What did I say? What have I done? was all I could think.

The door opened, and our teacher came in. "You are so quiet this

9. Everything passes, everything ends,
So will Adolf Hitler and his party friends.
The original second line read:
Every December is followed by May.

morning," he said in mock astonishment. Then we turned to our lesson, and I slowly regained my composure. Nobody thereafter ever
mentioned the incident again.

When I look back to my school days as I write these lines half a century later and ask myself what I then made of the incongruities and
contradictions, of the contrast between Parson Wille and Bodo Wacker
on the one hand and Paul Fuchtel and Helmut Adenstedt on the other,
I feel again the ambiguity that hovered over my life, in school as well
as outside of it, and made me feel suspended between two worlds.
One world drew its nourishment from talks about the past, its glories,
loves, and loyalties, a world whose memories flowed to us through
poetry and song and tales of bravery and fortitude. But another world
intruded on this past, a world whose spokesmen pointed to tomorrow,
called on us to be clear-eyed and hard-minded, to take from the past
only that which would make us masters of the future. It was the combination of the two worlds, their incongruities and contradictions, that
created the haze of ambiguity enveloping my years in the *Große Schule.*

Did our teachers realize the effect their teaching had on us? Parson
Wille clearly did. He tried to inoculate us against ambiguity by being
as unambiguous in his teaching as he dared. Bodo Wacker, I recognize now, followed a different path, the path of indirection. He planted
his lessons like time-bombs; they illumined, even delighted us, at the
moment of impact and they exploded their full force only later. Paul
Fuchtel and Helmut Adenstedt preferred to be as unambiguous as
Parson Wille was. But Fuchtel's Nazi lessons and Adenstedt's hymns,
informative and moving as they were, left no lasting mark. Their propaganda promises remain forever unfulfilled.

Throughout my school years I heard the messages of past and future and trusted that I could learn from them. I was sure that I could
find the good and the true in them both. What was so hard to bear, I
realize today, though I did not perceive it then, was that our teachers
could or did not tell us that that was impossible; that it was impossible
to find the good and the true in both messages; that, some day, each of
us would have to choose.

Teachers like Mr. Adenstedt and Mr. Fuchtel, who were so convinced they knew the path into the future, had no patience to listen to
anyone who suggested there might be ways other than theirs. Parson
Wille had to leave our school precisely because he told his graduating
seniors they could not live by embracing both ways. We *Sextaner* and
Quintaner, however, never had a chance to hear this from him. Bodo
Wacker and teachers like him who also could have told us did not
dare to do so directly. They tried to tell us by indirection through their

stories and charades, but we did not always hear them. Perhaps they, too, like my father, trusted that we would some day make our choice, and that it would be the right one. But they did not tell us that; only my mother did eventually, but that was when there was nothing else left to say.

Our teachers did not tell us because fear, fear for themselves and fear for us, closed their lips. That fear took on many shapes. It was the fear to betray your friends and to be betrayed by them. I and all my friends had to find this out for ourselves alone. For most of us this happened only after we had left our homes and school. Then that fear took on new shapes and became the fear that, one day, we would have to choose between the ways of the past and the promises of the future. My friends and I did not recognize and could not acknowledge that fear, though it was ever-present. For me, it broke through once on that day in class when the "What did I say?" sent its ice-cold fingers down my spine. But then I repressed it again unrecognized. What was most cruel about that fear for all of us was that it prevented us from confiding in and seeking comfort and support even from each other.

That unacknowledged, ever-present fear cast my schooldays in ambiguity, made me, at the same time, deny that ambiguity and attempt to manage the impossible, to live in both the worlds of Parson Wille and Paul Fuchtel at the same time. What else could we have done? What alternatives were there for us? The lessons of our teachers, taken together, created and ended in ambiguity. But they were the only lessons the school could give us.

4

Kristallnacht

I HAD JUST TURNED TEN WHEN, during the Easter season of 1938, I became a *Quintaner* in the *Große Schule*, that is, I began my second year. Having reached that milestone, it was now obligatory for me to enroll in the *Jungvolk*, the lower division of the Hitler Youth, intended for ten- to thirteen-year-olds. I was supposed to attend meetings of the group every Wednesday and Saturday afternoon, but, as I mentioned before, I was not then particularly excited about these gatherings. I was happy to have my mother cooperate often in writing excuse slips claiming I did not feel well or had a fever. I rather looked forward toward the summer when my parents and I planned to travel by train to the Baltic Sea and to spend our vacation playing in the sand and water at Kellenhusen. For me the excursion to the beach was a grand getaway from the drudgery of the *Jungvolk* meetings in the city gymnasium and the boredom of listening to yet another recital of the life of Adolf Hitler.

When we returned to Wolfenbüttel I still hated the thought of resuming the *Jungvolk* meetings but I looked expectantly toward going back to school and seeing my friends and teachers again. But I was to be disappointed. Though Bodo Wacker still greeted us as our homeroom teacher, he informed us that Parson Wille was gone and had been transferred to Braunschweig. My classmates and I were puzzled and wondered why, but Mr. Wacker told us only that such transfers happened sometimes, and we would have a new teacher for our lessons in religion.

I also sensed a change of atmosphere in our surroundings in the halls and in the school yard. There were strange comings and goings by men I did not recognize. These men all wore the party emblem on their coats and, with their briefcases under their arms pressed against their sides, went in and came out of Director Lampe's office at least every second or third day. Several times our recess was extended and all students were asked to stay outside in the yard until Mr. Manselmann appeared on the steps and called us back into our classes. At other times we had to wait for our teacher in the classroom. When he finally appeared, he would say only that he had been held back for an important meeting.

We also heard that some of our teachers and upper-class students were called to conferences that took all morning and were conducted by the men who wore the party emblems. We found out from some of the older students that the men were officials from the Education Ministry in Braunschweig and that they were interested in Parson Wille and had asked questions about his classes in religion. When these men appeared and conducted those all-morning meetings, substitute instructors showed up in our classroom. When we asked our regular teachers what was going on, most of them only shrugged their shoulders and said that whatever it was, we shouldn't worry. It had nothing to do with us. Only Bodo Wacker mentioned once that we should get used to these interruptions; they were bound to happen more frequently now. And Mr. Fuchtel, one of the few party members among the teachers, said mysteriously that we were witnessing a revolution and we should be proud that we were living in such important times.

That talk of revolution made very little sense to me, because when I thought of revolution I always remembered the picture in our history book that showed what was called "The Storming of the Bastille," with plenty of flags being waved on the street, cannons being fired, people falling over each other, and smoke rising from the big prison-fortress. There was nothing like that going on in Wolfenbüttel or in the *Große Schule,* even though we, too, had a big, fortress-like prison in town with big stone walls that bordered on the Herzogtorwall. But nobody attacked it, and there were no riots in town, no flag-waving crowds on the Rosenwall in front of our school, and no smoke rising from the prison. Mr. Wacker did not explain what it was that we should get used to and why, and I could never figure out what Mr. Fuchtel was talking about.

The months went by, September passed into October, the days grew shorter and grayer, and the routine of my school days—Mr. Berger's continuing explosions of cane-swinging outbursts during his English lessons, Mr. Pfaff's end-of-mathematics-class stories of America, Mr. Fuchtel's talk of Germany's good fortune under Adolf Hitler, and Mr. Wacker's accounts of World War I—appeared to have wiped my consciousness clean of the strangeness of those perturbing extended mid-morning breaks and absent teachers, until, on one of those early November days, when a chilly wind sent occasional gusts of dust over the cobblestoned streets and the clouds hung low and appeared ready to unload their watery freight any minute, all the vaguely felt threats of mysterious and unexplained events returned and overcame me with renewed force.

It was early in the morning, twenty or so minutes before eight o'clock, the time my first class began, and I was on my way to school, walking along the Lange. There were very few people hurrying past me, and only a few bicyclists rushed along on the pavement on their way to work. At one point I thought I heard fire engine bells ring in the distance, somewhere in the direction of the *Schloß* and the library where my father worked. But before I had time to let that thought sink in, my attention was caught by a broken display window of a leather goods store on the other side of the street. It was the only store window in which I had noticed before a red and white sign stuck in the corner which said: "Germans: Buy German—Don't Patronize a Jewish Business." Now, the jagged slivers of glass aroused my curiosity. Some pointed down from the wooden frame above as though ready to hurl themselves on the unwary passers-by, others clung to the sides of the window, trembling just slighly in the cold breeze as though afraid they, too, would lose their grip and join the others lying splintered on the sidewalk. I wanted to rush across the street and take a closer look. But I decided to walk slowly and watch carefully for the bicyclists who didn't seem to pay any attention and kept on rushing past as before. I also was afraid that, if I did not watch out, the pointed slivers at the top of the window might fall on me or the ones already on the ground would make me slip and cut myself.

Nonetheless, I walked across the street and then stared at the ladies' purses, shoes, and gloves that lay in the display area, covered with pulverized glass. And there, resting among the still well-polished pumps and slippers, lay half a brick, light red and ragged on the side where it had been broken off, and dark brown and smooth on its other surfaces. I wondered why nobody had come to pick up the brick, sweep up the glass, and install some plywood or something to protect the merchandise in the window. But, except for the speeding bicyclists on the street, there was now no one around besides me. So I figured an accident had happened in the night or a drunk had thrown that brick. Those things were not unusual, and the damage would soon be repaired. I moved on thinking that I had something to tell my friends when I got to school.

I turned off the deserted Lange, walked down the Altes Tor—the Old Gate—and then headed for the Gymnasialgasse, the little alley that led through some vegetable and fruit gardens to the Rosenwall and the *Große Schule*. As I emerged from between the wooden board fences that shielded the alley on either side, I noticed that something unusual was going on. There was the school building ahead of me on the other side of the Rosenwall and I saw some of my friends. But they were scurrying away from the school, not toward it. They ran in the direction from which I earlier had thought I had heard fire engine bells. They saw me and shouted: "Come along, come along, hurry, there's a fire down there."

I hesitated. School was to begin in fifteen minutes. Still, I couldn't resist. I started running, too. My book pack bounced along on my back: Thump, thump, thump. People on bicycles, pedaling to work, joined us. They, too, wanted to see what was going on. We ran down the Rosenwall, across the bridge by the old mill, then on to the Schiffwall, which continued the green belt, and turned right on the Leibnizstraße, realizing that, as we ran along, we were passing the source of the smoke that we could now see and smell on our left. So we turned again at the next side street and doubled back on the Lessingstraße.

And there we saw the synagogue or, more correctly, what was left of it. The red walls, the black slate roof, the well-kept lawn—the building as I had seen it time and time again when I had picked apples or raspberries in our family's garden behind the library—was gone. A burnt-out shell of smoke-blackened bricks, empty holes where the windows had been, a collapsed roof from whose splintered rafters plumes of blue-black smoke drifted upward—that was all that remained. What was left of the lawn had been trampled over and was strewn with plates of slate from the roof and broken pieces of marble.

Across the street from the smoking hulk a fire engine was parked. The hoses were rolled up; the firefighters sat on or leaned against their truck, dozing and staring wordlessly at the scarred ruin. Propped up against the sidewalk, close to where the synagogue's entrance gate had been, leaned a motorcycle, the SS markings on its license plate, an SS soldier in field gray uniform standing next to it. He was sucking on a cigarette and searchingly examined the gradually gathering crowd. Then, for a long while, he stared ahead at his feet. Suddenly, with an abrupt gesture of his hand, he tossed his cigarette on the dirty sidewalk, moved toward his cycle and sat down sideways, his back turned toward the crowd.

Everybody watched him, and nobody said a word. Finally, from somewhere in the crowd, a voice rose, male, clear, and distinct. It said, slowly, so we all could hear it: "*Solide deutsche Maßarbeit.*"

It struck me like the blow of a whip. Solid German craftsmanship. I wondered, what did that mean? A fire, after all, was not a piece of craftsmanship. It was an accident, a mishap, a disaster to boot, but not a piece of workmanship. I wondered what the man had meant.

"The firefighters were too late, I suppose?" another male voice asked, halting and timid, addressing no one in particular.

"Firefighters?" another voice replied, stretching out the word and weighing it, as though it was one never heard before, never known to exist.

"For such a fire you don't call firefighters," the voice added, "firefighters can't do much with such a fire."

Why can't they? I wondered. Why can't they put out such a fire? But the voice now was silent, and nobody else answered.

Some of my classmates stirred. We were going to be late for school. We ran back, not a one of us saying a word. I still remember the low gray clouds that seemed to reflect from above the smell of smoke and the air of desolation we had just witnessed.

As we hurried along, we all sensed that something extraordinary had happened. Why had all these people been so quiet? Why had the one who broke the silence spoken of craftsmanship? Why did the firefighters just sit and look? Why was there an SS soldier watching us and then turning his back on us? What was this all about?

As we arrived at school, we were late indeed. Mr. Fuchtel's history class had already begun. When I entered I heard one of my classmates report from Caesar's *De Bello Gallico* that the Germanic tribes used to light smoke fires on their mountains to warn of the coming of war. That made me sit up and pay close attention, the smell of the synagogue's smoke still in my nostrils. But I decided to keep quiet and not to respond to the talk of fire and war. I did not want Mr. Fuchtel to ask me what I knew of fire and war.

At mid-morning, when the bell rang for our fifteen-minute sandwich break, I stepped out into the school yard and noticed a group of *Sextaner* standing in a corner, pressed around one of their classmates who, gesticulating excitedly, was telling them something. A *Quintaner* like myself would not normally deign to join a group of *Sextaner* and listen to what these little boys had to say. But whatever it was that fascinated them was so obviouly unusual that I could not resist. I went over to the group and pricked up my ears.

"And there was this big, big noise on the stairway, and all of a sudden I saw a chair, and then a desk, and another chair fall out on the sidewalk, and men in brown uniforms were throwing paper out on the street, and then came a bunch of policemen who pushed Mr. and Mrs. Morgenstern and Albert, too, into a van and drove away with them; and the wind blew the paper all over the street, and there was broken glass and china . . ." The boy was so flustered and excited, his voice trailed off, and now the other *Sextaner* grabbed him by the arm and wanted to hear more.

71

"What else happened?" they shouted, "did Albert cry?"

I stepped aside, the words the boy had used—broken glass and china—in my ears. I had seen broken glass, too, in the morning on my way to school, and I had seen broken china also on the grounds of the synagogue. Did all this fit together?

I asked an older student from the *Tertia,* who had also come over to listen, what this was all about. He said that the one who had told the story lived on the ground floor of one of those big apartment houses on the Bahnhofstraße. He had watched from his bedroom window how the Morgensterns, the Jewish family on the third floor with their little four-year-old boy Albert, had been picked up in the night by the police, and how all their furniture and belongings had been dumped on the street. In the morning the Morgensterns' maid had been brought back by a policeman to clean up the broken pieces on the stairs.

Then the bell rang and I had to go back to class.

Later in the day I went home for lunch. My father had come from work and we sat around the table in my mother's sitting room eating our meal. Both my father and my mother seemed subdued. Usually they had things to say to each other and would ask me about my day at school. But not today. They remained silent except for the occasional, "Would you like some more meat," and "No, thank you, it's good, but quite enough."

I did not think it proper to volunteer an account of my day although I was sorely tempted. I felt conflicting sensations of excitement, curiosity, and bewilderment. I really wanted to tell my story and ask my questions. I wanted to hear what my parents had to say. But their demeanor that noon told me that I had better wait until I was asked. It did not come to that; not at the dinner table.

"I've got to run," my father said as soon as he had finished. "Director Herse wants to talk to me this afternoon. I'm not sure what's on his mind."

Several days later I heard him say to my mother that Mr. Herse, the director of the Duke August Library, had asked him whether, after the events that had happened that day, it wasn't time for him to join the party. Neither my father nor my mother then continued their conversation. Apparently they thought there was no need for that. From the continuing absence of the party emblem on my father's coat, I concluded that he had decided not to join.

But on that somber November day, when my father had left, I followed my mother into the kitchen where, as every noon, I was to help her with the dishes. As my mother bent over the dishpans, one with the hot soapy water for washing and the other with the hot clear water for rinsing, steam rising from both of them, and as I stood behind her, a dish towel in hand, I waited for the question I wanted to hear: "Tell me Jürgen, what was new in school today?"

And then she did finally ask it.

It was as though a dam had broken, and a torrent of words streamed out of me. I described my walk to school in the morning, the broken window on the Lange Herzogstraße with the half brick lying among the shoes, the burnt-out synagogue and the SS motorcycle, the strange remarks about *Maßarbeit* and fires for which no one would call the firefighters, and the story of the *Sextaner* about the Morgensterns on the Bahnhofstraße. All during the telling my excitement rose. It had been such an incredible morning. I had heard such unbelievable tales. My cheeks were flushed, I felt my ears burn. How could all that have happened and what in the world did it all mean?

My mother, her back still turned toward me and her arms in the hot, soapy water, suddenly straightened up from her dishpans. She turned around slowly and looked me in the face, her arms now hanging straight down at her sides, water and soap bubbles dripping off them and forming puddles on the tiled kitchen floor. And then she said: "Do you know, Jürgen, if you had been Albert Morgenstern, you would have been torn from your bed last night; you, your father, and I would have been pushed down the staircase, and all your toys and books would have been thrown on the street. Had you been born a little Jewish boy, this would have happened to you last night." She then turned back, grabbed the pan with the soapy water, poured it into the sink in the corner of the kitchen, and said I could go and do my homework.

I was stunned. I did not know what to think. I could not get the picture out of my mind, the picture of my parents and me being pushed down the stairs. It stayed with me that day as I withdrew into my room to do my school assignments. I tried to read some chapters in my book on German sagas, the stories of Siegfried and Hagen, of Kriemhild and Brunhild, the *Nibelungen* and their fabulous treasure. But I could not concentrate. The picture came back, again and again.

It would recur, also, again and again, in the following months and years. It would return unexpectedly and unannounced. It would keep me awake at night, when I lay in my bed, and it would rise before me when, at *Jungvolk* meetings or in Mr. Fuchtel's class, I would hear more about the "Jewish danger" and what it meant to be a German in a world that was "dominated by Jews." It became very clear to me that what had happened and what I had seen had something to do with Jews and Germans. But exactly what was it that made Jews so hateful to us Germans? I could not figure it out.

My mother was the first to answer at least some of my questions.

When, the day after I had seen the synagogue burn, I asked her why the Morgensterns had been taken away she said it was because they were Jewish. I thought about that a lot. My father, my mother, and I were Germans. The Morgensterns were Jews. The professor and his wife who had visited us three weeks before the synagogue was burned were Americans. Other people were Japanese, Englishmen, Frenchmen. But the Morgensterns were Jews, and my parents and I were Germans. What you were, Jew or German, made all the difference. It was that simple.

Or was it, really? I knew full well that my parents had not chosen not to be Jewish and that I could not take any credit for having been born a German. Had Albert Morgenstern and his parents chosen to be Jews? Did they deserve to be punished just for being who they were? Why was I supposed to applaud that punishment? My mother did not seem to think I should.

I decided to find out what my mother thought about that. I asked her whether she knew any Jews besides the Morgensterns. She looked at me wonderingly and said, "But, Jürgen, your piano teacher is Jewish."

I did not know what to make of that. I had been taught in the *Jungvolk* and by Mr. Fuchtel and my biology teacher that Jews looked dark and hook-nosed, always talked fast, and waved their hands when they did. Mrs. Lerner neither looked nor talked that way, nor did she wave her hands when she talked. After all, she was my piano teacher, and I watched her hands very carefully when she played so I could hold my hands and fingers the same way. Besides, Mrs. Lerner looked like all the other middle-aged women I knew in Wolfenbüttel. She was tall, straight, and blond, did not talk differently in any way, and always chatted with me pleasantly about school and my friends. To make matters even more perplexing, I liked her as a person and as a teacher as well. That she might have been Jewish had never occurred to me.

I now immediately wondered what had happened to her. Had she also been picked up in the night? Would I go back to her next Thursday for my piano lesson? But my mother said that Mrs. Lerner's husband was not a Jew; he was Aryan. Mrs. Lerner therefore would not have been picked up. And my mother was right. I went back to Mrs. Lerner the next Thursday and found her smiling at her door, ready to give me my lesson as usual.

But now I was uneasy about her. Should I take lessons from a Jewish woman, even if she was married to a non-Jew? Weren't all Jews dangerous for us Germans? Wasn't that what Mr. Fuchtel had said? Had I not heard over and over again at *Jungvolk* meetings and had I not read the big print in the glass-encased notice board of *Der Stürmer*, the SS newspaper: "Be proud you are a German . . . The Jews are your misfortune . . . send them to Jerusalem . . ."? Should I not therefore break off my piano lessons with Mrs. Lerner? I wondered out loud.

"Why?" asked my mother, "you are doing very well."

"But she is Jewish," I protested.

"Yes, so what?" asked my mother. "Your friend Dieter is taking piano lessons from her. He doesn't think there is anything wrong with that."

I adored Dieter, who, though almost two years older than I, was a classmate of mine in the *Große Schule* and already a *Fähnleinführer,* a leader of a hundred boys, in the *Jungvolk.* Besides—though my mother did not know that, and, in fact, nobody but I knew it, for I would rather have bitten off my tongue than to admit it to anybody—I had a crush on Dieter, one of those adolescent infatuations that are so common in all-boy schools and youth groups. I daydreamed of throwing myself into battle against gangs of other boys who had conspired to beat up Dieter, and I would suffer grievous wounds proudly and silently in defense of my hero. And now my mother reminded me that Dieter, my hero, also took lessons from Mrs. Lerner and did not seem to mind at all that she was Jewish.

Dieter not only was a *Fähnleinführer* but also an excellent student and athlete. The son of a Protestant minister, he served as a role model for many of us. We called him "The General" and were prepared to follow him wherever he might send us. As I mulled over my mother's response I could only think that if "The General" could take lessons from a Jewish teacher, then I could do it too. Besides, I reasoned, Mrs. Lerner didn't look like a Jew, and I could not think of anything that would turn her into an enemy of mine. With that, I dismissed the whole question from my mind.

Until, at night or in Mr. Fuchtel's class, the picture of my parents and me tumbling down the stairs would bring it back. And then, sometimes, the picture would blur, and it was the Morgensterns and Albert who fell down the stairs, and then Mrs. Lerner and "The General," "The General" in his splendid *Jungvolk* uniform with the green and white cord of a *Fähnleinführer* dangling from his shoulder. As the picture kept coming back in whatever form, it made me unsure of what to think and how to act. It puzzled and frightened me, because when I thought that someday I would be a soldier and ordered to push somebody down the stairs, how would, how could I do that? Should I someday have to push my own parents down the stairs, or "The General," or Mrs. Lerner?

I wondered how other people felt about all this. What did "The General" think? I never had heard him say anything in school or at

Jungvolk meetings about fighting Jews or burning synagogues and I never felt it right to ask him about it. Nor had my teachers in school ever mentioned pushing people down the stairs. Not even Mr. Fuchtel had said anything like that, though he always maintained that whatever the Führer ordered was the right thing to do. Bodo Wacker, on the other hand, had spoken glowingly and with feeling about his Jewish comrades in the trenches of World War I. He had relied on them to protect his life as he had been ready to sacrifice his for theirs. How did all this fit together?

The textbooks said that the Jews were our enemies and that we must always be on guard against them. In the bulletin board of *Der Stürmer* I read it every day: "The Jews are parasites. . . . The Jews are our misfortune. . . . There is no room for Jews in our Fatherland." There were signs in some shop windows that said: *"Juden Unerwünscht"* (Jews not desired), although—again the contradictions that made everything so puzzling to me—I heard my father speak at the dinner table of Mr. Bremer, the proprietor of the paper store on the Lange Herzogstraße where I bought my school supplies. Mr. Bremer had refused to put up such a sign, my father said, and that was very courageous of him. At our *Jungvolk* meetings and when we marched through town we even sang a song about sending all the Jews to Jerusalem and, by chopping off their legs, making sure they could not come back.

So the Jews, we were told, were "the enemy within." We had to learn to hate them as we were to hate all our external foes. There were many of them, though, as time went on, they appeared to change. There were, for example, the Chinese and the Japanese, who constituted the "yellow danger." Of the two, the Japanese were said to be by far the worst. They would overrun our fatherland if we lagged in our vigilance. I found that difficult to imagine. I knew from Mr. Kühnhold's geography lessons that they lived on the other side of the globe. I had a hard time imagining how they would come around and overrun us.

As it was, I need not have worried. Not long after we had first heard of this danger, we were told to forget hating the Japanese. The danger, so it was now said, did not come from Japan whose people were an industrious and capable race. In fact, they were the Germans of the Far East. The danger really came from England and France.

Englishmen, however much they had been praised as our Aryan, Anglo-Saxon blood cousins, we now learned, were a race of traders who cheated and exploited other people and enriched themselves at our expense. Had they not encircled us to keep us weak and enfeebled and then attacked us in 1914 to rob us of our colonies? Our fight was against England, the newspapers screamed. Death and punishment to perfidious Albion! My grandfather Felix in Chemnitz also did not like Englishmen. He had told me so. Had they not attempted to starve my grandmother and my mother by maintaining the blockade after the war had ended in 1918? "May God punish England," he said with great conviction.

And as for the French, they were the arch enemy. Everybody knew that. We had fought and vanquished them in 1870. But in 1918, through deceit and crookery, they had managed to deprive us of our justly won gains. Now we had to be prepared to battle them again and never ever forget our brothers and sisters who suffered under the unjust French rule in Alsace-Lorraine.

As I thought about all this talk about enemies I became ever more confused and puzzled. Some things made good sense to me; others did not. I could understand that we were a country beset by enemies, Jews among us, and English- and Frenchmen on the outside. After all, we lived in the middle of Europe, surrounded on all sides by peoples who envied us, and with many Jews as our next-door neighbors. So we had to be watchful, always ready to seek out and defeat our foes. That's what we learned in the *Jungvolk* and in school. It was only natural that we were being trained to battle Englishmen and Frenchmen in the field as soldiers and to keep an eye on the Jews among us. I had always wanted to be soldier, and battling other soldiers was a soldier's business.

But to be suspicious of Jews who lived next to me and taught me how to play the piano was another matter. As far as I could see, it had nothing to do with being a soldier. I was sure, though I didn't know it, "The General" felt the same way. Why else would he take lessons from a Jewish teacher? And now we were to hate not only our soldier enemies but also our Jewish neighbors and teachers.

I wasn't ready to hate anybody. From what I had learned from Bodo Wacker and my father, the German soldier never hated his enemies. He fought them bravely in valiant battles, but he knew that his adversaries were just as brave battlers as he. He knew that they, too, loved their families and their fatherland and were ready to defend it and die for it. Soldiers, no matter of what country, were supposed to respect each other. They believed in many of the same things like Christmas and honor and duty. I had heard stories how soldiers in the trenches, German and French, had ceased their mutual bombardments and celebrated Christmas together. Mr. Wacker had told us how fighting armies treated their prisoners with chivalry and placed bandages on their wounds; how they agreed to stop fighting for a while so that the wounded could be gathered and the dead buried. I had read how opposing airplane pilots saluted each other and dropped flowers from above on the downed enemy. None of this had anything to do with hate.

This business of hating enemies struck me and my classmates and quite a few of my fellow *Jungvolk* friends as rather unsoldierly. We all had learned that hate was the opposite of love, and we all agreed that we knew what love was. We thought of our mothers. But hate? What was it? How did one create it?

Hate was to us a curious thing. It was an abstract, empty word. I heard people talk about it on the radio. They praised hate and prayed to it as if it were a God. Newspapers were full of it: The German people have to learn how to hate, to hate from the depth of their souls. But that again I found troublesome. Soul was something that had to do with religion or with music like Beethoven's and Mozart's, or with poetry like Goethe's and Eichendorff's. My father sometimes spoke of the German soul that was somehow deeply filled with goodness and love. But now that soul was to switch from loving to hating, and I had no idea how that was to be accomplished.

There were pictures of Goethe hanging everywhere in homes and in school rooms, and busts of Beethoven standing on pianos in people's living rooms. To me, when I saw them, they still spoke of love, not of hate. Hate remained a puzzle to me. I never experienced it, not even later when the bombs began to fall on our homes, my father was killed, and I had to dodge bullets and shells and felt the full fury of war loosened on me.

Several years after the burning of the synagogue, when I was thirteen years old, I found out for the first time that I could not hate, even when I tried to, as I did one day because I thought I was supposed to. But I learned to my bewilderment that I could not do it; it did not work. My attempt at hating ended when compassion and then shame overcame me, such unexpected compassion and such searing shame that I wished I had never encountered the little man in the fog on the Harztorwall in front of our house.

I had just been given my first commission as *Jungvolkführer*, overseeing a troop of ten or eleven boys, and I was determined to prove myself worthy of the promotion. It was at the time when Jewish residents in Germany were forced to wear a yellow star on their clothing so that we Aryan Germans could recognize Jewish people easily and not offer them our seats on the streetcar or allow them into restaurants. It was then that I met the little man.

I had stepped out of our apartment to run an errand for my mother. I was walking along the Harztorwall when I noticed him, an old, bent, little fellow in a worn black overcoat approaching me on the street. Moist leaves had made the path slippery, and the old man limped along, unsure of his footing, a cane in his hand. Against his chest he clutched a packet wrapped in newspaper.

As he came closer I saw something yellow flash from underneath his packet. I recognized immediately what it was. It was the star of the Jews, and the man tried to hide it. I stopped and gazed at him. Thoughts raced through my mind. What should I do? What must I do? Could I as a German boy and *Jungvolkführer* let this Jew pass unchallenged? Was it not my duty to step up to him, tear his hand away from his chest, throw his packet on the ground, tell him that to cover up his star was a crime? Should I spit on his feet, order him to get off the street? Weren't they the duties of a German boy and *Jungvolkführer*?

I stood without motion, a whirl of thoughts racing in my mind. What would "The General" do? Would he know what to do, or would he be just as torn and indecisive as I was? I recognized that, indeed, I was indecisive; that despite all the thoughts that I considered I did not move; that something held me back and prevented my mouth from forming any of the words that I had contemplated. Now the man was next to me; now he shuffled past. I stared him in the eyes, made a last desperate attempt to look contemptuously. Then he had gone by.

I felt the blood shoot in my face. What had I done? A picture flashed through my mind—that of myself and my father and my mother being pushed down the stairs, our faces changing to those of Albert Morgenstern and his parents. I thought of Mrs. Lerner to whose home I would go the next day for another piano lesson. What had I done? What had the little, old man done to me? How did he deserve my contempt? Was he hungry, I wondered? Was he lonely? Did he have friends, a wife, children who loved him? Compassion overcame me as I watched him slowly fade away in the fog. There were no answers to any of my questions.

I felt a huge emptiness rise within me. I felt ashamed, horribly ashamed of myself as I blankly stared into the whiteness of the mist in which the man had disappeared. How could I hate a man like that? I turned to go. But I could not forget the little black figure, slowly dragging himself along with his cane, getting smaller and smaller until the mist closed in on him and he was gone.

Years later, in another country, I met the man again. It was a strange encounter. It happened in a movie house. I watched a film. At its end, Charlie Chaplin, in a black coat, limping along with a cane in his hand, faded away in the haze of a distant street.

The shock of recognition was overwhelming. In a flash I knew that I had seen him before, that it had been he, the little old Jew, whom I had encountered on that foggy day in my hometown. And it was he who then came to symbolize for me the enormity of evil that had over-come my life and against which I was protected only by what I could absorb of the lessons my parents, my grandfather Felix, and my teach-ers had tried to bequeath to me. As indirect and cautiously conveyed as these lessons were, they were all I had to keep my humanity alive in a time of evil, unspeakable evil.

5

Boy Soldier

T HE WAR BEGAN IN 1939 when I was eleven years old, a student of the *Tertia*, my third year at the *Große Schule*, and as yet a rather unenthusiastic *Pimpf* of the Wolfenbüttel *Jungvolk*. The smoke signals I had seen a year ago and whose message I did not want to discuss in class now revealed their truth in every newspaper headline. During the next few years, however, as the war intensified I became more involved in *Jungvolk* activities and rose gradually through the ranks until, by the time the declaration of total war closed the *Große Schule* in 1944 and I left home for other war duties, I led a *Fähnlein* of a hundred boys.

These years as *Jungvolk* leader were for me a most exhilarating time. The *Jungvolk*, I told myself, was my real school, the school that prepared me for my future career as an army officer. It gave me responsibility at a young age and taught me what it meant to become a leader of men. It was the comradeship of us boys and the awareness of the duties the war imposed upon us that sustained my enthusiasm and made life meaningful.

Throughout these years, too, there remained the memory of the Morgensterns and their son Albert, a memory I tried to banish as much as possible, because it made me uneasy and unsure, but which I could not totally repress. It accompanied my life as boy-soldier like a far-off, dimly heard dirge that was drowned out most of the time by the martial music of blaring horns and thundering kettle drums.

For me the war began in late August of 1939 when my father, a reserve lieutenant, was called to duty with the 17th Braunschweig Infantry Regiment for "an extended military exercise." I remember my mother wondering just what that meant, "extended military exercise," and asking a neighbor, who only shrugged his shoulders and said:

"We'll be lucky if it does not mean war." My father came home once more for an overnight stay on the weekend. He wore what I thought was the most splendid army officer's uniform I had ever seen. A few days later, after he had left again, we received word that his unit was to embark for service at the Polish border, and we could wave him off at the railroad freight station.

As an eleven-year-old I was excited by the prospect of seeing my father at the head of his company marching to the station. In my imagination he would be preceded by the regimental band and flag, and crowds of people would shower him and his men with flowers. That's how it was supposed to be, I thought, when soldiers moved out to maneuvers; that's how it had been when World War I began, and that's what I myself had seen a year earlier when the Wolfenbüttel anti-aircraft garrison had returned to town from their occupation of Austria. The soldiers in their blue uniforms with their red rank ensignia on their coats were sitting stiffly on their half-tracks, their helmets polished and glistening in the sun, and slowly rolled down the Braunschweig trunk highway. The trucks pulled 88-millimeter anti-aircraft guns, four-wheeled search lights, and generators. Interspersed between them soldiers drove heavy motorcycles, goggles over their eyes, and carbines with flowers stuck in their barrels slung across their backs. Every tenth or so cycle had a sidecar with an officer sitting behind a plastic windshield, the officer smiling and every now and then waving toward the crowd on the sidewalk. We boys, standing at the curb, held small paper swastika flags in our hands that we flung madly up and down, and the girls threw flowers on the trucks and cycles. I expected something similar of my father's regiment, although I knew that his men wore field gray uniforms and, being infantry soldiers, would march rather than sit on trucks.

But nothing of the sort happened. The departure of the Braunschweig regiment showed little of the enthusiasm and the waving crowds I had expected. It was an August afternoon without a cloud in the sky; the temperature was in the nineties; and there was no flag-waving and music-blaring parade. By the time my mother and I reached the railroad yard my father's regiment had already arrived. The soldiers were busy around the train, lifting vehicles and guns on the flatbed cars and throwing bales of straw into the covered freight cars in which they would ride. We found my father at the front of the train in one of the few passenger cars that were reserved for the officers.

I was exhausted and dispirited, overcome by the heat of the sun-baked railhead and the seemingly endless waiting. There were other mothers and children milling around, quite a few of the smaller kids crying for something to drink, others running back and forth to a faucet at the far end of the yard, bringing back water in mess kits borrowed from their soldier-fathers, and spilling a great deal of it on the way.

How I wished I could sit with my father on the soft cushioned seats of his railroad car! Not so much because I wanted to be close to him and the other officers but chiefly because I longed for a place in the shade. Despite the heat and the queasy feeling in my stomach I did not want to leave before I had seen the train, my father, and the soldiers begin their journey. My father urged my mother to get out of the sun and seek shade under some trees near the road. But I clung to her and begged her to stay and wait with me until the train pulled out of the yard.

After what seemed endless hours the locomotive sent a hiss of steam and a hoot from its whistle into the cloudless sky, and the train finally began to move. My father leaned out of the compartment window and waved; the soldiers in the freight cars blew kisses from the open doors; girls ran alongside and threw flowers. Slowly the train gathered speed and as it passed and curved away from us, we stood there, hot and exhausted, staring at the glistening rails, my mother unable to hold back her tears, and I feeling nothing but a yawning void inside me.

Where were these soldiers going? I wondered. Were they to come back soon, after another bloodless victory as they had in Austria in 1938 and in Czechoslovakia earlier in the year? Was it going to be war this time? I heard my mother and other wives anxiously ask that question, yet nobody had a confident answer. No one seemed to doubt that war was a very real possibility, but all the wives and sweethearts who streamed back with us to the streetcar stop expressed great confidence that, if war broke out, it would be brief and victorious, and their loved ones would come back home within a few weeks. Then the flags would fly again, the music would play, and everything would be as it had been before.

I felt grievously disappointed about the lack of enthusiasm, martial music, and waving flags, but most of all I was hot, thirsty, and tired. As my mother and I clambered on the streetcar to take us back to Wolfenbüttel I could think only that now all of us, my father, my mother, and I, were riding in shaded, cool comfort. I wanted nothing more than to fall asleep.

Except for the absence of my father the next few years at home brought little change in our daily lives. The need of supplementing our food and clothing rations through visits to the countryside or through cultivating good relations with merchants and grocers and the desire to find such necessities as soap, shoelaces, and leather soles demanded more and more of our time. In this search my mother and I came to depend very much on each other. Though we were never hungry during those early years of the war, there were shortages of coffee and chocolate, white bread, cakes, and sweets of any kind. My mother developed a craving for coffee that could not be stilled by the *Muckefuck* we were forced to drink, the *Ersatzkaffee* that derived its German name from the French *moka faux*. While my mother spent countless hours pursuing rumors of hidden sources of these now luxury goods and looked for them far and wide, I, too, found ways of "organizing," as we boys called it, rare goods beyond what was allotted to us on our rationing coupons and books.

My mother's forays into shops and vegetable gardens—Wolfenbüttel was known for its many commercial gardeners who raised vegetables and fruit for the city's canneries—delighted me. I loved the white asparagus and the strawberries my mother obtained from the gardeners on the Kleine Breite, the street we had lived on before I started school. White asparagus was one of Wolfenbüttel's specialties, and though we no longer had the ample supply of melted butter that we used to pour over it and of the raw ham that we ate with it before the war, it still tasted delicious to me with margerine and even without meat. I used to cover the strawberries with as much sugar as we could spare and let them stand until they had drawn enough juice with which, in turn, I then drenched the *Quark*, a kind of soft white cheese we made by letting milk sit on a warm stove. Strawberries and *Quark* was a favorite dessert of mine.

But, except for Wolfenbüttel's kale, also known as brown cabbage, I didn't really care for the green cabbage leaves that filled our soup pot all too often and the green string beans that were tough and leathery, and I certainly had no use for turnips, which to me always tasted just like paper. I could never understand why my mother brought home most often cabbage, beans, and turnips, particularly when I knew from her tales of World War I that she herself hated turnips with a vengeance. I sometimes couldn't help but wonder whether she did it to make me aware that there really was a war going on. But I dismissed that thought as absurd. Vegetables, I knew, were seasonal, and when the good-tasting ones like asparagus, carrots, peas, cauliflower, and brussel sprouts were gone, it was time for cabbage and bean soup and turnip stew.

The worst debacle, however, occurred when the owner of one of the clothing stores on the Kommißstraße let my mother have, without ration coupons, a poison-green short-sleeved polo shirt. While lying in his store window, the shirt had been bleached by the sun on its front to a dirty yellow while its sides and back remained the original green. On my way to school I had seen the shirt for several days on display and had thought to myself what a dreadful-looking piece of clothing it was and had wondered who would ever want to wear it.

My consternation and utter shock could hardly have been greater when my mother, her face beaming all over, met me on my way home from school one day and made me guess what wonderful news she had for me: She had found a shirt for me, without ration coupons, and I would have something to wear again when my old shirt wore out completely. With that she pulled the green thing out of her shopping bag.

As a result of the ensuing arguments there were tears on both our faces. But, of course, I had to give in and wear the shirt to school. For months I bore the nickname "Greeny," which my classmates bestowed on me. As far as I was concerned, the entire affair was an unmitigated disaster. I did my best to spill ink on the shirt and to get it torn. I would just as soon not have worn any shirt at all. Fortunately it was a summer shirt, and once fall began I claimed that it was far too cold outside to keep on wearing that shirt. By the time summer came around next year I protested strongly that I had grown and the shirt was now too small. My mother, who was not color-blind, after all, must have realized what the shirt had done to me. She accepted the argument without further words and suggested that, once summer and fall had passed, we donate it to the Winterhilfe, the party's winter relief fund.

I undertook my own "organizing", as we boys called it, usually in collaboration with my school and *Jungvolk* friends. On Saturday evenings, when the *Jungvolk* service was over and we customarily sauntered up and down the Lange, to see and be seen by the girls from the *Jungmädel*, we waited until five minutes before closing time at seven. Then we rushed into the bakeries to grab the unsold loaves, rolls, and cakes that would become stale over the weekend and therefore were given away without rationing coupons. My mother had come to depend on my success in this enterprise because *Semmel*—sweet white bread—and cocoa had become our customary Saturday night repast. Without me having been successful in the bakery there would not have been the expected meal. I don't recall that I ever failed her. *Semmel* and cocoa remained on our Saturday night menu until I left Wolfenbüttel in the fall of 1944.

Our other organizing activities depended on *Beziehungen*. "Connections" was the magic word, and we and anyone who hoped to get anything that was not otherwise available had to have connections. This meant I had to know somebody who had a kind heart or who owed me or my parents or my friends a favor. It was through connections that I could get tennis balls or bicycle tires, shoe laces, or leather soles, a bottle of peach liqueur, a canister of cocoa powder, or a carton of ice cream. Neither my friends nor I played tennis but we knew adults—some of my teachers, Mr. Fuchtel and Mr. Kühnhold—who did, and from whom we could obtain other favors for a tennis ball or two. Bicycle tires, shoe laces and leather soles always came in handy, for ourselves or for others. Without tires my bicycle was useless, and I hated nothing so much as having to tie my boots with a string or have Mr. Reinhardt nail some ersatz leather under my shoes. I'd much rather bring him a good leather sole and watch him sniff it approvingly and proceed to affix it.

Peach liquor and ice cream were our favorite ingredients for a good party, and here it was the *Jungvolk* connection that came in handy. The father of my friend Ulrich, our *Fähnlein*'s master sergeant, was the treasurer of Wolfenbüttel's Mast distillery, the maker of the famous Jägermeister. We boys didn't care for the bitter hunters' drink, but we sure loved Mast's sweet peach brandy. And as the father of one of our boys in the *Fähnlein* owned a dairy bar, at our parties we teenagers could indulge our taste for brandy-soaked ice cream.

As the war entered its fifth year these ice cream parties occurred fairly regularly. A group of us, all classmates in the *Große Schule* or fellow *Jungvolk* leaders, met in one of our homes to play Vingt-et-Un, or, as we called it, Siebzehn und Vier, the blackjack of American casinos. There was Ulrich, the *Fähnlein*'s master sergeant just mentioned, and Dieter, who by that time had become the head leader of all of Wolfenbüttel's roughly 600 *Jungvolk* boys. Etzel, who as *Fähnleinführer* was my immediate *Jungvolk* superior, always appeared, as did a few others and I, who now led a platoon of thirty boys in Etzel's *Fähnlein*. We sang ribald songs of cowboys and Indians, borrowed from the Wild West tales of Karl May and of other Germans who had never set foot in America, and embroidered our imaginations with scenes of wigwams and cattle drives that none of us had ever seen.

> *Als nun der Vollmond über'n Hügel trat,*
> *saßen beim Feuerschein,*
> *einsam ein Cowboy und sein Kamerad . . .*

and

> *Ja, die Sonne von Mexico,*
> *schien auf die wildeste Rothaut der Navajo.*[1]

1. Just as the full moon rose across the hill,
    there sat, by the fire's light,
    a lonely cowboy and his comrade . . .

The author's *Jungzug* standing at attention on the castle bridge

These were the songs that we also sang with our boys in the *Jungvolk* once we had left the *Schloßbrücke,* the bridge that led into the castle, our *Fähnlein*'s customary assembly place, and had marched down the Lange and out into the Lechlum Woods or the boondocks, the flood plain of the river Oker, south of town.

There were other songs, too, that we sang with our boys when marching through town, songs that evoked the German colonial experience in Africa:

> *Wie oft sind wir geschritten auf schmalen Negerpfad,*
> *wohl durch der Steppe Mitten, wenn früh der Morgen naht*[2]

or songs that reminded us of the battles of the World War I Free Corps,

> *hurtig sind, wie der Wind, Engelhardt'sche Reiter*[3]

---

and

> Oh, the sun of Mexico,
> shone on the wildest redskin of the Navajo . . .

2.　How often did we march on narrow bushmen's trails
through the midst of the Steppe in the cool of the morning

3.　Quick as the wind, Engelhardt's horsemen

or Nazi songs that were meant to stir us to martial enthusiasm. Of the latter, the song of the great war to come that made the rotten bones of the world tremble,

Es zittern die morschen Knochen der Welt vor dem großem Krieg

seemed to us especially rousing, though we could never quite decide whether we ought to abide by its closing line,

und heute, da hört uns Deutschland, und morgen die ganze Welt

or whether, in a burst of braggadocio, we should turn it into

und heute, gehört uns Deutschland, und morgen die ganze Welt.[4]

As for the parties, our parents—mothers, that is, for most of us, since fathers had long since left home for the front—did not object to them and did not interfere. They said we should enjoy our fun as long as we still could. There was so precious little of it. They all knew that Dieter's older brother had already been killed in the war, and none of them or us could ever know, given the nightly air raid alarms, whether we would be alive to see the sun rise the next morning. Besides, our mothers, more so than we ourselves, feared the day when we, too, would be called to arms and leave home. Thus we celebrated until the air-raid sirens would send us into the basement or, if the night remained quiet, we took off for home around midnight.

As I grew older and rose in the *Jungvolk* from a leader of ten to a leader of thirty I found it increasingly difficult to steer my way between what appeared to me as ever-growing, conflicting demands. There were, on the one hand, the expectations that as *Jungvolkführer* I take independent actions and accept responsibility for the boys under my command. I had war duties to carry out, I told my mother, such as standing fire watch during air raids and helping with clean-up work thereafter. Such tasks made it seem somehow inappropriate that I ask her for permission or promise to be back home at a certain time in the evening. On the other hand, I felt uneasy about running out on my mother when, as my father kept reminding me in his letters, she needed me for errands and work in the garden. I should take the laundry to Mrs. Frobart who had moved out of her farm house in the city

4. "And today, Germany listens to us, and tomorrow the whole world," or "And today, Germany belongs to us, and tomorrow the whole world."

and now lived at the edge of town, and I should weed the strawberry beds or pick apples and pears.

I also grew increasingly on edge listening to my mother's daily questions of whether I had done my school work. I became less and less willing to accept her directions for how I should spend my time out of school. I was particularly unhappy about her admonitions not to spend so much time on the Lange. I was afraid that my friends would ridicule me for being under my mother's thumb when I ought to be and behave like the "man in the house." So I came less and less frequently to confide in her or to respond to her requests for help with housework and shopping. I did not refuse to run errands for her, but I did it unwillingly and only after having been asked several times. It did not occur to me to volunteer such help. I thought I had more important things to do.

By the time I reached my fourteenth year my advancement as a *Jungvolk* leader made me find reasons to be away from home every afternoon. I left home around seven-thirty in the morning for school, stopped in briefly for lunch, and then did not show up again until dinnertime. Many an afternoon my friends and I spent parading up and down the Lange. We were on the lookout for girls, sometimes for the students of the *Lyceum* and sometimes for the vocational school girls. The *Lyceum* students did not customarily show up, except on Wednesdays or Saturdays when they walked home from the *Jungmädel* meetings. I had set my eyes on Ulla, who intrigued me with her long brown braids, her pretty head usually slightly cocked to one side, and her enticing smile. I saw her walking by on the opposite side of the Lange, but because her appearance always made my heart pound and my blood race, I never had the courage to cross the street and ask her whether I might accompany her. I always told myself afterward that that would have been the most natural thing in the world to do and I would do it next time. But I never did. I didn't have the courage.

Matters were not very different when the vocational school girls showed up. They looked across the street to us with an expression on their faces that was half contempt and half "I dare you." My friends made all sorts of lewd remarks about them, boasted of how "experienced" these girls were, and how they had come to know that when they had been out "hiking" with them in the Lechlum Woods or "visiting" them in somebody's home. But nobody ever went across the street to speak with them, let alone walk away with them. Our conversations about them remained remarkably vague and unspecific.

The only time I finally did meet with one of the vocational school girls was when I was fifteen years old. I was walking alone on the green belt not far from my home and encountered Brigitte. Brigitte lived not far from me on the Bahnhofstraße and, according to my friends, she was one of the "experienced" ones. She wore long black braids and a white dress as she came face to face with me on a narrow path that led between two overgrown lilac bushes, pushing her bicycle, which had a flat tire. Taken by surprise we both stopped, unsure how we could pass without touching. I stammered the obvious: "You have a flat tire, don't you?" and she responded, equally obviously, "Yes, I think so."

I offered to take a look at it, and she suggested that we move her bicycle to the basement of her apartment house. That we did, and I ended up in her living room for my first initiation into the mysteries and raptures of sex.

I never did talk to any of my friends about my encounter with Brigitte. I did not seem to have felt any need to engage in the competition of juvenile claims and exaggerations and to brag about my conquest. Rather, I experienced a sense of longing and affection and felt rather protective toward Brigitte. Ours, after all, had been a true rendezvous, not one of those make-believe stories or daydreams. I was not going to boast of having been with her. I promised myself I was going to defend her if I heard other boys speak disparagingly of her. But such occasion never happened. In the months thereafter I began to look on her as a phantom from another world that had appeared and vanished and left an unexpected gift, a gift I was not sure what to make of.

Brigitte remained that phantom only in my musings, because in the real world of Wolfenbüttel's everyday life I saw Brigitte occasionally, even spoke with her a few times when our meeting was by chance and none of my other friends were near. When I met her then I felt a deep longing for her but, at the same time, a very clear sense that I should never touch her again, that she was to remain forever the phantom she had become in my dreams, lovely, dear, unreachable. Needless to say, I never spoke to my mother about her.

In the meantime, my report cards in school began to reveal that I had entered on a slowly but steadily descending path. By Easter 1940 my overall grade was still "good"; a year later it had dropped to "almost good." Thereafter my teachers continued to testify that I had begun to slack off. Nevertheless, though I had also shown tendencies to become "disruptive," I still achieved "satisfying results."

Besides my time spent on the Lange, the cause of this decline was the disappearance of our best teachers, many of whom were called, like my father, to active duty in the armed forces. They were often replaced by men whose qualifications had little to do with academic learning or pedagogical expertise but who, like my mathematics teacher Mr. Schulz, had managed to gain the favorable attention of the party and thus found for themselves a cushy place that kept them out of danger. We boys were the first to discover these men's weaknesses and knew a thousand ways to throttle down our academic endeavors.

The other and even more potent cause of my academic decline was my growing involvement in the *Jungvolk*. As I passed my fourteenth birthday, I advanced in the ranks step by step from being responsible for a *Jungenschaft* of ten to heading a *Jungzug* of thirty and finally, as I turned sixteen, as Etzel's successor, to command a *Fähnlein* of a hundred. As the *Hitler Jugend* slogan had it that "youth was to be led by youth," we *Jungvolkführer* were free of direct adult supervision and interpreted the directives that were handed down to us from party headquarters to our own liking. We were aided by the fortuitous fact that the adult leader of Wolfenbüttel's Hitler Youth was a war hero who had lost his left arm in combat and was no more interested in Nazi ideology, party history, and Hitler's life than we were. Thus, with "the General"'s encouragement and under Etzel's leadership of our *Fähnlein*, the boring *Heimabende* on party-prescribed topics ceased. Instead we read to our boys adventure and war stories, played charades and guessing games, and acquired a vast repertoire of folk and military tunes, of hand-me-down rounds and hiking songs from the *Wandervogel* era of the Weimar Republic.

Outdoors, soccer matches and paramilitary exercises in the woods and hills surrounding Wolfenbüttel suited us just fine. Afternoons at a rifle range, with BB guns for the boys and .22-caliber rifles for us leaders, sparked our enthusiasm. As for physical education in the municipal gymnasium that I hated so much, I was now in a position to play games instead or, in the winter, ski in the city's parks and surrounding woods. When we marched through town we sang the songs of seagoing adventurers and *Landsknechte*, the mercenaries of the Middle Ages:

> *Wenn die bunten Fahnen wehen,*
> *geht die Fahrt wohl über's Meer,*

and

> *Das Leben ist ein Würfelspiel,*
> *wir würfeln alle Tage.*[5]

5. When the colored flags are waving
we shall cross the ocean blue,

and

Life is a game of dice,
we play it every day.

Etzel and his boys on the castle bridge

Our fondness for marching, singing, and music stretched farther than what party leaders could offer us in their official manuals and songbooks or would have permitted us to perform had they known about it. But when we left the city behind us and spent our Wednesday or Saturday afternoons on a clearing in the woods or at a hillside near the Oker, we loved to try out songs that we knew were strictly beyond the pale, such as, for instance, "The Internationale," the battle hymn of Communist parties everywhere. To this day I do not know how we ever got hold of text and music and which of us boy leaders managed to teach it to us. But I do remember how we first tried out the song on the banks of the Oker and how we then sang its rousing refrain,

> So comrades, come rally,
> And the last fight let us face . . .

as we marched down the Lange. I still see in my mind's eye some rather astonished passers-by on the sidewalk staring after us and shaking their heads, and I remember Etzel telling me that someone he did not know had stopped him as he walked back the Lange still in his uniform and asked him: "Did you boys know what you were singing?"

Etzel said he told him: "No, not really, but it was a rather fetching tune, wasn't it?"

Besides singing we also loved to put on all sorts of theatrical sketches of often outrageously comical and farcical content. Nothing pleased us more than to parody a Nazi-approved theme whereby, if we got called on it, we could claim to have acted in perfectly good faith. We did this with a song of the *Alte Germanen,* the Old Teutons, who, as the song had it, were sitting on both sides of the River Rhine and did a lot of drinking. In the second verse a Roman appeared among them who greeted them with "Heil Hitler" and introduced himself as Tacitus, to which the Teutons responded: "Heil Hitler, you Axis Brother, you are closely related to us," and they all together commenced another bout of drinking.

When Dieter had taken over the leadership of Wolfenbüttel's *Jungvolk,* the *Elternabend* became an annual event. It was a theatrical performance that we boys of the *Jungvolk* put on together with the girls of the *Jungmädel* on the stage of the city's Lessingtheatre for our parents and other interested citizens of Wolfenbüttel. It was during these preparations that I fell madly in love with Ulla, the *Lyceum* girl and *Jungmädel* leader whom, until then, I had only dared adore from across the Lange. At the *Elternabend* we boys and girls were to sing together

Etzel's *Fähnlein* marching on the Lange Herzogstraße

a series of songs and rounds and bring the whole evening to a close with a rousing rendition of *"Ade nun zur guten Nacht"* (Good Bye Now and Good Night), which included the lines,

> *Das hat Deine Schönheit gemacht,*
> *die hat mich zum Lieben gebracht,*
> *mit großem Verlangen.*[6]

These lines did it to me. Now, finally, when both we boys and girls disbanded after our rehearsals, I found enough courage to talk with Ulla and walk her home. My first great love swept me off my feet. For what would turn out to be the last few months of my life at home Ulla became the center of my world.

Jungvolk service during these months of 1944 brought us other war-imposed duties. We were asked to collect the blossoms of the linden trees for medicinal purposes or scrounge the city's neighborhoods for old iron, rags, and waste paper. We marched through all the city's side streets, singing loudly,

> *Lumpen, Knochen, Eisen und Papier,*
> *Ausgeschlag'ne Zähne sammeln wir,*[7]

and turned these for us boring occasions into competitive battles, not shying away from an occasional raid on the booty gathered by a competing group. We were more enthusiastic when it came to playing all sorts of indoor and outdoor war games. We horrified the good Bürger of Wolfenbüttel by chasing and beating each other in mock battles in the city streets. And we always loved, at the end of almost every meeting, to march down the Lange singing our songs of soldiers, pirates, medieval mercenaries, and African explorers, our flag flying ahead of us.

This was our world, we told ourselves, and not school nor church nor home could offer competing alternatives. During the winter break after Christmas, Etzel and I would gather our boys and teach them how to stow their gear into their backpacks and how to wax their skiis and carry them soldier-like over their shoulders. We prepared them for our annual skiing camp when we, under the leadership of Dieter, would

6.   'Twas your beauty
                     that made me fall in love
                     with the greatest of longing.

7.   Rags and bones and iron we pick up,
                     Knocked-out teeth and paper we collect

board the train to Bad Harzburg and, once there and disembarked, would set out on the twelve-mile hike to the St. Barbara Cottage at the base of the 2800-foot-high Sonnenberg Mountain. We would march, three abreast, through the town of Bad Harzburg past the tourist hotels and restaurants and one or two more miles on the highway until it was time to break ranks, throw our skiis on the ground, align ourselves in single file and begin the quiet, silent ascent, at first over the snow-covered highway and then over mountain trails, gliding through the trees, past the frozen waterfalls and lakes, with the snowflakes swirling above and around us.

For the next week in the St. Barbara Cottage we were guests of the Wolfenbüttel Anti-Aircraft Artillery Regiment. We were out in the mountains mornings and afternoons, honing our cross-country skills on ski patrols through the woods and proving our courage in racing down the mountain. Though none of us ever dared admit it, we all were glad the ski jump on top of the mountain had collapsed long ago, or else we would no doubt have challenged each other to risk legs and necks in flinging ourselves into the air. Even the mountain without the ski jump was scary enough, and I was not the only one who, halfway down its steep slope, sheared off the tip of one of his skis and ended up in a heap in the snow, a miserable bundle of shame and pain.

The high point of our week was the night combat patrol that served as a kind of graduation exercise and that earned us the right to wear on our uniform sleeve the Ski Instructor's ribbon. Dieter "The General" divided us into two groups, each instructed to pick up further orders at 11 o'clock at a location in the mountains that was defined only by the coordinates on our military maps. The orders both groups received there were the same: Move as fast as you can to the top of the Achter-mann, a 3040-foot-high bare and rocky summit; locate there a hidden metal box; and bring it to designated point on the cross-mountain highway.

It turned out to be a memorable night with many surprises. To reach our appointed pick-up point in time, Etzel, the leader of my group, had us leave the St. Barbara Cottage before our rivals did. It was a beautiful winter night, a three-quarter moon and brilliant stars shining through the fir trees and lighting our way past the frozen Oderteich and toward the old forester's home where, as we had soon surmised, "The General"'s adjutant awaited us with our orders. And so indeed it happened. Huddled at the edge of a mountain meadow we studied our maps and debated how far we might approach the top of the Achtermann on our skis, where the rocks would force us to begin the summit climb on foot, and who would climb and who would stay behind to guard the skis.

As we stared toward the mountain we noted how the stars had begun to fade and how clouds obscured the moon as they floated over its face. Soon a wind rose and snow flakes began to swirl. It then took only a few more minutes and we were hit by the full force of the storm. There was no point in trying to read our map. Etzel gave orders for us to stay in sight of each other, and we began to move off in the general direction of the mountain top. The gap between the trees gave us reasonable assurance that we were following a trail, and the rising elevation told us that we were moving in the right direction. So we glided along silently, eyes fixed on the tracks in the snow before us, anxious not to lose sight of the shadowy figure ahead of us, wondering where the other group might be and whether we would find the box on top of the mountain.

It did not take long before the blowing snow seeped into and under our uniform collars, covered our faces, and, with the darkness of the sky and the woods around us, made it more and more difficult to see where we were going. The wind kept up its monotonous whistling through the firs and allowed no other sound to be heard. Every now and then it would gust up into fierce gales of icy air, driving the snow into our faces so that it was hard to see anything.

After an hour or so of slow progression our column suddenly halted. I heard Etzel shout: "Take off your skis; run up to the left, up to the summit."

Before I had a chance to react, figures appeared out of the darkness in front of me. They were on foot, stumbling in the snow, carrying skis on their shoulders. Good Lord, I thought, they are the other group. Did they have the box already? I wondered. Who would carry it? Where were they going?

To my amazement the lead guy approaching me shouted: "Turn around, go back, its impossible. We've been on top. It's terrible. It's freezing. You can't see a thing. Nobody knows where the box is."

As I stood bewildered, wondering whether this was a ruse to have us give up the search for the box, a figure on skis loomed out of the darkness gliding toward me: "The General"!

"Put your skis back on, you idiots," he shouted at the other boys. "Turn around," he hollered at me. "Get off this mountain; meet at the highway. The exercise is finished. Move!"

And so we turned back the way we had come, the wind on our backs, the snow still falling, both groups now intermixed, following our own tracks until we hit the cut-off trail that brought us out of the trees onto the highway.

Though the storm had defeated us and we had not found the metal box that lay buried under the snow in some crevice among the boulders on the mountain top, we felt proud and elated. We had proved ourselves, had shown that we knew how to follow orders and that we were ready to move and persevere as soldiers. We were convinced that our adventure gave us a taste of what our lives and careers as soldiers and officers would be like. I thought I now felt the emotions teachers like Bodo Wacker had told me about in his stories of World War I. I believed that I now knew for myself what my father meant when he had spoken of manly comradeship in battle and of life among a company of soldiers in which each depended for his life on the other. We were soldiers. Soldiering was the life we desired.

But there were shadowy sides also to my experiences as *Jungvolk* leader and would-be soldier. My fellow leaders and I were rivals as well as comrades and competed against each other with our platoons. In our conversations we attempted to play great games of strategy, forging alliances among our *Jungzüge* and *Fähnleins*, and sought to finesse our strategic maneuvers so that we emerged with the strongest of the ever-shifting alignments. Most of the time, I seemed to wind up on the losing side, desperately seeking an ally with whom I might for once turn the balance of power in my favor. Yet I rarely succeeded and felt miserable and fearful a great deal of the time.

It was not until Etzel, in whose *Fähnlein* I advanced to the position of *Jungzugführer*, together with Dieter, who as head of all Wolfenbüttel *Jungvolk* units was well informed about these machinations, put an end to them that I felt free to endorse all my *Jungvolk* activities with unreserved zeal. Etzel, more than anyone else, pointed out to me and the other leaders in his *Fähnlein* that our real enemies were not to be found among ourselves but among the toughs of the *Hitler Jugend* and their followers from the working-class districts of the town. For them we *Jungvolk* leaders and high school students were their chosen targets. I already described how I had to watch my steps on my way to school or on errands for my mother in Wolfenbüttel's Old Town, and how I could expect to be attacked by the older boys and hooted at and bombarded with rotten apples by the younger kids under their sway. Through Etzel's advice I became aware that the comradeship and glory of the soldier's life was not to be taken for granted but had to be strived for and deliberately maintained.

Soldiers, I learned, also had to live with setbacks and defeats and with the realization that not everyone supported and agreed with us. I well remember the day in early 1943 when we were marching down the Lange, preceded by our drum and bugle corps blaring its piercing tones, and a man, wildly gesticulating, ran into the street toward our column and in an outraged voice shouted at us: "Stop that noise, get off the street, go home—thousands of our troops are freezing and dying at Stalingrad, and you can't think of anything better than bawling and blaring and rubbing salt in our wounds—go home, you fools!"

We were so shocked that our music stopped abruptly, and we trudged on toward the market, our usual place of dismissal, without a word or song on our lips. We did not know, then, how to deal with news of defeat. We would still have to learn that, and there was no one willing to help us with that lesson.

The war was like the ever-present atmosphere that enveloped us, invisible and quiet most of the time, but, when the sirens wailed and the bursts of anti-aircraft fire assaulted our ears, abruptly confronting us with thrusts of lightning and thunder claps. It confirmed us *Jungvolk* leaders in our self-image as soldiers. We all proudly wore the silver ribbon on our shoulder strap, the ribbon that announced that we had, at age fifteen, registered as volunteers for military service. I had signed up as officer's candidate for the army's elite unit, the Division Großdeutschland, the successor to the Berlin Guard Regiment of ancient lineage. Being a candidate for that position, I thought, would assure my father that I had given up all thought of joining the Armed SS. At the same time, it satisfied my ambition to join one of the country's most renowned fighting units, a unit that embodied the best of the Prussian-German military tradition.

That decision also relieved me of any further pressure from the recruiters of the SS. When they came, as they often did, to our *Jungvolk* meetings and I showed them my sign-up card for the division Großdeutschland, they knew they had lost me. If, as sometimes happened, a recruiter persisted in trying to persuade me to change my mind, I told him that after the war I intended to leave Germany for our African colonies and there become a farmer. In 1943 that statement sounded far-fetched even to an SS recruiter and I was dropped from their lists.

For me at age fifteen signing up for the division Großdeutschland, was an act of liberation. The die was now cast. My commitment to the army was sealed and my leadership position in the *Jungvolk* validated. I now was and would forever be a soldier. I steeped myself in book after book on German military history. I kept on leading my boys marching down the Lange, singing the songs of the Blue Dragoons who rode through the city gate, their bugles and drums accompanying them, and of the Red Hussars whose horses never slowed down, and I absorbed deeply into every fiber of my being the Prussian military code of *mehr sein als scheinen*—substance over appearance.

Yes, I had my questions and my second thoughts when in my life as a *Jungvolk* leader I encountered ambiguities and contradictions as I had at home and in school. I could not dismiss from my mind the unpleasant, even frightening experiences of internecine rivalry among our *Jungvolk* units. I could not rid myself of the nagging awareness that my commitment to my *Jungvolk* activities was the cause of my declining academic achievements and growing unwillingness to help my mother. I felt myself trapped when I sought to follow what I took to be the soldierly ideals of my father only to realize that he disapproved of much of what I did. Worst of all, there was the memory of that day in November of 1938; a memory that, every now and then, would wake me up at night with images of my parents and me stumbling down some stairs, a memory that, like the other questions and second thoughts, I tried hard to suppress. I found no way of dealing with them; I felt stymied when I could not find answers and explanations, when I felt myself lost in ambiguities and contradictions.

But I also would not let these unresolved questions deter me from pursuing what I took to be my destined path. I told myself they were part of everyday existence to be faced and overcome. A soldier had to remain steadfast and unperturbed, no matter what. I was, after all, going to be a professional soldier. In fact, in my *Jungvolk* uniform with its green and white *Fähnleinführer* cord on my left and the volunteer's silver ribbon on my right shoulder, the Ski Instructor's ribbon on my sleeve, and the sharp-shooter button and sports medal on my breast pocket, I already *was* a soldier and an officer, a boy soldier, to be sure, but a soldier nonetheless. My military career had already begun.

6

Assignment East

IN THE SUMMER OF 1943 the adult leadership of the Hitler Youth in
Wolfenbüttel asked nine of us *Jungvolk* leaders whether we were
ready during our vacation to spend four weeks in the areas of
Poland occupied by the German army. We were to carry out there our
normal *Jungvolk* activities with the local Polish boys, go camping with
them, teach them to march and to sing, play soccer, engage in athletic
contests, and tell them what life was like for our boys in the Reich.

For us there was only one possible answer. Of course we were
ready to go. We were impatient to travel and I wanted to see the for-
merly Polish lands I had heard so much about in Mr. Fuchtel's class. We
were eager to carry to Polish boys our enthusiasm for sports, parades,
war games, and all the other things we did at home. We saw that invitation as a great adventure, a once-in-a-life-time oppportunity. We told
ourselves that this was going to be the high point of our lives thus far.
We would be able to prove what we were capable of. We could see for
ourselves whether our ideals would stand the test on foreign soil, and
we could do our part to help the war effort. I cherished the additional
thought that I would now follow in my father's steps, would see the
country he had seen and written about in his letters and, if luck was
with me, perhaps have a chance to meet him there.

None of us gave it a second thought. None of us imagined, even
for a minute, that our hopes and expectations might be dashed; that
instead of introducing Polish boys to our ways of the *Jungvolk*, instead
of inspiring them with our ideals and aspirations, we might discover
with our own eyes the reality of the Nazi domination of Poland, the
misery it brought to the boys we had wanted to be with, and the corruption that clung to the occupiers who claimed to be Hitler Youth
leaders and our superiors.

But that is what we encountered. The cruelty we saw inflicted upon the Polish boys in the camp to which we were sent and the debauchery in which their tormentors indulged were so stark and so gross that we, at first, did not recognize them for what they were. We were astonished, then dumbfounded, and just as we were about to digest and understand what confronted us, we were thrown out of the camp, sent individually into widely dispersed towns and villages where we could no longer communicate with one another, and then shipped back home, decried as traitors, unworthy of the uniform we wore.

We were left to our own devices, unsure of our own reactions. Were the Nazi rulers of Poland, the professional Hitler Youth leaders among them, cruel and corrupt, or was it our naivete that blinded us to the necessities of war and occupation? Who would tell us? Who would answer such questions? Were we traitors, indeed, for having sought answers from the Polish boys we met in the camp? Would we, on our return home, be removed from our leadership positions in the *Jungvolk*, as the Hitler Youth men in the camp had threatened, and would our careers as soldiers and officers be cut off before they ever had really begun? We did not know; we feared the worst. As a result, on our return to Wolfenbüttel, we were all too ready to forget and suppress what we had learned if only no one was going to ask and remind us. We were going to continue leading our boys as though nothing had happened, as though we had forgotten what we had seen.

All this, of course, was far from our minds when we began our journey on the appointed day. With Dieter, "The General", as our leader, we nine gathered at the Wolfenbüttel railroad station early in the morning, resplendent in our uniforms, packs on our backs, canteens dangling on our sides, a new merit stripe *Osteinsatz*—Assignment East—stitched to our sleeves. The train took us to Braunschweig where we changed to the Berlin express. Our destination in the Reichshauptstadt was the national headquarters of the Hitler Youth. There we were to be briefed on our assignment and to get our marching orders.

We arrived at headquarters late in the afternoon and were met by a few officious-looking adult leaders who did not appear happy to see us. It was supper time, and they wanted to go home. Thus our briefing took all of five minutes. We were given train tickets for midnight on the second day after. Kattowitz, now Katowice, Silesia, was our destination, and we were asked to report to the local Hitler Youth office. Someone there would hand us our assignments. Then we were sent on our way to a nearby youth hostel.

We stayed in Berlin for two more days and embarked on a series of sightseeing excursions. On the first day, under a cloudy sky with an occasional cool, moist wind blowing, we walked through the Lust-garten, the great park that bordered the Reichstag and the Branden-burger Tor and looked up at the blood-red flags with their swastikas that hung limp from the tops of the buildings. Except for a lonely streetcar rolling past the Reichstag, the street at the park's edge was quiet. We walked along Unter den Linden and thought of Frederick the Great and the Kaiser's armies as they celebrated their victory parades on this historic ground. There were not many other people around. A few older men and women shuffled along or sat on benches. Soldiers on leave, their gas masks in their canisters hanging from their shoul-ders, stared with their girl friends at the Alte Wache, the famed memo-rial for Prussia's troops, at the other end of the Linden. The structure's entrances were now bricked up to protect it against bombs and fire. We turned toward the Wilhelmstraße and took pictures of the Füh-rer's Reichskanzlei with the SS guard in front and the huge stylized eagle spreading its wings over the entrance. These were the places we had been told we had to see, and we dutifully photographed them all. Somehow, we were not very excited about it and felt that we were doing what we were supposed to do. Our interest picked up only when we took a subway to see the Olympic Stadium with its two square towers guarding the entrance. We wanted to get inside, sit on one of the seats, and pretend we were watching the events we had seen be-fore in the movies and had read about in the papers. But the gates were locked, and the stadium was empty and silent. Berlin seemed a dead city.

The next morning we rode the train to Potsdam, visited the Garri-son Church where ten years before the old General Hindenburg had bestowed the chancellorship on Adolf Hitler, and wandered through the parks at Frederick the Great's *Schloß* Sans Souci. Once we had left the church with its austere surroundings of the wide, clean-swept parade ground behind, we liked it better in Potsdam. Perhaps that was because by the time we reached Sans Souci the sky was blue, birds sang in the park, and the loving couples, again soldiers with their girls, smiled and laughed. We, too, had our fun, hid behind the marble fauns and caressed the breasts of the nude statues in the park, and claimed the Chinese Pagoda as our, albeit temporary, headquarters. Back in Berlin we ate our supper at the hostel, and then took the subway to the Silesian Station where we caught the Kattowitz express at midnight.

The journey was a nightmare. On the platform we had trouble staying together in the masses of soldiers with their guns and helmets, bedrolls and packages. Most of them had been home on leave and were now returning to the Eastern front. They were not in the best of moods. Many of them were drunk, and we saw them press ruthlessly through the crowd to get away from the constantly patrolling military policemen whose silver sheets on their chests reflected the few beams of light that shone through the slit-like openings of the blacked-out platform lanterns. I was afraid that I might lose my footing and be pushed onto the rails of the track. A shrill blast from the locomotive's whistle announced the arrival of the train and the ear-tearing scream of the brakes made me wince. The wagons seemed already full with soldiers leaning out of the windows and mocking those on the platform trying to get in with sarcastic advice: "Stay home, fellow, don't be a fool. What do you want to go to Russia for?"

It did not take more than two or three minutes, and the crowd on the platform, including the nine of us, had been pushed and squeezed through the doors with a generous assist from the burly military policemen.

As the train began to move, the nine of us found ourselves in the aisle that ran alongside the car's compartments. In the compartments soldiers drank and talked or lay snoring, pressed into corner seats or against their neighbors. We nine spent the night half lying, half sitting on the floor of the passageway, trying as best as we could to keep our uniforms from getting soiled on the dirty floor, awakened every few minutes by a soldier trying to make his way to the restroom at the end of the car. There were no lights in the train as enemy planes could be expected at any time, and a total blackout was by then the rule all over Germany.

I don't remember how often the train ground to a halt, as all the stations, blacked-out and deserted for the most part, looked the same. As, toward morning, the sky began to lose its blackness and filtered its lightening gray through the dirty windows, we entered the Silesian industrial area with its coke ovens and gas flames shooting up into the air all along the track. A penetrating smell of gas and coal pervaded everything, and soot and coal dust seemed to have settled everywhere and painted everything outside a water-streaked dark gray. When the train slowed down again a soldier called to us, "Hey, boys, get ready, next station is Kattowitz," and we wearily roused ourselves from our cramped positions on the aisle floor, strapped on our backpacks, and waited until the wheels, after much screeching and bucking, finally came to a stop. One of us flung open the wagon door, and we clambered down the steps to the platform. We had arrived in Poland.

It was between eight and nine in the morning, and we made our way to the local Hitler Youth headquarters. As we entered what looked like a fashionable, middle-class home and were led to a basement kitchen, we were treated to a breakfast of hard rolls and cocoa by some Polish girls and then ushered upstairs into an office room. There again we encountered some very officious-looking, unsmiling adults in Hitler Youth uniforms who gave Dieter written instructions to report forthwith to a tent camp called Birkental. We would like it there, one of the men said, because it was pretty and we would not have much to do. I wondered just what that meant. I didn't mind if it was pretty but we had come to do our jobs, not to loaf.

We walked back to the Kattowitz railway station and, after a short wait, climbed on an almost empty local train. With its belching locomotive and its antiquated cars it chugged along slowly with many stops along the way. At our point of disembarkation, a station whose name I have now forgotten, the instructions read we were to march four to five miles to the Birkental camp along a country road planted with beautiful birch trees that, no doubt, had given their name to the camp. It was a pleasant walk. Meadows and forests extended to the right and left, and swallows darted along our path and over the fields. Eventually we saw in the distance white tent tops in rows of ten or twelve gleaming in the sunshine, set off against another patch of dark green woods. As we came closer we made out the red and white Hitler Youth banner hanging limply from a flag post and a wire fence stretching between rows of wooden posts to the left and right of the entrance.

When we reached the gate we were met by a young man in Hitler Youth uniform, a small caliber rifle slung over his shoulder. He stepped out of a wooden guard house painted with red and white stripes and raised a similarly painted metal barrier to allow us entry. As we stepped through the gate we saw that the fence on either side was not, as we had assumed, made of simple wire strands to keep cattle out of the camp but consisted of double strings of barbed wire. Our greeter pointed to a tent behind the entrance and said: "We have been expecting you. Get your orders in the tent from the commander of the guard."

We looked at each other, somewhat puzzled, shrugged our shoulders and moved toward the tent. We had been to many a *Jungvolk* camp at home, but Birkental was something else. We never had posted armed guards at our tent camps, and we never surrounded them with barbed wire. We wondered what was going on here.

We had little time to consider that question just then because we entered the tent and met another adult in Hitler Youth uniform, a revolver strapped to his belt, sitting behind a table and looking at us quizzically.

"So there you are, you boys from the Reich," he said. "We are glad you have come to help us, but don't think you can tell us what to do. This is *our* camp"—and he stressed the word *our*—"and you will fit in and do things our way, I am sure. Now, Scharführer Lange, here," and

105

Camp Birkental

he pointed to a lanky fellow who lazily pushed himself out of a camp stool, "will show you to your tents. After that you grab your rations, and then report back here to me for guard duty." With that he rose and waved us out of the tent.

We followed Scharführer Lange through the meadow with its rows of tents until he stopped at the far corner of the ground and pointed to two tents that, he said, were to be ours. He suggested we stow our gear, pick up our rations from a long table that stood a few feet away underneath a row of trees, and then return to the guard tent for further orders.

Once he had left us, we looked at each other, and one of us said, wonderingly, "Guard duty? Is that what we came for?"

"We shall soon see," Dieter replied, "but let's keep our eyes and ears open to learn what this is all about."

Sure enough, when we came back to the guard tent the man with the revolver told us that our task for the next four weeks was for three of us to be in charge of the camp's guard detail every third day. We were to devise our own system of rotation and, on our two off-duty days, had no particular functions to perform. However, we were not expected to leave the camp, unless with special permission of the camp leader. Our duty, the man explained, consisted of assigning to guard duty and supervising a group of specially chosen and trusted

Polish boys. They were to patrol the camp day and night along the barbed wire. The boys, he told us, had orders to challenge anyone who approached the wire from inside the camp. If their challenge was ignored or they were attacked, they were to make use of their small caliber rifles and fire. As he noted our incredulous stares, he added: "This isn't the Reich, you know. You are in Poland. Now, go, and take up your duties."

We could hardly believe our ears. Here we had come all the way from Germany in order to introduce Polish boys—who we expected to be much like our own at home—to camping and sporting events, games and scavenger hunts, and to the fun of singing folk songs and rounds. And now we were to be used only once every third day for guarding a camp whose inmates were suspected of wanting to escape any moment they got a chance? What kind of a camp was this?

We returned to our tents and took council. On the way back we had noticed other strange goings-on. We had seen an adult leader in Hitler Youth uniform, a revolver strapped to his side, order four or five Polish boys to jump in a squatting position across the length of a narrow sand pit. The boys, in brown fatigues without any of the customary symbols indicating rank and home area, were loaded down with back packs and held heavy wooden beams, resembling railroad ties, on their outstretched arms. Each jump made them sway precariously on their haunches and sink deep into the sand. The uniformed man constantly harassed them with shouted curses to hurry up and threatened them with a whip when they slowed down. As one of the boys slipped, toppled to the side and let his beam fall to the ground, the leader cracked his whip over the boy's head, kicked him from behind, and shouted at him to pick up his beam and catch up with the others. We were aghast. This was not our concept of Hitler Youth service and certainly not of our *Jungvolk*. This was more like what we had read of punishment routines in an army penal battalion. We realized that we had entered a different world from what we had expected, but we were not sure just how we should react. We agreed that we needed to find out more about this camp and its inmates and leaders.

So we decided that during the night Dieter and two others would leave our tents and try to make contact with the Polish boys in theirs. Those of us who did not go gathered in one tent to hear the report of our emissaries. It was a cloudy night with raindrops falling at intervals. We lay silent in our sleeping bags on the straw straining to hear whether we could make out any sounds of our comrades. But everything remained quiet. I must have dozed off because I sat up with a start when the tent flap was jerked open and Dieter and our two friends appeared and slipped in a little after midnight.

They reported that at first they had been received with suspicion by the Polish boys but that after they had stated their mission and had been asked to enter one of the tents, they had engaged in a long conversation. The Polish boys had told them that almost all of them were between fifteen and seventeen years old and worked all year long as apprentices in the coal mines of Silesia. They were entitled to two weeks' vacation during the year but were forced to spend this time in the Birkental camp. They hated the camp with a passion but detested even more their so-called "leaders," adults from the Reich who, through party membership and other connections, had found protected jobs that kept them from being drafted into the army. The Polish boys described them as corrupt and vindictive, a gang of war profiteers who lorded it over them with sadistic abandon. Dieter suggested that, as it was late and there was not much we could do that night, we all mull over what we had heard and seen and keep our eyes and ears open during the next few days and take notes of everything we observed in the camp.

Just how corrupt the camp leadership was and how much these men profited from their cushy position we were to find out the following night. A few minutes after lights-out had sounded we were aroused by one of the local German leaders, who ordered us to come to the kitchen of the camp commander's compound in the woods at the far side of the camp: *"Führerfraß"* (leaders' banquet), he said.

Again, we could hardly believe our ears. What were we going to experience now? The man led us away from the tent area past the woods at the far edge of the camp to a large blockhouse half hidden in the trees. As we entered we stepped into a brightly lit dining room where we confronted a huge table loaded with sausages, hams, and breads, with cakes and tortes, apples, pears, peaches, strawberries, bananas, and pineapples, the latter being fruit we had not seen since the beginning of the war. We were treated to cigarettes and coffee—cigarettes that to us *Jungvolk* leaders, and presumably to all Hitler Youth members, were strictly forbidden—and coffee that, for most Germans, had become unobtainable. The feast continued until midnight and into the early morning hours, and we returned to our tents incredulous and more at a loss than ever to know what to do.

As it was, the camp leadership relieved us of the burden of our indecision. The next day all nine of us, those on guard duty and those whiling away the time by reading or exploring the confines of the camp, were called back to the camp commander's compound "on the double," as we were told by a messenger. Until then we had seen the commander only through the dense cigarette smoke of the *Führerfraß* the night before. Now he awaited us in that same dining room where he towered over us on a raised rostrum. It was obvious that something dramatically threatening was brewing. He could hardly contain himself and trembled as he let loose a string of profanity and shouted at us: "You traitors, you swine, you dirty bastards without honor and loyalty. You are not worthy of the name German," and on and on he bellowed.

He had found out about our night talks with the Polish boys. That, he told us, had been high treason. That had put us beyond the pale in the camp and, as far as he was concerned, beyond the pale everywhere and forever. He was going to make sure that our treachery was reported to the Hitler Youth headquarters in Berlin and in Wolfenbüttel, and he was going to make an example of us. Back home, he shouted, we would be relieved of all rank and position in the *Jungvolk.* To make sure that we would never again gain influence or honor, he would report us to the armed forces as unworthy of any future commissioned or noncommissioned career. With that he confined us to our tents and said he was going to find a different assignment for us.

We were stunned, to say the least. We had no idea to what extent he was in a position to do us lasting damage and whether his threats would follow us on our way back home. But we had to fear the worst. In his fury he had lectured us that, as participants in the Hitler Youth's Assignment East, we stood under military orders and, back home, we would have to face the equivalent of a court-martial. There was not going to be a military career for any of us. He was going to see to that.

A day later we were asked to report back to the Hitler Youth headquarters in Kattowitz. We gathered our gear, marched back past the silvery-green birches, and chugged into town on the local train. The staff in the office stared at us with a mixture of curiosity and contempt. The head man, obviously seeking to get rid of us as fast as possible, pushed travel orders and train tickets into our hands. He split us up into groups of two or three and told us that, at our assigned localities, we were to conduct meetings with the local Hitler Youth and *Jungvolk* units. As far as he was concerned, we were on our own. In three weeks we should report back to him and he would hand us our return tickets to Berlin. With that we were dismissed.

Etzel and I were dispatched to the small mining town of Radlin where we were to stay in the house of the town's Nazi party leader and his wife. The Beutlers were *Volksdeutsche,* that is, ethnic Germans who had lived in German settlements in Hungary and now had agreed to move into occupied Polish areas whose native population had been expelled. They were supposed to get us in touch with whatever Hitler Youth groups existed in the area. When Etzel and I arrived in Radlin and found the Beutlers' home, our hosts suggested that Etzel meet with the boys in Radlin and I seek out my contingent in a neighboring village. They added that a carnival had set up its booths and merry-go-rounds there on a field, and all I had to do was to follow the sound of the music and I would surely find the boys.

It was in the early afternoon that I, dressed in my *Jungvolk* uniform, set out on the two-mile hike through fields of rye, looking and listening for the carnival. I could not fail to find my destination. The sounds of the steam calliope and the bells on the merry-go-rounds were un-mistakable, as were the sights of tents billowing in the breeze and the sweet smell of Turkish toffee and burnt almonds, even though the wartime "toffee" was made of barley and the "almonds" were really hazelnuts from last year's harvest.

As I turned into the fair grounds I saw plenty of boys standing and walking around, none of them in uniform, and all of them, as soon as they spied me, turning toward me and staring at me. They probably had never seen anyone in a *Jungvolk* uniform before. From all I could tell, they were a varied lot. By the looks of their clothes they worked on farms and in the coal mines. Many of them wore shirts with their sleeves cut off, showing arms that were the size of my thighs. They were laughing and saying things I could not understand, not only be-cause they spoke Polish but also because of the tinkling bells of the carousels and the shouting of the barkers. I began to wonder whether, perhaps, I had made a big mistake to walk, all by myself and in my *Jungvolk* uniform, into this rough-looking crowd that reminded me of nothing so much as the Wolfenbüttel working-class toughs—only in Wolfenbüttel I could understand their language, knew what they had in mind and how I could escape. Here I had nothing but my wits to rely on.

I instinctively knew that I could not turn and run, as I might have wanted to. I would have demonstrated not just my own cowardice but, even worse, I would have let down Etzel and Dieter and all the boys at home. So I screwed up my courage and walked straight to a group of boys that had gathered in front of a shooting gallery.

"Are you the boys from the Hitler Youth?" I asked.

They stared at me and said nothing.

"Wasn't I supposed to meet you here?" I added.

"Who are you?" finally said one of them in German. "What do you want here?"

I told them who I was and that I had come to meet them and show them what we did at home in our *Fähnlein*.

There were a couple of guffaws and a few words in Polish, which, from the smirks on the speakers' faces, I could guess meant something like "just what we have been waiting for."

"All right," said the guy who had asked me who I was, "then let's start right here." He spoke in German and challenged me to get a gun and show him what I could do.

This was the acid test, I knew. If I failed it, I would not like what would happen next. I knew I had to get back home to Radlin through those fields of rye. It would be getting dark by then. I might never make it. Those boys knew the countryside, but I did not.

I stepped up to the shooting gallery, tossed the man a few coins and asked for a BB gun, loaded it with its magazine of ten pellets, compressed the air reservoir, and took aim at the moving cutouts of deer, bears, hares, and pigeons that, fastened on little white sticks of plastic, passed before me. I squeezed my left eye shut, peered over the rifle barrel with my right, took a deep breath, and murmured silently, Lord, help me, and pulled the trigger.

The first bear fell off its pedestal. I pumped up the air once more, took aim, pulled the trigger again, and a hare tumbled to the ground. I repeated this procedure until the magazine was empty. Ten little animal figures lay in the saw dust, and the man behind the counter gave me a stuffed teddy bear.

I had passed the test. The boys nodded and grinned sheepishly, asked me whether I would come back the next day. I quickly seized that opportunity to bow out gracefully, saying I probably would, but couldn't promise, and moved off to the path that led back to Radlin. Even then, when I was on my way, I couldn't help but look back frequently, making sure I was not being followed. Something told me I had better get home before darkness set in. It was not a good idea, I thought to myself, in the summer of 1943 when dusk fell to be a lone boy in a *Jungvolk* uniform in the midst of a Polish rye field. When I got home Etzel, too, had returned from his meeting with the boys in Radlin. He told me that not one of his boys had shown up. We both decided that we weren't going to go to any further such appointments.

The rest of my stay in Radlin was memorable only for two events. Mr. Beutler received permission for Etzel and me to visit a coal mine. When we showed up in the morning, Etzel and I were told to change into miners' clothes, including hard hat and head lamp. Our guide took us to the elevator and we descended to the 300-meter level. Down there in the darkness, with only widely spaced lanterns and our bobbing head lamps shedding a dim, yellowish light on the black walls of the eight-foot-high tunnel, we followed a narrow-gauge rail line until our guide halted at a small hole in the floor to our left. It was the entrance to an inclined shaft, five feet wide and five feet high, that descended at an angle of 30 degrees into the ground. It was pitch-black in there, and the blackness seemed ready to lacerate the unwary passserby from all sides with its ragged and sharp protusions of rock and coal. But there we were, with no choice for Etzel and me but to follow our guide, who had now begun to crawl on his back, feet first, down to the next opening at the 500-meter level.

We now had nothing left by which to gauge our progress but the points of light from our head lamps that caressed the sides of the shaft. I thought the blackness would never end, and I fought with myself to suppress attacks of claustrophobia. Once along the way we came upon miners at work as they bored their compressed air hammers into the massive coal beds over our heads. The noise of their hammers was deafening, and the coal dust that swirled around them and us stopped up my nose and made me sneeze and wheeze. Our guide used a flashlight he carried in his hand to signal to the miners to stop their work and let us slide alongside them on our backs. The miner next to me bumped my arm a couple of times and pointed to his hammer and to me, inviting me to try out for myself how much coal I could scrape loose from the bed. I was foolish enough to take him up on it and, as he pushed himself upward from where he lay, I slid over to his former place, grabbed the hammer and sought to lift it up and press against the coal bed overhead. The hammer seemed to weigh a hundred pounds and nearly crushed me as it lay on top of me. I could not even lift it, let alone press it against the coal above me and pull its trigger. The miners laughed, and our guide motioned for Etzel and me to move on. As I continued sliding downward on my back, my hands pressed against the ground, I could not help but think of the Polish boys at Birkental for whom this was their daily routine fifty weeks out of the year. I could now understand even better their anger and desperation at being ordered to go to camp during their vacation and there be brutalized by their German masters.

The second event was my father's visit. My father, who had been stationed in Poland and the Ukraine since he had left us in August of 1939, had managed to get a pass to the resort town of Zakopane in the Carpathian Mountains. From there he had made his way to Radlin and had found me at the home of the Beutlers. We did not have much time to be together, and as I remember it, we spent most of the Saturday afternoon and the Sunday morning in the Beutlers' garden. I had many questions to ask, most pressingly those that concerned my experiences in the Birkental camp. What did my father think of all that?

My father did not seem too surprised by what I related, mainly saddened and angry. In response he told me some of his experiences in Poland and the Ukraine. But he did not speak much of his military assignments. He spoke mainly of his soldiers; how he had come to cherish the confidences and trust of his men, Silesian farmers and

The author with his father in Radlin, Poland

simple peasants and woodcutters from the Bohemian Mountains; how they had wives and children; how they loved them; how they suffered from being separated from them; how they felt sorrow and pain when they got news of illnesses, deaths, unfaithfulness, and divorces at home. He said that his own soldiers were not really different at all from the Polish families he had been with and the Ukrainian and Russian peasants in whose simple cottages he had been quartered. Over and over he returned to the sameness of simple pleasures of simple people, no matter whether they were Poles or Germans, and he spoke feelingly of the hospitality of Ukrainian and Russian peasants.

And then it became clear to me how in all his narrations he was answering my questions about Birkental. He told me not to be surprised that his Ukrainian and Russian hosts had received him so warmly. When the first German troops had arrived in their villages the people had been thankful, he said, deeply grateful because they looked upon him and his men as their liberators and protectors. He told me how he had listened to them at night in their shelters tell their tales of starvation and persecution under the Soviets; how brutal Stalinist terror had been, and how they prayed that it would never return.

And then my father looked at me and asked me: "Do you now know why I am sad and angry? Because we are now doing the same to them." After a second or so, he continued: "Oh, not all of us. My men don't do it, and our fighting soldiers on the front line didn't do it either. We know what we are fighting for, and it is a better world, a world without terror, without brutality, not a world of hate and murder and death."

"But there are others, who came later, who had other aims in mind, who came to enrich themselves, and who looked down upon the people and terrorized them, just like the Bolsheviks had done. You now have seen some of them for yourself. The ones you call corrupt and brutal. They defile our cause; they besmirch our name; they drag us all down in the dirt with them."

He was silent then for a while, and so was I. And then he added: "The people you met in the camp, those so-called leaders, sabotage and undercut our own cause. They alienate the Polish people when we should and could persuade them to be our friends. But you don't have to be afraid of them. You can be sure, they will not whisper a word of your 'treason' to anyone. They are far too afraid that word of their corruption and misdeeds will spread, and that's the last thing they want. Put them out of your mind, they are not worth your thoughts." It turned out that my father was right. When my comrades and I came back to Wolfenbüttel our local adult leadership knew nothing about our difficulties in the camp. When we tried to tell them, their response was a curt, "Forget it."

After my father had left, time dragged on in Radlin. It was clear that the Hitler Youth leadership in Kattowitz was not eager to send us back before our allotted four-week term was up. Mr. Beutler, too, did not press me or Etzel to meet with the local youths. But he did arrange for us to visit the steel and iron works near Cieszyn at the Czech border. He took us by car to one of the mills, and we walked with him into that roaring plant where tongues of red-hot glowing steel came shooting out of the ovens, where iron workers clad only in leather pants and leather aprons grabbed these tongues with oversized steel pliers and spun them around heavy steel posts so they would dart off in the opposite direction and then pass on rollers to the next set of pillars, to be turned around once more until the white glistening steel gradually cooled. We saw the cauldrons of glowing liquid iron slowly tip and pour their contents into molds, sending clouds of steam and superheated air through the halls of the plant. The combination of the deafening noise, the stifling temperature surrounding us, the bitterly pungent smell of the steam that swirled around us, and the shifting play of colors—the red-hot of the ingots, the glistening silvery-white of the steel rails, and the black of the slowly tipping vats—was the closest to hell I had ever come.

But it wasn't the last and the most-lasting of all the views into the abyss that we saw that day. That view came as almost an afterthought, unplanned and surely not desired by Mr. Beutler. It came when we were on our way out of the plant and a vista opened over an immense open-pit mine. We looked down into a vast hole, dug into the ground, a hole in which dozens of gray-clad men and women, each wearing strips of yellow cloth on their backs, were pushing small carts loaded with black coal up the winding rails that led from the pit to the plant. The constant slow-moving procession winding in switchbacks up the side of the pit, here from right to left and there from left to right, looked like a giant ant hill with coal-dust-covered insects running hither and thither. Down at the bottom there were other "ants" at work, clawing and scraping with pickaxes and shovels to loosen the coal and throw it into the carts.

We asked Mr. Beutler who these people were and he told us they were Jews from the concentration camp who were "helping" to keep the plant productive. There was little we said at the time, but I could not help wondering: Would Albert Morgenstern or his parents be among them?

Soon thereafter our four weeks came to an end, and we took the train back to Berlin and home. In Wolfenbüttel no one mentioned or asked about our expulsion from the camp. The Hitler Youth leadership did not want to hear about it, and we were not eager to spread the word either. For the boys in our *Fähnlein* I wrote a report in which I attributed our leaving the camp to our displeasure with our guard duty and our being plagued with body and head lice. I wrote that we finally succeeded in getting transferred to other duties. I taught my boys in the *Jungzug* a song about a beautiful girl that lived in a little Polish town and never allowed anyone to kiss her:

> *In einem Polenstädtchen*
> *da wohnte einst ein Mädchen, die war so schön.*
> *Sie war das allerschönste Kind,*
> *das man in Polen find.*
> *Aber nein, aber nein, sprach sie: Ich küsse nicht.*[1]

That song seemed to satisfy the boys' curiosity about my trip to Poland and they asked no further questions. If I had learned a lesson from my Polish experience it was how to turn people's attention away from scenes I did not want them to see and to keep them from asking questions I did not want to answer. I had learned how to keep silent on issues such as corruption, cruelty, and steel mills with concentration camp labor, which I knew nobody wanted to hear about.

Still, I felt uneasy about what I would tell or ask my mother about my experiences in Poland. My mother, of course, was happy to see me back and was full of questions. Most of all she wanted to know about my father. I told her all I could remember about my meeting with him, how well he looked and how much time we had had to talk. But I related very little of what we had talked about. My father had asked me not to worry my mother, and I took that admonition as a convenient excuse not to talk about things like the camp and the steel mill, which I did not really want to speak about anyway. I was not sure in my own mind what all these things meant, and, being unsure, I did not want to have to face that question.

But however reluctant I was to talk about these things with others, I could not suppress my own thoughts and questions that kept pursuing me. What *did* all this mean? Were my experiences just examples of the unavoidable dirty underside of war that had to be tolerated for the

1.   In a little Polish town
              there once lived a girl who was so beautiful.
              She was the most beautiful child
              that you would ever find in Poland.
              But no, but no, she said: I do not kiss.

greater good that was to emerge, or had I uncovered part of a ghastly horror play that had made all of us willing or unwilling, witting or un-witting participants in evil?

And what about my father? He had, for the first time, admitted to me that there were things not right in our country, that there was cor-ruption and brutality, that not all our leaders were honorable men and brave soldiers. In fact, he had said more to me than I at first wanted to admit to having heard. But the memory of what he said stayed in my mind and kept popping up. It was when he spoke of "the others, . . . the ones you call corrupt and brutal; they [who] defile our cause; they [who] besmirch our name; they [who] drag us all down in the dirt with them," that he added, "and the Armed SS are among the worst of them. We in the army shall have to call them to account. But," he con-tinued, "that will have to wait until the war is won. Then will come a day of reckoning."

"Then will come a day of reckoning"—that phrase took on a life of its own in my mind. When it burst to the surface, as it did periodically, I thought of corruption and brutality. I saw again in my mind the barbed wire around the Birkental camp, the laden table at the *Führerfraß*, the boys with the beams on their outstretched arms, the antlike people in the open pit mine. I thought of the Ukranian and Russian peasants who were now being exploited and oppressed by the very same men they had greeted as their liberators. What was I to make of all that? How were these sights going to shape my future? Where did they fit in a world that I had assumed was governed by love of country and of people, of loyalty and of honor? I felt doubt invading my thinking. To the ambiguity of my life in school and in the *Jungvolk* now was added doubt about the honorableness of my country's cause.

7

St. Mary's Tower

MY FATHER'S WORDS IN RADLIN had made it clear to me that he, too, struggled with the ambiguities that surrounded me, and that honorable men had good reason to be upset with the course their country pursued. I asked myself how a soldier like my father could remain so steadfast in the performance of his assignments when he questioned the righteousness and the honor of the cause he fought for. Was it true that duty came first and above everything else? And by what yardstick did he measure and condemn the actions of the SS? And what was it that gave him strength to hold fast to his sense of duty when he recognized the compromises with evil that this duty demanded of him?

As I pondered these questions I thought of his and Bodo Wacker's tales of World War I and "Parson" Wille's prediction to us boys in the *Sexta* that a time would come when we would fall back on the hymns of our Lutheran songbook for comfort and support. My thoughts turned to my grandfather Felix, the Protestant minister and Latin schoolmaster who had married my parents and baptized me, and to my grandmother Alma, who personified for me the Lutheran minister's faithful wife and helpmate, and I wondered just what their faith had meant and did mean to them and my mother.

When I was a small child my grandfather Felix had been a figure of imposing authority and control. By the time I came to know him, he had given up his pastorate and served as a professor at one of the municipal Latin schools in Chemnitz. He ruled over his family by the sheer power of his commanding eyes and his gravelly voice. He never had to raise it. A quick and threatening, *"Na, was soll's?"* a stare of his steel-blue eyes, and a knock with his fingers on the table top, and everyone did as he was bid.[1] My uncle Gerhard, my aunt Mausi, my mother, and my grandmother seemed to take it for granted that in his house his will was to be done. They did not question it and they did not seem to resent it. They also knew, as I did, that they could turn to him with their worries and requests, and that he would listen and comfort them.

Because my grandfather was no tyrant. His authority was tempered with affection for us all, and an irrepressible humor pervaded his talk. When he refused my requests for a piece of his chocolate which he kept locked in the drawer of his writing desk, he would quote Wilhelm Busch,

> Abstinence we call the pleasure,
> from things we cannot have as treasure.[2]

By the time I had reached the age of six or seven, he also taught me the Latin version of Busch's Max and Moritz stories and the poems of Christian Morgenstern, such jewels as

> The Picket Fence
> One time there was a picket fence
> with space to gaze from hence to hence.

and

> The Sniffle
> A sniffle crouches on the terrace
> in wait for someone he can harass.
>
> And suddenly he jumps with vim
> upon a man by name of Schrimm.
>
> Paul Schrimm, responding with "hatchoo,"
> is stuck with him the weekend through.[3]

---

1. In tone and effect, my grandfather's, *"Na, was soll's?"* is more like the English, "Hey, what's that supposed to mean?"
2.   *Enthaltsamkeit ist ein Vergnügen*
       An Sachen, welche wir nicht kriegen
3.   *Der Lattenzaun*
       Es war einmal ein Lattenzaun
       mit Zwischenraum, hindurchzuschaun.
and
            Der Schnupfen
       Ein Schnupfen hockt auf der Terasse,

Grandmother Alma and Grandfather Felix

At the dinner table where he presided over the whole family he laced his banter with learned references to Biblical phrases and classical myths, which he intentionally mixed up. When we then laughed at the wrong time, he took a fiendish delight in confronting us with our ignorance. He also loved to play cards with me—Sixty-Six or some such game that required thirty-two cards and whose rules I have long since forgotten—and demanded that I first deal out the deck, one card at a time, while we both recited a little rhyme that went like this:

> Two little birds sat on some trees,
> It was so cold, they'd almost freeze.
> But then the sunshine warmed their way,
> And we have thirty-two to play.[4]

I always loved to listen to the story of how my grandfather Felix married my parents on May 30, 1925, in the Church of the Cross in Chemnitz, Saxony, a church, with its square brick tower and the raised cross on the top of it, I had come to know well on my vacation visits. I knew that, as a Biblical quotation to guide them on their way through life, Grandfather Felix had chosen Revelation II: 10—*"be thou faithful unto death, and I will give thee a crown of life"*—the same words that my parents chose seventeen years later for my confirmation in the Church of St. Mary in Wolfenbüttel. Neither in 1925 nor in 1942 could he or my parents have known what life-sustaining power these words would come to possess for me; how they would help guide and steady me on my path through the depths of desolation and despair; and how my grandfather's and my parents' legacy would provide rod and staff that comforted me in the midst of sorrow, pain, and evil.

My confirmation in 1942 made me realize for the first time the abiding influence over my life of my grandfather and St. Mary's, the Church of the Beatae Mariae Virginis. Every day in my room in our home on the Harztorwall I had looked out of my window at St. Mary's

---

> *auf daß er sich ein Opfer fasse*
> *—und stürzt alsbald mit großem Grimm*
> *auf einen Menschen namens Schrimm.*
> *Paul Schrimm erwidert prompt: Pitschü!*
> *und hat ihn drauf bis Montag früh!*

Both German and English version are from Christian Morgenstern, *Galgenlieder*, trans. and selected by Max Knight (Berkeley: University of California Press, 1964), 16–17.

4. In German the lines ran like this:

> *Ein Vöglein auf dem Baume saß,*
> *Es regnete und es ward naß.*
> *Da kam der liebe Sonnenschein,*
> *Es müssen zwei und dreißig sein.*

The author's parents shortly after their wedding, 1925

tower as it thrust into the sky over the tiled roofs and brick chimneys of the houses on the Krumme Straße. St. Mary's tower had always watched over me and Wolfenbüttel, day after day and night after night, like a mother hen over its chicks. I had accepted it and its sonorous bells as part of the ever-present surroundings of daily life. Of course it was there every time I looked, just as I would see the blueness of the sky and hear the song of the robins on a summer day, and just as, in the fall and winter, these were replaced by the grayness of the clouds and the twittering of the sparrows. St. Mary's tower was part of existence, and it spoke to me, if I was ready to listen, of the ever-presence of our religion, the Christian faith of Martin Luther. It was our faith, the faith of my mother, my father, my grandfather Felix, and my grandmother Alma. It was so much a part of our daily life that we took it as given and, except for reciting a blessing at meal time—

> *Komm, Herr Jesus, sei unser Gast,*
> *und segne was Du uns bescherest hast,*[5]

—we spoke little of it in my home. Perhaps that was because both my father and my mother believed that if they had urged religious obser-

5.   Come, Lord Jesus, and be our guest,
     and bless the gifts you bestowed on us.

vances on me, they would only have alienated me from a faith that meant little to me when I was young. Perhaps it was because both my parents were shy in speaking of things that were dear and sacred to them. Perhaps it was because my grandfather had said once when we were on one of our annual visits in Chemnitz that he did not think much of the hypocrites who loved to pray in the synagogues and on the street corners. "When you pray," he said, "go into the room and shut your door and pray to your Father who is in secret."[6] Perhaps it was because Luther's faith was present like the air we breathed, unnoticed by us but surrounding us everywhere and sustaining us in every step we took. It was there when I was born and it was there when I was baptized and when, in the spring of 1942, a month after my fourteenth birthday, Propst Rosenkranz, our family's pastor, confirmed me as a member of Wolfenbüttel's St. Mary's church. Only then, for the first time, did I become aware that I could not take this faith for granted; that it was not like the air that I breathed whether I wanted it or not; that it was not a part of me like my parents and my grandfather had been part of my life; that, if this faith was to be my staff and my rod, I would have to accept it and commit myself to it, and it would then make demands on me that I could not evade.

My mother tried to tell me this on the day of my confirmation. She said that I now left my childhood behind and officially became an adult. There would be no further such family celebrations as my baptism and my confirmation when my parents and my grandparents took care of me and when I alone stood at the center of attention. The next occasion would be my wedding, and I would have chosen my mate. Then, she said, the family would again gather around me, but those present would no longer honor me alone. They would honor me and my wife with whom I would share my life and start a family. And, she added, she fervently hoped it would be peace again and my father, too, would witness the event.

On that morning in March of 1942, my father was far away with his troops in Poland. Only my grandparents had come from Chemnitz. They and my mother had accompanied me to St. Mary's. We boys and girls in our Sunday best stood under the towering height of the white columns that stretched to the vaulted ceiling high above us. We looked up at Propst Rosenkranz on the pulpit and at the agonized face of the bent-over Moses who held up the pulpit with his back and grasped in his hand the stone tables with the commandments. It was such a familiar sight. Why, I always asked myself but never anyone else, not even Propst Rosenkranz, did Moses have to suffer so much when he

6. Matthew 6: 6.

bore the weight of the world on his shoulders? Was not religion to be a balm for those who labored? Why could I not look into a smiling face? And far off, at the distant altar, the crucified Christ looked down on me, too, with anguish on his face.

It was, indeed, a familiar sight because on many occasions I had sat in the back of the church where my mother and my grandparents were sitting now. On Sunday mornings, before the war began, I had listened with my parents to the sounds, the music, and the words that reverberated through the immensity of the stone-enclosed space. After the war had begun and when my father came home on leave, he had taken me there. And there always had been those Christmas evenings when with my parents I had tromped through the snow on the Harzstraße and Kleine Kirchstraße, impatient because I thought of the presents that would await me after our return home on the dining room table with the tree and its flickering candles. But when we then climbed up the stone steps at the entrance of St. Mary's, the big bells above ringing out over the town, and when, before stepping through the door, we shook off the snow from our overcoats and hats, and finally faced the two huge glittering fir trees before the altar, with their candles all aglow, I was fully absorbed by the spectacle before me, the crowd sitting on the benches and standing in the aisles of the church, the organ and the choir sending their messages from behind us, and Propst Rosenkranz climbing on top of Moses to read us once again the familiar Christmas story,

> And it came to pass in those days, that there went out a decree from Caesar Augustus, that all the world should be taxed.[7]

The high point for me came when the old organist and the choir burst into

> *Es ist ein Ros' entsprungen, aus einer Wurzel zart,*
> *Wie uns die Alten sungen, von Jesse kam die Art,*[8]

Michael Prätorius's beautiful Christmas carol that he wrote in Wolfenbüttel and that had rung out for the first time in St. Mary's Chapel, the predecessor of St. Mary's Church, over three hundred years ago. All of this, I knew, was part of my history, part of my legacy, and today, on

7. Luke 2: 1.
8.   Lo, how a rose is blooming from tender stem hath sprung!
       Of Jesse's lineage coming, as those of old have sung.

this March Sunday of 1942, I was asked to affirm it and commit myself to its preservation.

I no longer recall what Propst Rosenkranz said in his sermon that morning, but I do remember the thundering and vibrating rise of the

Ein feste Burg ist unser Gott,[9]

as it swelled behind and above us from the organ and from the voices of our families and the members of the congregation. This was Luther's hymn, and it was his spirit that pervaded this congregation to which I was now called. It was the same spirit that I encountered in the *Aula* of the *Große Schule* with its inscriptions under the ceiling,

Die Furcht des Herrn ist der Weisheit Anfang,

and

Ihr Seid Christi—Christus aber ist Gottes.[10]

Now, on this day when I left my boyhood behind and became a man, I realized just how deep my roots went into the soil of Lutheran Protestantism, how thoroughly I had absorbed my grandfather's faith, and how much that faith had been the bond that had held our family together.

Later, at noon at home, my mother, my grandparents, and a few family friends gathered in our dining room. The presence of my grandfather, who seventeen years earlier had married my parents and three years thereafter had baptized me, reminded me once more that it was now my part to carry on the family's commitment to our church and our God. This was the meaning, my grandfather Felix said, of the Bible verse he had chosen when he married my parents and which now Propst Rosenkranz had handed to me. "Don't ever forget it, Jürgen," he said, "faith holds us together, all of us, through the generations. If your father were here, he would tell you the same thing. Keep the faith, Jürgen, keep the faith."

The next day, after I had accompanied my grandparents to the railroad station, a small package arrived from my father. It contained a little book, *Prussian Chorale: The Faith of German Soldiers through Three*

9.   A mighty fortress is our God
10.   The Fear of the Lord is the Beginning of Wisdom
        You are of Christ, and Christ is of God

Family portrait, 1935. In front (*left to right*): Grandmother Alma with her first grand-child, grandfather Felix, and the author; in back: Uncle Heini, Aunt Mausi, the author's parents, Uncle Gerhard.

Centuries. This, I realized, was my father's way of telling me that there was no contradiction between being a Christian and being a soldier. The book showed that the traditions of the Prussian and German mili-tary had always endorsed and relied upon a strong faith in God. It told me that my life as a soldier was to be guided by steadfast faith in my God. This I took to be the message and the legacy my father be-queathed to me on the day of my confirmation.

It was a year later when I returned from Poland that I gradually and dimly began to grasp the book's entire message. The book not only assured me that my father endorsed my desire to lead a soldier's life; it also answered the question I was asking: What was the source of the strength that had carried my father through the horrors of trench war-fare in World War I and that sustained him now as he led his soldiers in Poland? What allowed him to remain steadfast in the performance of his assignments even when he had begun to question their righ-teousness and the honor of the cause for which he fought?

The book contained the answer: It was my father's Christian faith that had given him the yardstick by which he measured and con-demned the actions of the SS and that had led him to speak of the day of reckoning. It was that same faith, buoyed perhaps by desperate hope, that had made him willing to wait for that day until the war was won. It was that faith also that gave him strength to hold fast to his sense of duty when he recognized the compromises with evil that this duty demanded. It was a faith that God's eternal justice would prevail in the end.

For me there was only one question left: Could my father's faith also become my bulwark and anchor as a member of the profession I had chosen and in the afflictions and tests that were certain to lie before me? I did not know then that within little more than a year I would have to put that question to the test. I could only look up at St. Mary's tower and hope that it would stay against the sky, firm and forever.

8

The War at Home

DURING THE FALL AND WINTER OF 1943 the war made itself felt in Wolfenbüttel with ever-growing frequency and intensity. It was, as the Nazi slogan proclaimed it, a total war. It was a war that engulfed us every hour of the day and every hour of the night, a war of which we heard through our newspapers and radios as it was fought in the Arctic waters of the North Atlantic, in the heat of the Italian peninsula, and in the snowy wastelands of the Russian steppe. It was a war that we experienced firsthand when the sirens shrieked and made us jump out of bed and scurry into shelters and basements. Except for the martial strains that poured out of the radio, it was a war without regimental bands and flying flags. It was a war in which news of retreats replaced news of victories, in which telegrams arrived in our town that told of husbands and sons who had been cruelly hurt and disabled and of others whom we would never see again. It was a war that would bring death and destruction to Wolfenbüttel and confront us boy soldiers with scenes of desolation and premonitions of defeat for which we had not been prepared. It was not the war of the textbooks, the war of glory and heroic death, but the war of blood and gore, of terror and shame, and of bodies torn and mutilated. It was a war in which I, my classmates, and my *Jungvolk* friends, boys that we were, were expected to behave as adults and soldiers and were treated as such.

The wail of air-raid sirens had become an almost daily occurrence. Hundreds of British bombers flew over Wolfenbüttel at night on their way to and from Berlin, and we listened to the distant hum of their engines as it announced their coming and passing. On other nights, when searchlights lit up the sky and the voice in the radio warned of scout planes and waves of attack bombers turning toward Hannover, our

128

provincial capital some fifty miles away, we heard the rolling thunder of the hundreds of bombs detonating on the city and felt our house vibrate with the shock waves that traveled through the ground.

The attacks on Hannover called for us boys in the *Jungvolk* to don our uniforms and gather the next morning at the Wolfenbüttel headquarters building of the party. We were picked up by buses and rolled to Braunschweig and then over the Autobahn to Hannover. Our usual place of disembarkation was on a beach of the Maschsee, a big lake that stretched south of the city center. There trailers of moving vans had been set up and we received shovels and pickaxes for a day's cleanup in the ruins of the devastated city. We were supervised by army engineers and received army rations for our lunch. By five o'clock we were on our way back to avoid being caught in the next night raid on the city. We received little schooling during those weeks of almost incessant air raids.

Back home at night, my mother and I got up and dressed when the sirens howled and usually waited, sitting around the radio, for the all-clear sign. One night, as the rapid staccato and sharp bursts of the anti-aircraft batteries stationed around Wolfenbüttel had become particularly menacing and my mother and I had taken refuge with neighbors in our basement, the roar of a low-flying bomber returning from Berlin made it seem as though the plane was directly coming toward us and about to crash down on our house. As my mother and I pressed fearfully against each other, our boarder, an actor of the Hannover Light Opera Company whose personnel had been evacuated to Wolfenbüttel, burst out in his Viennese accent, *"ahn ahngehackter, ahn ahngehackter"*—meaning a plane that had been damaged by having been "picked at"—and broke the spell of fear that had caught us. He made us laugh despite the terror that had gripped us.

When the sirens sounded during the day while we were in school, we were sent home or, when there was not enough time for us to get there safely, we were herded into the school's basement. We hated to be confined in the air-tight shelter where we sat on uncomfortable wooden benches, stared at the straw-sack beds along the far wall on which we had slept on the nights we had been on fire duty, and could hear nothing but the monotonous radio announcements about enemy planes turning this way or that. We much preferred alarms in the afternoon when school was finished. Then we could run out in the open and watch what was going on, and no teacher or policeman would send us into air-raid shelters.

One summer afternoon, as I led my *Jungvolk* platoon toward the army's training ground at the edge of town, the sirens began to scream and we took cover in the ditches and under bushes. With awe we

An oil painting by Otto Bücher. The author second from left and Etzel center. (Courtesy of Hans Jürgen Fricke)

watched the dozens of fluffy contrails that streamed against the bluish whiteness of the sky high above us. Then suddenly, to our astonishment and excitement, four German Messerschmidt 110 fighters, looking like little black toy planes, appeared seemingly out of nowhere and darted toward the American planes. White rocket contrails shot out from them and into the American formations. Within seconds planes were plunging downward, though we could not make out who had shot down whom, and the falling planes disappeared from sight beyond the horizon.

One afternoon, in the early fall of 1943 when the leaves had not yet changed their colors, I learned that an enemy plane had been downed during the night and had crash-landed in the Lechlum Woods. I rode my bicycle to Etzel's home on the Lange Straße, and the two of us took off to see for ourselves. As we entered the woods and pedaled on the narrow footpath through the trees we soon came upon a spot where broken branches blocked our trail. We dismounted and left our bikes behind. Making our way slowly around the sheared-off, fallen treetops, we saw before us, half buried among the bushes, the remnants of a British Bristol-Blenheim, its broken fuselage and wings charred and twisted. In a clearing not far from the wreckage we noticed a freshly dug grave, the earth still moist and dark brown. Two branches nailed together in the form of a cross were stuck in the earthen mound. We could see no name or other form of identification and had to assume that there lay buried a British pilot.

We both turned to the bushes and broke off twigs with fresh green leaves and pressed them in the soft ground of the grave. We stood silent and gazed at the brown of the soil and the green of the foliage. I tried to imagine what the airman's mother looked like, whether she resembled my own. I wondered whether we should speak a prayer. I looked over to Etzel, but he didn't notice. He only looked at the grave. I did not say anything then. I felt the twigs expressed better our feelings than anything we might have stammered. We were somber and sad and thought of ourselves and the fallen pilot as comrades, soldiers in a world of war. It didn't really make much difference on which side a soldier fought and fell, I thought. His God and ours, was he not the same? How long would it be until we, too, Etzel and I, would be in the midst of battle? And, if it came to that, would someone, like ourselves, stand by our graves and say a prayer?

Our day of battle was to come sooner than we thought. It was the night of January 14, 1944, a month before my sixteenth birthday. My mother and I had spent another Christmas without my father, a Christmas when our thoughts and talk centered on our hope that he would come home on leave early in the new year. The news from the Eastern front had become steadily more discouraging and made our hopes appear unrealistic, indeed, though we did not admit that to ourselves and each other. My mother was at work in the kitchen, cleaning up the supper dishes. I sat at my father's desk in the living room doing my homework. The sirens' wail penetrated the air and was followed by an unearthly silence. My mother joined me in the living room, and we made sure that the black shades were carefully tucked against the windows to keep any sliver of light from escaping into the night. The radio announcer's voice continued monotonously: "Large enemy bomber groups approaching Hannover and Braunschweig. Take shelter immediately."

"I think we should go to the basement," my mother said.

"I hear nothing yet," I replied. But it wasn't true. The distant hum of hundreds of airplane engines intensified and became unmistakable. Anti-aircraft guns opened up, and then the unearthly scream of the first bomb made us jump up and run to our apartment door. I heard a thud outside where, as we later found out, a canister of phosphorus or a dud had hit the grass in the park in front of our house, right in the middle of a clump of beech trees. As my mother and I stepped from our apartment into the entrance hall of the house, an explosion blew open its heavy wooden door and pushed gusts of air into our faces. Glass from the transom crashed around us, and, as another ear-shattering explosion burst outside and sent a blast of air and debris into our faces, I felt the unstoppable urge to run to the toilet. I turned back into our apartment, raced for the water closet at the end of the hallway, and, as I sat down, watched with awed fascination through the window the blue, red, green, and yellow markers—Christmas trees we called them—drifting earthward from the sky. I finished my business as fast as I could and joined my mother and other housemates in the cellar.

There, in its darkened, catacomb-like hallway we huddled on the rickety garden furniture that had been set up for just such occasions. The basement windows had been blown out, and our shelter was illumined only by the yellow-pinkish glow of a radio dial that shone from underneath a woman's chair. "Jürgen, oh Jürgen," my mother whispered and grabbed my hand. Another explosion. The house rocked, the radio dial went dark for a few seconds, came back to glow, and we heard more windowpanes splinter. The noise of bursting shells and exploding bombs filled our ears. An acrid smell made it hard to breathe.

"My god, my god," a terrified voice muttered over and over again, and somebody shrieked: "No, no, no . . ."

"Be quiet, be quiet, only quiet," said the man from the third floor to his wife and pressed her hand. With each new explosion he pulled his and his wife's hand violently toward himself. Each time a bomb sent another gust of air through the basement we bent forward and tried to make ourselves ever smaller as though this would lessen our chances of getting hurt.

The crackling and sharp explosions of the flak guns continued for another twenty minutes or so, the rumbling of airplane engines slowly diminished, and we noticed the cold January night breeze with its acrid smell of explosives that seeped into the basement through the shattered windows and mingled with the heavy, moisture-laden air. From the radio under the woman's chair now came a well-modulated voice: "Enemy bomber groups turning away. Be careful of anti-aircraft shrapnel and time-bombs."

I was angry at the voice. It sounded so satisfied, so pleased with itself. It could have belonged to a cigar-smoking gentleman in a hotel lobby. We got up to make our way upstairs and inspect the damage.

"Didn't I say so," said the man from the third floor.

"You said nothing, Richard," said his wife. "What could you have said? They will come again. We have heard them flying every night. Now they will come for us, tomorrow and the night after tomorrow, then again, tomorrow and the night after tomorrow, they'll come . . ."

And we all knew it, too, but nobody but the wife of the man from the third floor said it.

Once back upstairs in our apartment my mother and I checked for damage and found only the hallway window broken. Everything else was well and undisturbed. My mother wondered about Mrs. Fink and her children in their house at the northern end of town. Would they have been hit by the raid? I said I would go and see. I took my bicycle out of the shed in the back of our house and rode along the Harztor-wall past the theater, turned into the Lange Straße, past Etzel's house, crossed the Saarplatz and rushed down the Breite Herzogstraße until I reached the trunk highway to Braunschweig. As I pedaled through town I saw a few people out on the streets looking at their houses, sweeping up broken window glass and staring at fallen telephone wires. They stood in groups and talked about the raid. On the high-way I noticed for the first time the reddish glow that came from the clouds at the northern sky ahead of me. It was the reflection of the burning city of Braunschweig. It and the narrow beam of white light that danced before me on the road supplied the only illumination I had. The beam came through the small slit I had cut in the black paper with which I had covered up my bicycle headlight. Moon and stars were hidden behind the clouds. As I came close to the Finks' house the big chestnut trees overhanging half the street now blotted out even the pinkish glow. I stared into the darkness, looking for the Finks' garden gate when my bicycle handlebars suddenly jumped upward. Before I could slam my foot on the coaster brake, I was thrown into the air and flew across the bars and over a mound of dirt and stones and rolled halfway down into a huge black hole. A bomb had blown a crater right in the middle of the highway in front of the Finks' house.

When I realized what had happened I climbed out of the hole, dragged my bicycle back to firm ground, brushed myself off, and walked slowly toward the Finks' garden gate. I leaned my bicycle against it and approached the huge red beech tree and the house that loomed behind it in the dark. As I came closer I could make out that not a window was left intact. Many of the wooden shutters were torn loose and dangled crooked and misshapen from their hinges. Bomb fragments had scarred the walls, and tiles from the roof lay all around the foundation. I slowly clambered over the bricks and tiles, found the house door half-open, its glass inserts splintered. I stepped inside over the dust- and debris-covered stairs and climbed to the first floor. I heard a voice call from above, "Is somebody there?" and I shouted back, "Yes, it's me, Jürgen, Mrs. Fink. Are you and Nucki and Helmut all right?"

"Yes," came the answer, "we are all right and have gone to bed. There's nothing we can do as long as it is dark. We have no electricity. How are you and your mother?"

I told her that we were fine and that I would do a little cleaning up downstairs and then would go home again. I found a broom and swept away some of the most obvious dirt, window shards, and pieces of the ceiling fallen onto the living room floor, but gave it up soon because I figured the noise would keep the family awake. I got on my bike, noted that it had not been harmed by the crash, and rode back home, knowing that the next day I would have to report for clean-up duty.

At 7:30 Etzel and I together with another twenty or thirty of our boys gathered at party headquarters. Police and other officials distributed shovels, pickaxes, and fire-fighting equipment, loaded it all on a truck, and ordered us to march toward the village of Groß-Denkte. Even though Wolfenbüttel had been hit that night, it was nothing compared with what had happened in the city of Braunschweig and the surrounding countryside. Braunschweig's old city center with its half-timbered houses had been burned to the ground. Because a strong wind had blown the colorful markers gradually away from their intended targets over the city, hundreds of second-wave bombers had dropped their loads over a wide swath of agricultural land, hitting the outskirts of Wolfenbüttel and wiping out entire villages.

We did not know it as we marched that morning, but we were to stay in Groß-Denkte for the next five days. For five days we shoveled and carted sand, pulled stinking cow cadavers by their tails and hind legs from underneath the smoking ruins of collapsed stables and barns, carried human corpses shrunken by phosphorus fire to half their size to the village church whose roof had been blown off and whose benches had been pushed to the side to make room for the corpses. At night we slept for ten or twenty minutes at a time, rolled in blankets that soldiers had given us, trying to stay as close as we could to the warmth of a still smoldering barn or house to protect ourselves against the cold of the January frost. When daylight broke Red Cross nurses fed us sandwiches, hot ersatz coffee, and cool lemonade; soldiers came over to us and offered liquor, cigars, and cigarettes. The coffee kept us warm and awake; the liquor made us feel stronger than we were; the sweet lemonade made us thirstier still, and the sandwiches made us gag and throw up.

When we were called back to work we dropped the cigarettes after a puff or two. You cannot dig out a basement with a cigarette between your lips. You don't carry a corpse to the village church with a cigar in your mouth, even though the church was a burnt-out ruin and there was no organ music. Those things we learned awfully fast, and we needed neither parents nor teachers nor Hitler Youth leaders to tell us. Age mattered little; whether we were twelve or sixteen, we had two hands, and that was enough. Only the stomach mattered. Had it once been used to Sunday's steak and gravy, it now protested only if you sat on the ground next to a foul, stinking cow and tried to eat your bread. Had it been weak all along, intolerant of whipped cream and sugar and butter, it made you retch and choke even without lemonade and bread. Then we threw up again, rolled in the dust of the street and the ashes of houses trying to suppress the pain of stomach cramps. Among the village ruins, our stomachs became the measure of all things.

Etzel stayed with me as much as he could. We had marched side by side, and together we extinguished fires and shoveled sand. I climbed up the slippery rungs of a ladder and crawled through an open second-floor window of a smoking house. I wore a gas mask and helmet. Etzel had followed me and now stood outside on the ladder and handed me pump and hose. As I moved into the room, thick smoke engulfed me. I could not see much. The room seemed empty of furniture, at least in the middle where I stood. The sides were hidden by smoke. With my right hand I began pushing the handle of the pump, down, up, down, up, like a machine. My left, grabbing the muzzle of the hose, directed the stream of water at the glowing floor boards before me. I felt sweat collect at my chin. Moisture began to fog the inside of my mask and, together with the smoke outside, to cloud my view. But I kept pushing and pulling the pump handle and pouring water ahead of me. I found it harder and harder to see where the stream of water hit until suddenly the hose went limp in my hand and the water stopped coming.

I heard Etzel shout from the window, his voice seeming to come from far away. I felt hands grabbing me under my armpits and pulling me backward so that I lost my balance, my feet now scraping the floor I had sprayed. Somebody tore the gas mask from my face, and it felt as though cold, fluid ice poured into my lungs. As I wildly flung my arms around to grasp a hold somewhere, I felt my feet and my body glide over the rungs of the ladder until I hit the ground and the hands that had pulled me let go of me. I sat on the earth, dazed, leaning with my back against the still burning house that I had just left. As I closed my eyes I heard the fire crackle above me, and I thought how nice a sound that was.

Then another shout, and I felt myself being torn away from the house, striking my shins on piles of wood, bricks, and stones and falling heavily forward, pain shooting through my legs and my rib cage. As I fell I could hear the thundering crash of the collapsing house behind me. I lay still for a few moments and then opened my eyes. Before me, immediately under my face that was touching the ground, I saw a few green leaves of grass, nothing else. What had happened? How could the grass be so green, the air so cool, the pain in my body so far away and so unreal when just a few seconds ago I had seen and smelled nothing but acrid smoke, felt nothing but the dampness of my face under the mask and the automatic pushing, the ups and the downs, of my pump? Where was I? What had happened?

As I lay there, still and as if in a trance, I felt someone grabbing me by the shoulder, pressing a shovel in my hand, and saying to me: "Here, Jürgen, take this. There is work to be done over there, the basement and the stable." It was Etzel. He had already learned that the best medicine for pain and exhaustion and the only way to prevent me from realizing and thus succumbing to the danger I had faced was to keep me going, was to stop me from giving way to self-indulgence and self-pity. I was not to be another horseman on Lake Constance whose heart, the story went, gave out when he realized he had just galloped across the half-frozen water.

And so we struggled on, five days, in sunshine and rain, by the light of still burning houses. Our oldest was sixteen, our youngest twelve. When, on the evening of the fifth day, we were ordered to hand over our shovels, pumps, and gas masks to the soldiers and to march back to our homes, we were exhausted and tired, too tired to react with any emotion. Like automatons we lined up in our usual column of three abreast and started on the way home. No one in our column spoke. All we heard was the bump, bump, bump of our feet, and the occasional shuffle when someone lost his balance and tried to regain his place in the line.

As we trudged along the country road I could think only of two lines I had read somewhere:

> So we make our way, a defeated army,
> extinguished are our stars.[1]

I could not get these words out of my mind. They struck at my self-concept as a soldier, as a soldier who had never himself experienced the emotions of accomplishment and victory in a real battle, as a soldier whose first engagement with the enemy had brought him face to face with defeat and death. Was that what lay ahead of me, defeat, desolation, death? Was that what the war would mean for me in the end? Was this what would lie at the end of my career as a professional soldier?

It was only the pebble in my left shoe that succeeded in tearing me free of my thoughts. A piercing pain shot through my foot and woke me up from my shuffling. I stumbled, noticing dumbly that the sole of my left boot now flapped open with every step I took, filling the shoe with sand and grit. It kept me from thinking of extinguished stars and of defeat in battle, and it prevented me from falling asleep.

The night was dark. Rain clouds hid the moon and stars. The wind carried the tangy smell of burnt wood across the fields. It was like a balm. It covered the stench of phosphorus and smoldering and rotting corpses. The wood smell, our exhaustion, and our longing to forget gently covered the acrid taste in our mouths, the terror and the horror of our memories.

When I got home I collapsed in my bed. Sleep, only sleep, was all I wanted. My bed was white and soft and clean. It had been waiting for me, five nights, and it was as though nothing had happened in between, as though I had just entered the house, returning from school or, perhaps, the playground. But when I woke up in the middle of the night and opened the curtain and looked toward Braunschweig I saw in the reddish sky the reflection of fires still burning in the piled-up ruins of great department stores, churches, and blocks and blocks of apartment houses. Starkly outlined against the sky's redness stood, silent and unwavering, the tower of St. Mary's. Did it have a message for me?

1.   *So zieh'n wir dahin, ein geschlagen Heer,*
      erloschen sind unsere Sterne

When my mother came in, she sat on my bed and asked me how it had been in Groß Denkte. I did not tell her much. I just said I was too tired to remember. She then reminded me that, over a week ago, I had bought tickets to the Braunschweig opera, tickets that were good for tomorrow afternoon. Would I, perhaps, want to go with Etzel? The opera, supposedly, was going to perform, and it might help us to forget Groß Denkte. I said I would think about it. She kissed me and wished me another few hours of deep sleep. Then, she said, I would be ready.

The next day Etzel and I decided that we would go. There were no trains, no streetcars, not even trucks running from Wolfenbüttel to Braunschweig. The rails were torn up from their beds, the highway pockmarked with craters. So Etzel and I walked the eight miles to Braunschweig, two hours by foot, following the broken surface of the once-concrete highway through the Lechlum Woods and the fields, carefully stepping around the huge craters that were now beginning to fill with water.

As we approached the city, the smell of phosphorus and burning lumber wafted toward us. Fires still flickered over the bomb-scarred valleys of streets and avenues. Eerily entangled electric wires, burnt-out shells of cars, salvaged dirty remnants of writing desks and wardrobes, a bed here, a box of toys there, guided our path through the silent waste. Clouds hung low, and gusts of wind blew dust, soot, and smoke in my face. People moved through the ruins like shadowy puppets in a long-forgotten mystery play, one holding a book in his hand, another carrying a featherbed on his back, standing and staring wordlessly at what once had been their homes, their faces empty of emotion, their eyes wide open. Two little girls were playing on what had been the sidewalk, pushing a small wooden truck in which they had placed a doll, dirty and without arms. "Carting away the corpses, mommy," one said to her mother, who only stared and said nothing.

Etzel and I reached the Opera House. Miraculously, neither bombs nor fire had touched it. There it stood, dark and blacked out, like a fortress on a hill, overlooking the city. There was a wooden board pushed in the ground near the street: Verdi, Aida. That's all it said. One of the great entrance doors stood barely open. As it began to yield to my pushing against it, it scraped against the grit and sand on the broken tiles of the foyer floor. It was dark inside; only a candle flickered near a little booth. A small, heavily bent old man in blue coat and yellow brass buttons approached us.

"We'll begin at four," he said. "We want to be out of here by seven, in case there is another raid." I looked at my watch. It was half past three.

Etzel and I decided to go upstairs and walk out on the balcony. It was still light outside for us to see a black column of smoke rise over the forest of chimneys that reached out of the ruins toward the rain-heavy sky. There were no people on the broad avenue that led from downtown toward the Opera House. Round patches of molten asphalt pockmarked its surface, like the abscesses of a leper, I thought. To the left and the right, nothing but piles of rubble, and all around us in the air the heavy, sweet smell of phosphorus.

We were tired from our long walk and decided to find our seats and sit down. Our tickets directed us to the uppermost gallery, the seats for students and music lovers who could not afford any better. As we looked down from up high we saw that, except for several soldiers on leave from the front with their sweethearts, a few elderly invalids and lone widows, and us two, the house was empty.

We looked at each other. Without saying a word we turned and descended the stairs to the first balcony. We headed for the center loge, the best seats in the house. They were empty. We sat down, looked around, and saw that we were all but alone. In the dim yellow light of the few functioning bulbs in the chandeliers we could see perhaps two dozen or so other guests, sitting widely dispersed in the other front-row seats and below on the main floor. We drew the side curtains of our loge, sank back into the heavy, upholstered armchairs, and the opera was ours, and ours alone.

Celeste Aida—*himmlische Aida*—the overture swept us up and carried us away from the death and destruction outside. Down on the stage a different world unfolded and made me drunk with its splendor, its lights, its glitter, its love, and its pain—a different love, a different pain, though it was love and pain just the same. It was a love and a pain for me alone to behold. There was nothing said and sung, nothing displayed and nothing portrayed, that did not seem directed just at me, and me alone. The conductor's baton leaped at and for me, his music cast a spell of heaven and of hell, asking me to surrender and join in the High Priest's final prayer, *pace t'imploro,* imploring a better world of love and peace for all of us.

As we left, the plea for peace ringing in our ears, we stood once more on the outside balcony. Now the sky resembled a velvety black curtain that hung over the city. The clouds had cleared and myriads of stars glistened icy and distant. Down below us, flat and crouched, the bizarre forms of a stony death. Between the blacked-out wasteland and the night-blue sky, painted across the horizon, a band of pinkish reflection of invisible fires.

Etzel and I walked through the silent streets, picking our way among the rubble and craters, over the torn highway, and past the silent fields and woods. By the time we reached home, the memory of the sounds, sights, and smells of Groß Denkte had fused into one with that of the love, pain, and peace of Aida.

This, then, was war. This was what the life of the soldier was all about. This was a war of defeat, not of glory and victory. And throughout the darkness, the pain, and the death rang the words of Aida's priest, *pace t'imploro,* I implore you, peace. Was that a soldier's prayer? Could it be a soldier's prayer? Where would my commitment to the profession of arms and my faith in a God of soldiers lead me? I did not know; I could not know. I could only think of the tower of St. Mary's as I had seen it stand against the fiery sky and reiterate my promise to myself that I would remain faithful unto death.

9

Etzel's Tale

AFTER THE BOMBING RAID IN JANUARY 1944 the tempo of alarms and of summons to special relief actions for us boys in the *Jungvolk* increased measurably. Night- and daytime attacks on Hannover occurred once or twice every week, and we *Jungvolk* boys continued to board specially chartered buses to Hannover to dig out basements and air-raid shelters, clear rubble from roads and streetcar lines, and help bombed-out families pack up their few rescued belongings and load them on trucks to be taken out to relative safety in the countryside.

When we were home in Wolfenbüttel, Dieter, Etzel, myself, and a few others, all *Jungvolk* leaders, drew together ever more closely. The evacuation of the Hannover Light Opera Company to Wolfenbüttel and the quartering of its personnel with families on the Harztorwall had given me a wonderful opportunity to get to know some of the actors and actresses. The story of the *ahngehackter* was only one of many that made the rounds among us boys and showed how our nightly involuntary meetings during air-raid alarms in our basement had forged close friendships. As a result I received free tickets for myself and my friends for every new performance the company gave in Wolfenbüttel's Lessing Theater. Strategically placed throughout the theater, a couple of us on every balcony, we were expected to start the applause after every aria and act. That duty and, for one of us, at the end of the performance, the leap from the first balcony's front right seat to the stage, with a bouquet for the lead actress in hand, was our price of admission. We hummed and whistled all day long melodies of Emmerich Kálmán's *Csárdasfürstin*, Leo Fall's *Dollar Princess*, Fred Raymond's *Mask in Blue*, and Franz Lehar's *The Land of Smiles*. We had become enthusiastic operetta connoisseurs.

141

Etzel

When we weren't in the theater or on relief missions we spent many a night at the blackjack and peach brandy ice cream parties that lasted until the sirens would drive us in the shelters or, if the night was quiet, until way past midnight. We were conscious of the fact that for all of us this might come to an abrupt end any day or any night. Our mission in Groß Denkte and our trips to Hannover had told us that.

School itself had become ever more meaningless for us. For most of my classmates in the *Große Schule* regular classroom activities had ceased already in the spring of 1943 when they were sent to man the anti-aircraft batteries around the nearby industrial centers at Salzgitter. Our teachers followed them, and instruction for us "three-year boys" who stayed behind continued on an on-again, off-again schedule until, later in the year, we were sent to school in Braunschweig. That proved to be a disaster since I quickly found out that, compared with the Braunschweig students, we transfer students from Wolfenbüttel were at least a year behind in our knowledge of mathematics, Latin, and the natural sciences. I began to dread my daily streetcar trip to Braunschweig and threw myself into my *Jungvolk* activities with even greater enthusiasm than before. It became for me a virtual life-saver.

In these months my friendship with Etzel deepened. Etzel, two years older than I, was my *Fähnleinführer*, and I served under him as one of his platoon leaders. I often met with him in the afternoon and evening in the house on the Lange Straße where he lived with his mother on the second floor. His uncle, the artist Otto Bücher, had his studio down below on the ground level and lived with Etzel's aunt Elli Bücher on the top floor of the building. The house itself, built of half-timbers filled in with straw-lined bricks, was old and dilapidated. The wooden steps creaked when I climbed up to Etzel's room. The room itself was just large enough to hold a sofa, two easy chairs, a bookshelf, a gramophone, and a coffee table. Its window looked across the narrow street onto the plastered wall of a building on the opposite side. With its entrance separate from the main apartment and no possibility for anyone to watch us through the window, Etzel's room afforded us the greatest possible privacy, and we made the most of it.

When we met there, Etzel used to sit in his worn, faded easy chair and I on the lumpy sofa. We faced each other, and, when they were available, ate cookies and drank tea his aunt would bring. Sometimes we played chess or listened to the kind of sentimental music Etzel liked to play on his gramophone. "As beautiful as today, so shall it ever be"[1] was one of his favorite tunes. At other times, some of our *Jungvolk*

1.   *So schön wie heut,*
       so soll es bleiben,

friends would join us and we would plan activities for our Wednesday and Saturday afternoon meetings. But most of the time, it was just Etzel and me.

And so it was on that Friday afternoon that was to remain indelibly imprinted on my memory. We were alone in the room. Etzel's mother had gone to visit relatives out of town. Mr. Bücher was painting in his studio and let it be known that he did not want to be disturbed, and Mrs. Bücher had briefly looked in to leave us a pot of tea. Then she, too, had left the house.

"What are we going to do with our boys tomorrow?" I asked Etzel. We hadn't made any particular plans, and I felt that time was running out for us to make any special preparations. "Shall we go on that long-postponed scavenger hunt or shall we begin rehearsing for that play you wanted to put on for the *Elternabend?* Or is it time for another collection of rags and bones?"

"Collection of rags and bones?" Etzel responded and spit out the words as though they made him gag. He sat up and looked me squarely in the eyes. "Shut up with that crap, Jürgen. Rags and bones. I've had enough of them. There are better things we can do with our boys."

"What's the matter, Etzel?" I asked, taken aback by the vehemence of his words. "Of course there are better things to do. I don't like collecting rags and bones any better than you do. But you know damn well that the party insists on us meeting our quota, and we are a long way from it. I'd much rather go on a scavenger hunt, play soccer, put on a play, or listen to stories. You know that."

Etzel didn't seem to hear. He pushed himself forward in his chair, his eyes fixed on the floor before him. His fingers dug into the chair's soft sides and he kept on muttering, "rags and bones, rags and bones.

"We are rag pickers, aren't we?" he suddenly said and looked up at me. "We pick up rags from the dirt of the street, throw in a few bones, and pretend we can build a new and better future with them. Don't tell me you believe this."

"I don't know what you are talking about, Etzel," I said. I felt very uncomfortable because Etzel didn't sound like himself. "I just wanted to know what your plans are for our boys tomorrow. You haven't told me."

"Tomorrow?" Etzel responded, and cocked his head to one side. "Shall there be another meeting? A meeting in the service of our Führer, our beloved Führer?" Etzel's words sounded bitter and sarcastic. He stood up abruptly, shook his head and added: "Forgive me. I am

---

so soll es bleiben,
für alle Zeit.

144

tired. I didn't sleep well last night. Forget what I said. It's of no account."

But I would not let him go. This sort of outburst had happened before, but I had dismissed it when it occurred as a passing attack of ill humor. I didn't think this was the real Etzel I heard talking. I did not know what to make of it, but I also wanted to get to the bottom of it. I didn't want to dismiss it again. Something bothered Etzel, and he tried to keep it hidden from me. I wanted to know what it was.

"Listen," I said to Etzel, who by now had sat down again in his easy chair and had buried his face in his hands. "Listen, your story of rags and bones does not make sense. What's the matter? There is something else bothering you besides us collecting rags and bones, and you better tell me. You can't go on like that forever, letting it, whatever it is, eat at you all the time."

Etzel looked up at me. "Yes," he said softly, "there is something else the matter, and it is eating at me. But it doesn't just concern me alone. It concerns all of us, you, the boys, everyone, but few know it. Few even have as much as an inkling. And it will catch up with all of us some day when it will be too late for us to do anything about it."

"What are you talking about, Etzel," I said, now thoroughly disquieted. "What in the world are you talking about?"

"Well, I am talking about rags and bones, or more precisely, the rag and bone pickers who run our lives and want us to become rag and bone pickers, too. It is they who drive us toward a catastrophe." Etzel described an arc with his outstretched right arm. "I mean the adults who run the Hitler Youth, the guys we met in Kattowitz and in Birkental, the superintendents and the county leaders here in Wolfenbüttel, the ideological trainers, the relatives and teachers like Mr. Fuchtel who spout phrases of our thousand-year Reich, the big fellows and the little ones."

Etzel looked straight into my eyes as though he would not allow me to escape from the spell his words had cast. "Now, Jürgen," he added, "you wanted to hear this, but you must promise me never to speak about this to any person. No one, you hear? Not even your mother. Not even your father when he comes home on leave next time. Keep your mouth shut. If you don't, it will be all over with me, with my aunt, my uncle, my father, my mother, with the boys, with you, with us all. Promise me you will not talk about this ever."

His eyes bored into mine, and I stammered: "I promise. I never will. I promise."

"All right," he said, "listen, then. You know my aunt, don't you?"

I nodded silently, thinking of Etzel's aunt Elli who had brought us tea earlier in the afternoon and wondered why Etzel asked me about her. I also wondered why he had earlier referred to his father whom I had never seen and who was divorced from his mother.

Etzel remained silent. I saw his Adam's apple move up and down his throat. He seemed to wrestle with himself, to fight for air to continue speaking. I waited, likewise silent and very anxious.

Then, the words fell out of his mouth, like silvery rain drops, one by one, hitting the ground with sharp little pings, six pebbles clicking on the wooden floor, then, bursting open with thunderous explosions, wiping everything from my mind: "My aunt, she is a Jew."

I could not take in Etzel's message. His aunt, a Jewess? That was impossible. That could not be. I had never seen on her the yellow star all Jews were forced to wear. I had never, in my wildest dreams, ever entertained any such possibility among all my friends and acquaintances. That Dieter, as I, took piano lessons from a Jewess I had accepted because Dieter and my mother seemed to think it natural and a matter not worth debating. That Jewish people, the Morgensterns and Albert, were thrown out of their houses and sent to a concentration camp, had bothered me and made me uneasy. It had threatened me when, in my thoughts, I put myself and my parents in their place. That I, that day in the fog, had almost attacked an old, frail man had made me ashamed; but, then, I thought, I had not attacked him, had only thought about it. But now I was told that my best friend lived under the same roof with a Jewess; had a Jewish woman be around him every day, every night. I could not comprehend it.

In my consternation I grasped at straws and said: "But what about your uncle? Is he Jewish, too?"

"No," said Etzel, "he is not. But never mind my uncle. I did not tell you this story because it concerns him, but I told you because it concerns you, me, the boys, and all of us. Do you know what I am saying?"

And again his eyes bored into mine. I could only shake my head.

"Look," Etzel said. "It isn't just a simple question: Are you a Jew or are you a German? It's much more than that. I guess if it weren't for my aunt, I would not realize that either. I owe that knowledge to her, and I thank her for that." And again he looked me in the eyes: "Jürgen, you never said much about my aunt. You were nice to her, ate her cookies, drank her tea, answered her questions when she asked you about your mother, our boys, or about school. I remember only once, when you said to me: 'You know, your aunt is a nice woman. I like her.' But that was before you knew what you know now, that she is Jewish. I, on the other hand, have known it all my life. And I love my aunt. I, the Aryan, the leader of the town's best *Jungvolk Fähnlein*, I love my Jewish aunt."

Fragments of sentences and thoughts whirled through my head. "I . . . the Aryan . . . the *Jungvolk* leader . . . I love my Jewish aunt . . .

before you knew she was Jewish . . . it isn't just a simple question . . ."
I gathered my thoughts and finally said: "But you, you, Etzel, nephew
of a Jew, you came to us in the *Jungvolk* and are one of the best leaders
we have. One hundred boys look up to you; think you are their model.
Why did you do that? Why do you wear that uniform with the swastika when your aunt is Jewish?"

I did not really think there was an answer to that question, and I
was sorry I had asked it. But Etzel only smiled, reached for a cookie,
looked at it as though it was an object of intense interest to him, placed
it back on the table, and said: "You know the answer very well, Jürgen.
Why did *you* come to the *Jungvolk*, why do *you* march with us? Why
do *you* do it week after week? I will tell you why, Jürgen. You do it because you, like I, love our boys. That's why I joined and stay with the
Jungvolk, that's why you did it, and that's why we are here together.
We are friends, we are comrades, we love our boys, and we have made
our *Fähnlein* our world and the best of all of them in town.

"But," and the smile on his face disappeared, "in my case that's not
the whole truth. I don't know about your family but I suspect it is the
same as in mine. There is no Nazi in my family. I don't think there's
in yours either. My father was, and still is at heart, a Communist. Back
in 1919, he was one of the founding members of the party. His party
membership had much to do with his divorce from my mother. Not
that my mother disapproved. She was and is a Communist at heart
as well. But the party's demands on their marriage were greater than
they could tolerate. So they divorced, and my mother moved in with
my uncle and aunt.

"So what do you think? A family of Communists and a Jewish
aunt? How were we to survive under the Nazis? I was the only one
who could give cover. I knew that very quickly, all by myself. My parents and my uncle did not have to tell me that, and they did not tell me
that. From early years on I was left to myself to form my own opin-
ions. And I did. I had read the Biblical story of Benjamin ransomed to
the Egyptians. I recognized it as my own. I don't hold it against my
father or my uncle. What else could they have done?

"Well, yes, they could have left Germany with us years before the
war began. But they refused. Jobs, old friends, party comrades, career,
and always the final, decision-stopping thought: Things will never get
that bad; not in Germany; surely not in Germany. So they stayed, and I
became—as my uncle jokingly says—the family's honorary Nazi. I pay
our tribute, and it seems to work. So far, at least, my father, mother,
uncle and aunt have not been bothered."

There was a long silence between us two. Finally I said, "That may
well be so, Etzel, but it does not explain your enthusiasm, your devo-

tion, your joy for and with our boys. You didn't just pretend all that, did you? You could not possibly have put on a theatrical show for us, could you? That's quite impossible. You do not hide from us your true self when you are with us?"

"Of course, not, Jürgen," Etzel replied. "Who do you take me to be? My enthusiasm is real. I would never have had the strength to put on such a charade. Besides, have you forgotten? I love our boys, and I have led them my way, not the Nazi way.

"Judge for yourself: Are the boys of our *Fähnlein* a bunch of convinced, fanatical Nazis? Did we participate that night in 1938 when the shop windows were broken? Did we spit on Jews with the yellow star on their coats? Come on, Jürgen, you can't deny that? You have never seen our boys do any of these things, have you?"

I knew Etzel was right, but I could not help but feel a wave of shame flow over me again as I thought of my encounter with the little Jewish man on that day in the fog. Now Etzel praised me for not having done what I had considered doing, and I was more confused than ever.

"No," Etzel continued, "so long as we stay with our boys, so long as we can keep them as our friends and comrades, so long as we can fight with them, can inspire them, can win soccer games, so long they will never think of hating Jews.

"But we shall not always be there," Etzel went on. "Did you never notice that we rarely followed the official plans of the party? When they wanted us to carry out paramilitary service, we took the boys out of town into the woods, played cops and robbers and sang folksongs. When they called for ideological training, we told our boys how to care for a backpack and how to wax their skis. Have you ever heard of another *Fähnlein* that marched through town singing "The Internationale"? You yourself took the boys on a field march of three kilometers that day when we were to have discussed the 'race problem.' When I joined you out there in the boondocks, I read you all the story of Huck and Jim on the raft from that paperback I found among my uncle's books. I told my aunt about that later, and she couldn't stop laughing. But you and the boys had no idea what went on that afternoon. If the Nazis had found out—that is, if they had had the brains to understand the irony of it all—they would have accused us of 'sabotaging the war effort, and mocking the Führer's pet doctrines.' And you know what would have been the consequences of that.

"No, Jürgen," Etzel rose, "we still can love the boys and ignore the Nazis. I am not unhappy as a *Fähnleinführer* with a Jewish aunt. Boys are boys, and I love them. Don't get your eyes stuck at the uniform. Know there beats a boy's heart under the brown shirt.

148

"But," and the glow in Etzel's eyes grew dim again, "it's true, there are times when my double-life threatens to extinguish my enthusiasm. It isn't easy to live in two worlds. And there is always the knowledge—and I am sorry to burden you with it—that all this will come to a disastrous end. In the meantime, however," and Etzel smiled again, "there are our boys, and we shall be out in the woods with them tomorrow. That's worth all the trouble.

"So here's your answer," Etzel said while moving toward the gramophone: "We are not collecting rags and bones tomorrow. We are going on a scavenger hunt." Etzel stepped forward and cranked up the machine: ". . . as beautiful as today, so shall it ever be . . ."

"Records like these are a godsend," he said. "You can start them when you want to finish a conversation and can't find the right words to do it. They spare us embarrassment. You have to smile about this sentimental kitsch. And a smile always does us good after a serious conversation."

That evening my friendship with Etzel was sealed to last a lifetime.

Not long after our conversation, Etzel received his call to arms and left us to join the navy. I was promoted to *Fähnleinführer* to take over his place. I felt sad and honored at the same time. The day Etzel had to leave, I ordered *Fähnlein Blücher* to gather at the station and surprise Etzel with a send-off. Blücher—a field marshall of the Prussian army during the wars of liberation in the early nineteenth century—was the name we had selected for our *Fähnlein* several years earlier. By this choice and by the names we had given to the *Fähnlein*'s three platoons—Schill, York, and Zieten, Prussian military commanders of the eighteenth and nineteenth centuries—we announced who our heroes were and whose traditons we had pledged ourselves to honor.

The send-off was a sad and poignant occasion. All the boys had come and stood at attention in front of the railroad station. For Etzel it was a surprise. He walked slowly past his boys and shook everyone's hand. Tears glistened in his eyes. As he disappeared in the station entrance we marched through the baggage gate across the tracks onto the platform. By the time Etzel reappeared out of the tunnel that led from the station building to the platform and moved toward the waiting train, we had lined up again, our flag fluttering in the wind. Etzel boarded one of the cars and leaned out of a window. As the train began to move I started off our *Fähnlein* cheer: *"Blücher,"* I shouted, and *"steht,"* the boys responded.

"Blücher," I called once more, and *"kämpft,"* came the reply.

And finally, *"Blücher,"* and *"siegt,"* shouted the boys. Etzel waved out of the window, and we began to sing our *Fähnlein*'s song:

149

Fähnlein Blücher auf der Fahrt,
zieht durch deutsche Lande . . .[2]

Etzel kept waving until he disappeared from our sight as the train pulled around the bend.

I ordered the flag rolled up and dismissed the *Fähnlein* on the platform. The boys crowded around me and kept saying how they wished to see Etzel again, how they would never let him down and would remain the town's best *Fähnlein*. As we slowly walked through the tunnel Etzel had come through on his way to the train I heard them talk to each other excitedly: *"Remember when Etzel . . ."* and *"Remember how Etzel. . . ."*

Despite the boys around me I felt depressed and lonely. I wondered whether I could ever live up to the legacy Etzel had left me. There were the boys, with their enthusiasm and loyalty, as yet unaware of who Etzel really was and of the double-life he had lived among them. And there was I with my promise never to let anybody know what Etzel had told me about himself and his family and with my own growing doubts about the righteousness of the German cause. To what goal and what end would I lead Etzel's boys? To what goal and what end could I lead them? I did not know.

However dejected I felt on the day of Etzel's departure, in the coming weeks I devoted all my waking thoughts to the boys of the *Fähnlein*. I thought Etzel deserved no less. I thought of that each time I met with them every Wednesday and Saturday afternoon at three o'clock on the bridge to the Wolfenbüttel castle and ordered the *Fähnlein*'s flag unfurled.

Our flag, the black flag of the *Jungvolk* with the white lightning rune at its center, was indeed a very special flag, and it owed its specialness to Etzel. I do not know whether it had been Etzel's idea or that of his uncle. But his uncle, the artist, had designed bright-red stylized letters that spelled the name "Blücher," and Elli Bücher, Etzel's Jewish aunt, had stitched these letters across the flag's black cloth. When we marched down the Lange for the first time with our *Blücher* flag, we took the town by surprise. We were aware that we shocked and offended many. By adding a name to the flag we had, in many people's minds, defiled the flag. Even more, we were telling everyone who saw us marching that we followed ideals that we had selected for ourselves

---

2. In English the cheer would be equivalent to: *"Blücher* stands firm, *Blücher* fights, *Blücher* is victorious." The song says, *"Fähnlein Blücher,* on the march, hikes through German lands. . . ."

The Blücher flag

and that these were not those of the party. Our new flag expressed to perfection our self-image as boy soldiers, our loyalty to the traditions of the Prussian army, and our disinterest in the party. And we could not be sure that we would be allowed to thus flaunt our commitment. Would we be accused of flag desecration and forced to remove the name? Would the party and the adult leadership of the Hitler Youth risk antagonizing a hundred boys who loved their *Fähnlein* and their leader? They did not. Though there were some angry remarks directed at us, nobody demanded that we tear off the letters. We kept the flag flying and marched with it every Wednesday and Saturday afternoon.

Today I realize that—whether it had been Etzel's or his uncle's idea to place "Blücher" on the flag—showing that flag on the street had been another way of Etzel's tweaking the party's nose. Only we boys did not know it. I had not known it until that Friday afternoon when Etzel told me his story. And then, when I knew it and when Etzel had left us and I had taken command of his *Fähnlein*, I felt committed to continue flying the *Blücher* flag. I did it because of my friendship with Etzel and because I knew the boys would feel betrayed had I ordered the letters removed. I did it also because, after my experience in Poland and after what I had learned from Etzel, I had come to feel that it was the right thing to do, that ours was to be a soldiers' flag, not a party

151

flag. What I could not be sure of was whether it was only youthful bra-
vura that drove me to thus make public my rejection of the party or
whether, if called to account, I would be ready to defend that rejection
and suffer the consequences. I did not know. I could not tell. I secretly
wished I would never have to tell.

10

Death Enters

I N AUGUST 1944, when Etzel had left and I had taken over his *Fähnlein*, I was formally admitted as an officer's candidate to the army's elite Division Großdeutschland. I had been summoned with a dozen other boys to a country day school outside Wolfenbüttel for a three-day examination that was to probe my health and physical and mental abilities. As I sat in the train taking me to the examination, questions beset me that foreshadowed the unreality and ambivalence that I was to experience later in life when I thought of my father and what his life had meant to me.

Here I was about to enter upon my career as a soldier, a career for which I thought my father's life had set the example. But this was August 1944, barely a month after the news of the unsuccessful assassination attempt on Hitler had hit us with a shock wave of disbelief and bewilderment. How was such treachery possible? was my mother's and my immediate reaction. When Hitler announced that his survival was proof of providential protection and that it was to assure us of ultimate victory, we were at first inclined to believe it. This had not been the first unsuccessful attempt on his life. Hitler had survived earlier bombs that had been set by political foes and, during the early years of the war, had managed to surround himself with such an aura of infallibility and invincibility that many believed he was destined to win in the end. But deeply tucked away in the recesses of my memory were the words of my father in Radlin: There would come a day of reckoning and the army would call the SS to account. I knew that the July bomb was set by an army officer, and that army units were involved in the plot. The newspaper headlines and radio bulletins had made that very clear. Had my father known this was coming? Was this what he had referred to in Radlin? Did he sympathize with, perhaps even support, the plotters? Then I also recalled that he had said the accounting would occur only after we had won the war. So he could not have meant the July plot. But how could I be sure?

As I sat in the train, alone in a compartment, I began to compose a letter in my head, a letter I wanted to send to my father after I had passed the examination and returned home again. I wanted to tell him my feelings and thoughts and I wanted him to respond and settle my uncertainties. I intended to write him that the die had been cast, that he would no longer have to worry that I might choose the SS, that having joined Großdeutschland I had thrown in my lot with the army. I wanted to let him know, too, that I remembered what he had told me in Radlin; that, despite what had happened, I was going to take my stand with the army, to be with him, on his side; and that I trusted in what he had told me. I knew that I could not be explicit in my words, that I could not openly say what I meant by being on his side, but I was sure he would understand. One word of his would be enough of a reply to finally lift the uncertainty that I still felt. I could then commit myself fully to my career as a soldier and know that I was following in his steps. As it was to turn out, I never had the opportunity to send my letter; my father never had the chance to reply and end my uncertainty.

On the first day after my arrival at the boarding school an army physician looked us over, and we then assembled in a classroom for tests in mathematics, language, and history. I was anxious because of my low achievements in the Braunschweig school I was then attending. But I need not have worried. Except for some of the more advanced mathematics problems I had no difficulty with any parts of the exam. I wrote confidently about my desire to become a professional soldier and I found the questions in literature and history easy to answer. The next day the officers challenged us in the gymnasium to show our courage and agility on double and single bars and probed our endurance by sending us on a five-mile run through the wooded hills surrounding the school. After lunch we were to assemble in the gymnasium where we would be told whether we had passed the examinations and whether we would be assigned to the particular unit for which each of us had volunteered.

And so we stood at attention as the commanding officer, an infantry colonel, the German Cross in Gold, the Iron Cross First Class, the Infantry Combat Medal, and a Purple Heart on his tunic, came slowly down the line, followed by a lieutenant who pushed a small wheeled table with a stack of parchment documents and small red cardboard boxes that held the army's silver eagle pin. With a handshake the colonel confirmed our admission, handed each of us document and silver pin, told us we were now members of the German army, and pronounced the name of the regiment or division with which each of us was to serve. As he approached me and was about to grasp my hand, the ground seemed to turn upward under my feet. I heard a ringing in my ears and felt the blood rushing out of my head. As from far away, out of another world, sounded the colonel's voice: "Großdeutschland." Then it was all over. The colonel had passed. I looked at my hand in which I held the document and the small box with the silver eagle.

I was deeply shaken and frightened. What had happened to me? Why had I nearly fainted at the exact moment when I had been assured that my dearest wish had come true, that I was confirmed for a lifetime in the career of a soldier? Was it a loss of nerve just when I had placed myself on my father's side in the confrontation with the SS that he had predicted would come? I could not think clearly, and I stumbled out of the gymnasium, oblivious of the congratulations that swirled all around me as my fellow officers' candidates slapped me and each other on the back and cheerfully shouted their hurrahs.

On the train ride home I relived the incident over and over in my mind trying to uncover what had happened and what it meant. I was still very shaken. As the train neared Wolfenbüttel I could no longer bear it. I told myself to forget it, to deny it. It had never happened, I assured myself, my imagination was playing tricks on me. I now was an officer's candidate in my favorite army division. That was all that mattered. The incident, as I came to think of it, had not been real. I was going to shut it out of my mind and forget it.

The examination had taken place in mid-week and ended on a Thursday. On the following Saturday I met again as usual on the castle bridge with the boys of *Fähnlein* Blücher. When I approached, Ulrich, my adjutant, had already called the boys to order, and they were lined up in formation and looked at me expectantly. Ulrich saluted and reported that everyone was present and accounted for. As I received his message and was about to order that the flag be taken out of its sheath and unrolled, I noticed a woman coming across the castle square toward the bridge. She waved at me and motioned that I come and meet her. I recognized her as a functionary in the party's women's auxiliary. I hesitated for a moment but thought it best to find out what she wanted. So I asked Ulrich to take over the *Fähnlein* and march with it to the soccer field where I would catch up with them later. Then I walked toward the woman.

When I came up to her she apologized for calling me away from my duties and asked me to come with her to her home. It was urgent, she said, because she had some very important papers to give me. I was puzzled and vaguely uneasy but decided to comply. She remained silent as we walked, which did nothing to allay my uneasiness. Once we reached her home and entered she asked me to sit down at a table while she reached into a desk drawer and pulled out a telegram. She had some bad news, she said, but I was the one who should hear it first so I could pass it on to my mother. With that she gave me the telegram. It was the notification that on the previous Thursday my father had been killed in Serbia in an American air attack on a train he was accompanying on its way to Greece. How, she asked, were we going to break the news to my mother? Was there anyone who might help with that?

Her question did not allow me to fully grasp what I had just learned but made me stammer that we should probably call for help on my mother's best friend, Mrs. Fink. "Why, then," she said, "why don't you do that. Take the streetcar and get Mrs. Fink." With that she directed me to the door. Obviously, she wanted to get rid of me as fast as she could.

I don't remember much of the next twenty minutes or so, except that I still held the telegram in my hand as I climbed on the rear platform of the streetcar. I stood there, dimly recognizing people staring at me in my *Jungvolk* uniform, the new silver army eagle and my sharpshooter's medal on my chest, the green and white *Fähnleinführer*'s cord on my left shoulder, Assignment East and Ski Instructor's ribbons on my left arm, and tears streaming down my face. I was oblivious to what went on around me.

I found Mrs. Fink at her home where the crater in the road had been filled in and smoothed and the blown-out windows had been replaced. "My God, Jürgen," she shouted when she saw me as she opened the door, "what is the matter with you? What has happened?"

I showed her the telegram and told her my story. She took me in her arms, the tears now streaming down on both of our faces, and all she said was, "Your poor, poor mother; your poor, poor mother."

With that we both set out on foot to our house. Mrs. Fink suggested that we walk instead of taking the streetcar because then we had time on our way to decide how we would break the news to my mother. And so we two sad figures wended our way back to town, along the Braunschweig highway, over the Breite Herzogstraße and the Lange Straße. Just as we turned the corner into the Harztorwall we saw my mother coming, shopping net in her hand, on her way to the grocery store. She was only a few feet away from us.

"What are you two doing here on the street?" my mother asked, perplexity in her voice. "Why aren't you with your boys?" She looked quizzically at me.

It was obvious from the look on her face that she was alarmed. I don't remember any more just how we answered her. I only recall that, without having had a chance to talk about it, both Mrs. Fink and

I knew that we did not want to give her our message on the street. Somehow we found a way to persuade her to turn around and go home with us.

Once home, we told her what we had to tell her, and all I remember was the cry through her tears and mine, "Oh Jürgen, now you are all I have left."

The day I received the news of my father's death and witnessed my mother's grief I knew I had entered on another phase of my life. Now that I had lost my father I had to come to resolution of my questions on my own. The memory of the incident at the officer's examination rushed back into my mind. I could not help but believe that my moment of near fainting was related to my father's death. Was it his last message to let me know what he thought? And what did that message say? Did it confirm my expectation that when I chose the soldier's life I followed in his footsteps or did it forewarn me that he had been a soldier not by choice but out of duty? Did it tell me that a legacy had passed from him to me, a legacy that would join us as soldiers and as officers? Or did it warn me that my hoped-for life's career was to be cut off before it had even begun? Had I been right in seeing my father as a soldier-scholar, or was he at heart a scholar whom only circumstances had forced to don the officer's uniform? That's what my mother said when I asked her: "Your father was a scholar and he served his country; he had no choice." What did all this mean for my hoped-for career as a soldier? If I could ask my father all of these questions now, what would he say? And as I asked them of myself, what could I say? I had no answer. All I sensed was that I became more and more uncertain of what I had believed was to be my life's destiny.

During those days and weeks of my searching for answers a letter arrived from the town of Semlin in Serbia. It was addressed to my mother and came from a soldier, an artist in civilian life, whose portrait of my father I described at the beginning of this book and which hangs today over my desk. The soldier wrote to console my mother and express his condolences for the death of my father. His opening lines were: "In my life I have had to write many a letter for which my heart's blood should have served as ink, but rarely has it been as difficult for me as it is now." He went on to say, "a gracious fate gave me, the simple soldier, your husband as superior." From the very beginning of his acquaintance with my father, the writer continued, he had been "fortunate not only to serve under a captain to whom I could look up because of his high sense of ethics and his exemplary conception of duty but also because I had found a warm-hearted friend. . . . I shall always be grateful to my creator that throughout three full years of an

The author's father as sketched by his soldier friend, 1942

ever more oppressive war he gave me a man like Captain Herbst as my companion. Walking in our free hours through a foreign country or sitting at night in his room, we shyly reached out for each other's heart in our conversations. More and more he laid aside all thought of rank and allowed me, as also I did him, to look into his soul. And it was Germany that shone in him, for, for me, Germany means goodness."

The letter writer touched on the presence of evil among human beings, and in writing of my father's reactions to it, he allowed me a glimpse into my father's struggle with the ambiguities that surrounded us all. "For people to forget themselves," he wrote, "and sink into human meanness caused Captain Herbst deepest sadness. He found it especially hard to bear the corrupting influence of war on the character of all peoples."

The next sentences, it seemed to me, led to the heart of my own questions and uncertainties that, as I now could see, had also been those of my father. They illumined how my father had managed to live with the tensions and ambivalences of the scholar-soldier. They showed me that he looked on the constraints and impositions of the soldier's life as unavoidable necessities that, as cruel and destructive as they were, had to be endured if there was to be hope for a better and truly humane future. They made it clear that his hope and faith lay in the eternal divine goodness of people everywhere. "My captain," wrote my father's friend, "fled into the iron compulsion to have to persevere throughout these times in order that later, in peaceful years, men's good qualities could flourish again to new benefits. . . .

"Untouched by contemporary party and social positions and demands he believed in the divine eternal of our people and of mankind. As a scholar, he penetrated deeply into the essence of things and appearances, even though he spoke about this with only a few. As recently as last Sunday evening when I showed him a poem, 'Lament over Germany,' he said softly, deeply moved, after a long silence: 'Does one have to say everything?' "

As a child I had perceived dimly from the words of my grandfather Felix and my parents that the greatest love and the deepest pain remain hidden to the eyes of the world, unsung and unuttered. Now I could find that message verified in the words of my father's friend. That which mattered most could be communicated only among those who shared and understood. And, at the deepest level, my father's hope and trust for the future, the writer told my mother, had focused on me: "Captain Herbst believed in a better future led by a young generation born of purest love, even though we Germans who think thus are numerically few."

There it was, the answer and the message I had been searching for.

159

My father's friend had described my father as a soldier, a soldier who "brushed aside the thought of possible danger with the simple sentence: 'We are soldiers,'" and who died the soldier's death. But he also showed him to me as the scholar who, he wrote, "with a simple order" took along his artist friend "on this journey [through the Balkans] across classical terrain to the early centers of European and human culture," and who found the true source of his strength, his compassion, and his love in his scholarship.

My father's friend ended his letter by writing, "Christ taught us that the father's will shall have to be done, and Selma Lagerlöf prays in 'Death's Teamster' that God may not call us away before we have reached the stage of perfection attainable to us. But, of course, only real human beings, that is, God's children, can pray like that. I am convinced that my captain, Dr. Herbst, could have lived for many years to your joy and love. But I am also convinced that as a human being and within his potential, he had attained his full ripeness. . . . His unextinguishable self will be with you and your son and all he loved spiritually, because for such human beings there is no death, only a step into another existence."

I looked in my mother's eyes as we read the letter for the first time, and I could see there through her tears and mine the love the writer had referred to, the love that now showed through the pain and grief that enshrouded us.

In the few weeks that were left to us before I, too, was to leave home for war duties my relationship to my mother began subtly to change. I came to recognize the indomitable will that kept my mother on her feet when malnutrition and illness sapped her strength. I will never forget her saying to me one cold winter night when there was hardly any heat in our kitchen and she had made me eat the last herring she had been able to bring home, "You don't know, Jürgen, how tough I am, but we will never succumb to hunger, cold, and illness. Not us, not us."

I realized how all her efforts for years had been directed to only one goal: To keep me fed, healthy, clothed, and protected, as much as that was possible for her, from the evil that engulfed us. I saw now how she had denied herself food and warmth and comfort that I might thrive, and how her love for me and my father had woven an invisible blanket of protection around me. It wasn't only, as my father's friend had written, that my father had placed all his hopes in me, but so had my mother, with great sacrifice to her own well-being and health.

I now felt a strong obligation to be at my mother's side as often as I could. I now was, indeed, the man of the house. I no longer had to claim and assert that position boastingly. It had been thrust upon me. I knew my mother needed me. I knew it wasn't just a matter of running errands and helping with house work, tasks I now undertook without her having to ask me. I sensed that my mother needed my presence more than anything else, and that, if I did no more than my father had done in the past—sit in the same room with her and read a book—this was enough.

I was strengthened in my renewed resolution to be close to her by remembering my father's admonitions in his letters and seeing them now as expressions of his trust in me. Though I had resented these admonitions when I first received them, now I reread them as sacred obligations. If I really loved my father and admired the course he had followed, then the least I could do was to live up to the expectations he had placed in me. It also helped, I am sure, that as *Fähnleinführer* I no longer needed to "prove" myself among my age mates. I could now turn down challenges to be out at all hours without having to fear ridicule or to regret the absence of shared experiences. With Dieter and Etzel having left town and serving in the armed forces, I had, in the eyes of many in Wolfenbüttel, taken their place as model *Jungvolk* leader. As long as I could rely on the love and loyalty of my boys, I could be their model and leader just as my father had been his soldiers' captain, companion, and friend.

Death now had become a reality for me. As I had read my father's soldier's letter and as I watched my mother's grief, death took on a new dimension for me. It was no longer a matter of heroism and bravado, of patriotic poems and defiant songs. Death was an ever-present, all-pervasive reality that clouded our lives and made us draw more closely together with those we loved most. My mother, Dieter, Etzel, his aunt and his uncle, the boys of the *Fähnlein*—I became aware how vulnerable we all were, how an act of war or vengeance could strike us down at any moment. I learned how much we needed each other, and how hollow the world around us was, the world that besieged us daily with its exhortations and slogans to be indomitable, brave, and persevering. Death, I now knew, was part of our lives and loves, and, though I still fought to admit the thought, some day, perhaps soon, it would extinguish us all.

11

The Choice

URING THE WEEKS FOLLOWING MY FATHER'S DEATH my friendship with Ulla deepened and ripened. She became my confidante and shared my anguish and my concern about my mother's declining health. She would wait for me at the streetcar stop when I returned from school in Braunschweig, and we would walk home together talking about our worries and plans. Not all of our talk was somber and serious because we both knew that soon I would have to leave, as Dieter and Etzel already had, and we hoped that before that happened we could attend dancing school together. We middle-class youngsters were to be instructed by a private dancing master in a Wolfenbüttel restaurant. *Tanzstunde,* as the lessons were called, was to teach us the art of the waltz, the fox-trot, and the tango, and the instructor was to train us in proper table manners and the social graces generally. We thought that would be fun and, provided no air raid would interfere, would give us a chance to meet and be together on a fairly regular schedule.

It all began with me having to call on Ulla's mother to formally request her permission to invite her daughter as my partner. That ceremony was intended as the grand rehearsal for the one eventually to follow when the boy would have to go to his future wife's home and ask her father for his daughter's hand. I dreaded the occasion and was quite intimidated when, on a sunny afternoon, dressed in my Sunday suit, I set out on my errand. Ulla's parents lived in an apartment above a jewelry store they owned, no more than a ten-minute walk away from my home. As I marched through the streets, a bouquet of flowers wrapped in white tissue paper in my hand, I hoped nobody would see me, least of all the vocational school boys of the Krumme Straße whose social status saved them from such bourgeois rituals as I was engaged in. My heart beat high in my throat as I entered the store. To my dismay I was greeted with effusive mock-politeness by Ulla's little brother, who happened to be standing behind the counter. I can still see the big grin on his face and hear his sweetly ingratiating voice— "And what, dear Sir, may I show you of our latest acquisitions? Are you interested in these nice new wrist watches, or is it perhaps a ring for some lady's finger?"—he, of course, knowing full well what I was there for. Happily for me, Ulla's mother stepped into the store from the workshop in the rear and, before I could get myself to stammer my request, she graciously admired my flowers and asked me to come upstairs. She was sure, she said, I had come to see Ulla, but Ulla, unfortunately, was out on an errand, and would I not mind talking with her for a few minutes? When I assured her that the flowers were for her and when I stated my request, she only smiled and said, "Of course, Jürgen, Ulla has been talking of nobody but you lately."

As it turned out, that was the beginning and also the end of my dancing lessons with Ulla. A few days later the government's declaration of total war closed down all schools and public amusements. No longer was there to be any private or public business that was not directly related to the war. The school in Braunschweig was closed, a development that I greeted with immense relief, but our dancing lessons in Wolfenbüttel also were canceled. The Braunschweig students were summoned to leave for the Dutch–German border to dig trenches and thereby help stem the advance of the Allied armies. Again I was exempted, this time not because I was too young but because I belonged to the *Jungvolk* in Wolfenbüttel, and the adult leadership there had different plans for me. I was now told that I was to hand over my *Fähnlein* to Ulrich, my adjutant, and report for duty as an instructor in a Hitler Youth Leadership Training School in the Harz Mountains. In the intervals between training courses I was to serve as a railroad courier, carrying confidential messages throughout northern Germany to various party and military offices.

My parting with Ulla and my mother was bittersweet. While I had shared with Ulla my worries about my mother, I had not talked with her or with my mother about Etzel's tale and about the questions that I had planned to ask my father. I had promised Etzel never to mention to anybody what he had told me and I did not want to burden Ulla with knowledge that could only endanger her life. I did not want either her or my mother to know that my signing up as an officer's candidate involved more than the simple act of chosing a career, that having selected the division Großdeutschland I had, prompted by my father's words and my family's faith, committed myself in any future confrontation with the party and the SS to the side of the army. I thought of my father's words in Radlin not to worry my mother about the dangers he faced and I never mentioned to her what he had told me. Besides, I did not want Ulla or my mother to know that while I had, in my mind at least, taken this step, I was still full of uncertainty about it all. There had not been time to send my father the letter with my questions; his death now made it impossible for him to assure me that I had understood him correctly. As always when I was uncertain in my own mind, I found it difficult to talk about things that concerned me, and I kept them to myself. So when I said goodbye to my mother and to Ulla, I did so with a heavy heart, feeling sad that we could not talk about the things that mattered most, while trying to be cheerful and encouraging, persuading them that I was taking off in high spirits for new adventures.

And adventures I encountered aplenty, most of them during the railroad trips I took as a courier. By the second half of 1944 the trains, no matter where they ran, had become favorite targets of Allied fighter bombers that would swoop out of the clouds and strafe everything that moved. Local as well as express and freight trains usually had a flat-bed car attached with light anti-aircraft guns placed on them. Though I was fortunate in never experiencing a direct attack on any train I was riding in, I felt myself very much a real soldier. Dressed now in the smart field gray uniform of the Training School, my army eagle and other medals affixed to my breast pockets, the Assignment East and the Ski Instructor ribbons stitched to my sleeve, on my shoulders the two stars indicating my rank as a *Jungvolk Führer,* I hobnobbed with the gun crews as much as I could, often riding with them in the train's last car.

All this boosted my self-esteem. Here I was, a sixteen-year-old boy, having an official pass for any railroad train I chose to enter, carrying important messages—it all seemed very exciting and flattering to me. Besides, I soon learned that there were lonely women aplenty, in military or civilian clothes, who sought the company of soldiers and uniformed boys like myself. Layovers in smoke-filled waiting rooms and long journeys in cushioned second-class railroad compartments gave opportunities for many a pleasant hour. I also learned to my surprise that for traveling soldiers and their female companions there was no shortage of candy, chocolates, and coffee, wine, liqueur, and cigarettes. When, as I sometimes succeeded in doing, I routed my travels through Wolfenbüttel and stopped over for a night at home to bring my mother coffee and chocolate, she would sadly shake her head and sigh: "Jürgen, if I knew how you got these presents, would it make me happy?"

All I could say in reply was, "Mother, there's a war going on, and these are military rations."

Still, the heart of my assignment was at the Training School, and it was there that the questions I had evaded in my report on the Assignment East and that beset me after my father's death came to haunt me again with renewed force. Now I found myself at the heart of an elite party institution in which Nazi indoctrination formed the center of its program. While my daily duties in the school consisted of leading cross-country runs, supervising boxing matches, and conducting singing lessons for the trainees, usually boys of fourteen who were to be groomed as Hitler Youth leaders, I absorbed enough of the ideological teaching through my daily contact with the school's leader to wipe away the unsettling uncertainties that I had experienced over the meaning of my father's words in Radlin. My exposure to the school leader's monologues on Nazi theory and plans had the surely unintended effect of confirming me in my assumption that I had not misunderstood my father; that the confrontation between party and army would have to come; and that, when that time arrived, I would take my stand on my father's side.

Of my duties in the school I considered the cross-country runs to be my most exacting, the boxing matches my least favorite, and the singing lessons my most pleasurable task. I was determined, however, to do equally well at all of them. The school's leader and the drill sergeants, highly decorated and partly disabled noncommissioned army officers, evidently regarded the cross-country run as a kind of qualifying test for the trainees. Thus, when I arrived to take over my duties, I was first assigned to join the then current group of trainees and told to participate as one of them in their initial run. That way, one of the drill sergeants said, they would have a chance to judge whether I really was the right man for the job, and I, in turn, could find out for myself what was expected of the trainees.

When the trumpet sounded reveille on the first morning of my life in the school, I lined up with the trainees in front of the flagpole on the school's parade ground. The rocky slopes surrounding the school cast back the tones of the trumpet, and the dark fir and spruce trees stretching down the valley swallowed them. We thirty boys stood in formation, dressed in our black-belted gray jackets and gray pants which were tucked into our boots. A step ahead, slightly to the left of us, stood the bugler with his trumpet now secured to his belt.

A small, heavyset figure emerged from the school building and walked toward us. It was the school leader. He wore the same gray jacket as we did, but his legs were clad in black riding breeches and highly polished knee-high boots. Under his jacket one could see his brown shirt and black tie. His head was covered with a brown officer's cap. On the breast pocket of his jacket were affixed the Iron Cross First

Class, an infantry combat medal, and a purple heart. A small pistol in a black leather holster stuck to his belt.

The boy with the trumpet stepped forward, turned to us and shouted: "Attention—I report to the School Leader."

His words echoed back to us from the trees. He turned again, and boy and school leader saluted each other, their arms outstretched, fingers pointing into the sky. Then it was the school leader's turn to shout, and two trainees stepped forward toward the pole. The trumpeter raised his instrument to his lips, the piercing tones bounced back from the silent trees, and the red and white Hitler Youth flag rose into the sky.

"Heil Hitler, boys," the school leader's voice came to us, and "Heil Hitler, school leader," we shouted back.

At ease, he ordered, and announced the plans for the day. We were to get ready for a cross-country run in the morning, and he was to lecture in the afternoon.

Fifteen of our group took off together. We jogged along a narrow footpath at the base of a steep wall of cliffs. Soon we began to jump over broken-off branches and fallen trees, and I cursed my bad luck of being the last of the column. When those at the head of the line climbed over a tree trunk I bounced against the boy before me, and when those in the lead had overcome their obstacle, I still struggled with rocks and branches and then had to speed up to keep the pace with the disappearing line before me.

Soon I saw the boy ahead of me turn off the path and climb up the mountainside on the right. The morning sun had gained strength, and I felt the sweat gather on my forehead and upper lip. My whole body began to itch. On the loose ground and gravel of the hillside small stones and sand slipped into my boots. I felt the debris slide past my ankles and gather under my insteps. I kicked with my foot against a rock to dislodge the pieces but it did not do much good. My feet hurt; I felt my heartbeat in my throat; sweat and saliva ran down my chin.

Once up on the mountain we followed a logging road. It was torn up and full of sand-filled holes that made my feet sink into them and my boots fill up with more sand and stones. Soon we started downhill, following the switchbacks of the path. A mountain stream blocked our progress, tossing its water over rocks and boulders. I saw those before me jump into the water, saw them slide, fall, pull themselves up again, and climb up on the other bank. Then I was in the water, jumped for a flat boulder in the middle of the stream, slipped, felt the coldness rise up to my hips, slipped again, and pulled myself with arms and legs through the roaring foam until I climbed on the bank and tried again to catch up with those before me. Boots and clothes all were wet, and between my toes I could feel the cold, grainy paste squish with every step I took.

Then up again we ran along a mountaintop path. By now we moved like machines, feeling little, unconscious of our burning feet, aching legs, and whistling lungs. The descent to the school led over a stone and boulder field over which we slid, slipped, and jumped as best as we could. I looked out for treacherous cracks between the rocks, pushed and pulled myself over crevices and fallen tree trunks, until we finally reached the bottom of the slope. Now we ran again, coughing and panting and sweating, more slowly than at the beginning, but running nonetheless until, at the edge of the school ground, we encountered the obstacle course.

I dropped to the ground, made myself as small as I could, pulled arms and leg together, and crawled along underneath the barbed wire. At least, I thought, we did not carry any backpacks. Once out from under the wire, a rocky escarpment, ten feet high, fell off perpendicularly before me, and from it, at a right angle, stretched a brick wall, eight inches wide and twenty-five feet long. The balancing act, I thought, and was already hastening along on the narrow ledge when the ground began to weave before my eyes, the grass below appeared to shoot up toward me. Go, go, I heard myself mumbling, and then a voice from below: "Jump, jump now." I did, and I felt the stones and the sand in my boots pierce my feet like hundreds of little flames, pushed myself off the ground and hurried on toward the slick wooden wall. I jumped at it, felt again the hundred little flames burn into my foot and toes, pulled myself desperately across the polished top of the wall. As I tumbled down on the other side I had the releasing sensation of falling into a void. It lasted for a fraction of a second only and then I felt the crunching crash of my body on the ground, heard the harsh, commanding voice of the school leader: "Only the hanging beams left, boy, and you'll have done it!"

The beams were placed across a muddy pond. A few running steps, a jump, and I dangled in the air. Keep your arms bent, was all I could think. . . . Don't let 'em straighten out . . . don't let 'em . . . for heaven's sake, don't let them straighten out . . . or all is lost. The musty smell of the stagnant water rose from below. I pushed my hands, right, left, right, left, keep your arms bent, each push a little less far, with each push a heavier weight pulling on my hands and arm muscles. Ten more feet, six more, three more, now three more times with each hand, now two, only one more, push and swing and . . . let go, a deep breath while I hit the ground. It was finished. I had done it.

As I got up on my feet a sensation of pride and accomplishment overcame me. I knew the school leader had watched me and that I had proved to him and the drill sergeants that I was no weakling. I could do what I was supposed to demand of my future trainees. I tucked in my uniform and walked toward the school building. Then I heard the school leader call out from behind me: "Herbst, at dinner time today, report to the leader's mess hall. That's where you'll take your meals from now on."

I glowed with pride. I had been accepted. I had been found capable of carrying out my new job.

At the mess hall table I joined the school leader and the drill sergeants. There was little conversation. The school leader loved monologues. "Yes, school leader," "Quite right, school leader," "That's just what I think, school leader," the drill sergeants said.

I kept silent. I did not know what I could say. It was the first time I sat in this company. Meat, potatoes, gravy, and vegetables were passed around. Outside, the boys were served stew. I knew. I had read the daily menu. The food tasted good. I was hungry from the morning's run, but I did not quite dare to take as much as I would have liked. The second time round I passed the vegetable. The school leader spoke about the lecture he wanted to give that afternoon. "Ideological training," he said, his hands holding knife and fork pointing upright into the air, "is our most important duty, more important even than military training. It is the depth of conviction that keeps the soldier at his task even when his bodily strength gives out. We soldiers," and he leaned toward the drill sergeants, looking straight at them, "know this, don't we?"

"Indeed, school leader," they said as with one voice. I thought I saw their eyebrows twitch.

"The unconquerable faith in the rightness of our idea," the school leader continued, still holding the silverware in his hands, "the knowledge of the national socialist fighter about the infallibility of the Führer and his teachings that cannot be shaken by anything are the best guarantees for our final victory. That is why we have to drum our creed again and again into the minds of our trainees until it has become their own unerasable conviction. Ideological training, every National Socialist should know this, is the alpha and omega of our movement. We believe in the power of the idea. That is why we are so much stronger than the Bolsheviks and the Western materialists. Idea, faith, and fanatical will to translate our creed into reality are the pillars of our National Socialism.

"By the way," the school leader smiled confidingly and laid down his fork and knife, "I had a chat the other day with Helmut, the little, weakly guy from the third platoon, the pastor's son. I talked with him for a long time in a fatherly, confidential way. We discussed matters seriously, and he told me what his father had taught him. If it weren't so incredible, so downright criminal, today, when we are in the midst of our greatest struggle for survival, one might be inclined to smile about such naivete, such stupidity.

"This man, this father," the school leader went on, having again picked up his knife and fork and about to move a piece of meat into his mouth, "he is a pastor. With criminal and stupid brazenness he has fed this boy with all these stories of little Jesus and this other Biblical nonsense. The boy was on his way to believing it all!"

There was a slight pause as the school leader chewed on his meat, and then he continued: "Well, I will have to say that I succeeded in beginning to cure him. I talked with him seriously and logically. I forced him to start thinking, to really analyze what he was mouthing. Yesterday, when all the boys went down to the firing range I ordered him to the library to read *Der Mythos des Zwangzigsten Jahrhunderts* and *Mein Kampf.*"

The school leader paused again to pay attention to his meal before him and, after having scraped some cauliflower and potatoes off his plate and having shoved it into his mouth, he added with great satisfaction: "There you see the practical side of what I said: Ideological training is our most important task! This morning I talked with him once more. His reading shows results. The boy takes on some sense. But, gentlemen," and the school leader sat upright, put his knife and fork down again, glanced quickly at everyone, and then let his eyes rest on me: "One thing, gentlemen, we shall have to keep in mind always. We shall never succeed in building our national socialist Reich as long as these ridiculous blabbering idiots of the church are able to shoot off their mouths in our midst. It became again clear to me yesterday that the churches are the most reactionary elements in our state. As long as churchmen can mislead our Germans with their false doctrine we cannot afford to let down our guard; we cannot allow ourselves to tire.

"Gentlemen," and the school leader raised his voice, "we all shall have to be clear about one thing: A National Socialist can never be a Christian! Christianity is treason against the German state! The church is a plague boil on the body of our people!"

I tried to look up from my plate. I felt how the school leader's eyes moved away from me and swept over the others. For a few seconds there was absolute quiet. Seemingly out of nowhere, a Bible verse shot up in my mind: *"Be thou faithful unto death, and I will give thee a crown of life"*—the words that my grandfather had given my parents at their wedding as a guide for their lives and that they, in turn, had selected for me at my confirmation. My thoughts drifted to St. Mary's in Wolfenbüttel with its tall, gray-white gothic pillars, and, in my mind's eye, I saw our pastor Rosenkranz on the pulpit above the bent-down Moses, heard him recite the Lord's Prayer, remembered how my thoughts wandered and how I sought to concentrate on the prayer and did not succeed.

Then the voice of one of the drill sergeants broke the silence: "School leader, I request permission to rise."

"Please, of course," replied the school leader, "we all may rise."

For days thereafter I could not rid myself of that minute of silence after the school leader's monologue. I kept on seeing the church, the cold gothic pillars; I heard the voice of Pastor Rosenkranz; I felt the shame over my inability to concentrate; I saw the dinner plate before me, felt the eyes of the school leader, heard his shrill voice: "A National Socialist can never be a Christian," and I listened again, as if to a muted refrain, to that small, still voice that said: "Be thou faithful unto death, and I will give thee a crown of life."

In the weeks following the school leader's table talk my thoughts returned again and again to his words: "A National Socialist can never be a Christian." Quite often, as I lay in bed at night, the scene in the dining room appeared before me but then it became blurred: I heard the school leader pray, saw Pastor Rosenkranz in riding boots and breeches, heard him shout orders in a shrill commanding voice. What was I to do? How could all these pictures and voices come together again and blend harmoniously with the world I had lived in—the world of Dieter, our chief *Jungvolk* leader who was a pastor's son; the world of Etzel and our boys at home; of Etzel's aunt and uncle; of my mother and my grandparents who had been with me two years ago in St. Mary's at my confirmation; the world of my father who, as his confirmation gift, had sent me *The Prussian Chorale* and, when he had come home on furlough from the war, had taken me to St. Mary's every Sunday?

I had lived in a world in which, until that day in the leader's dining room at the Hitler Youth school, all these pictures and voices had somehow managed to coexist together. Yes, there had been questions and uncertainty. I had remembered Albert Morgenstern and his parents who were torn out of bed at night and had been carted off in a police van; I had witnessed the Birkental camp; I had wondered at Cieszyn whether Albert was among those whom I saw suffering there; I had met the little man with his yellow star in the fog; and I had listened to Etzel's tale and had been sworn to everlasting secrecy.

And in that world, encouraged by Etzel, I had nevertheless been able to lead my boys, and I had been able to go to church at the same time. In that world when I was ten years old I had asked questions of

170

my mother and of some—not all—of my teachers and I could accept their answers even though I dimly felt that they were not answers, only words. When I was fifteen I could still tell myself that all this was required by the necessities of war. Until that day in the school leader's mess I had been able to live with these incongruities and evade the questions they asked.

But now, in my sixteenth year, the school leader had told me I could no longer live that double life. I could no longer wear the brown shirt of the *Jungvolk* and go to church on Sundays. I could no longer remain faithful to the bequest of my grandfather and my parents. I had to make a choice.

As I saw it, the school leader had confronted me with a simple, direct challenge: Choose the party, the brown uniforms, the Hitler Youth, or cast your lot with the army, the field gray uniforms, the church.

Now it was up to me. I had to decide. I thought of my father, of Dieter, of Etzel, of my boys. All of a sudden, it seemed an easy choice. The uncertainties that had for so long surrounded it vanished. If I was to live with myself, I told myself, if I was to remain loyal to my ideals, my family, my friends, and my boys, there really was no choice to make—the choice had been made long ago, when I was not aware of it. It had been made for me as much as I might think I was making it now.

I could not help but think of Dieter and Etzel. Both were gone now, serving in the military. Dieter, the son of a Protestant pastor, and Etzel, the nephew of a Jewish aunt—did not they have to face the same choice? Had not their choice been made for them, too, long ago? What would they say were I to ask them this question? Had they come to the same answers I had? I saw them both before my mind's eye in their uniforms, Etzel leading us boys of *Fähnlein* Blücher, and Dieter standing in the marketplace before the 600-some boys of Wolfenbüttel's *Jungvolk*. But they were gone now and I could not ask them. I could only assume that their answers had been the same as mine, just as I was sure now that I had understood my father correctly.

That realization came to me as an immense relief. I no longer had to worry what I would do when I was asked to choose between leaving the church to keep my rank as a *Jungvolkführer* or remaining a member of St. Mary's and repudiate my life with the boys of *Fähnlein* Blücher. I knew it would not be easy to leave the boys, knowing they would be told I had betrayed and abandoned them. But I also knew that I was not deserting my boys; that when I sided with the church and the army I was showing them the way into the future, a way with honor and decency that would, one day, wipe out—I was certain of that—the villainy and infamy that those who, my father had said, defiled our cause and besmirched our name had brought upon us. That way would allow us all, my father, Dieter, Etzel, myself, and our boys, to believe again in the honorableness of our country's cause. The only question that now continued to nag me and for which I knew there was no answer until I gave it myself by my actions was whether, when the moment came, I would have the courage to follow through with what I intended to do.

12

Baptism by Fire

MY DAYS IN THE HITLER YOUTH TRAINING SCHOOL came to an end in mid-January of 1945 when I received orders to report for basic military training at the National Labor Service camp Rodewald near Hannover. I was glad that the call had come and I could leave the Training School behind. Though my last weeks there had been uneventful, the school leader's challenge had been on my mind most of the time. As I lay in bed at night and thought about it, I had prepared and rehearsed my response to it countless times. The challenge followed me at Christmas when the school had closed and I went home on leave for the holidays.

On Christmas Eve I walked with my mother to the service at St. Mary's. I tried hard to push all thought of the school leader's words from my mind. I was determined not to let them come between me and my mother, not between me and Propst Rosenkranz, who stood on the pulpit above the anguished Moses and delivered his Christmas Eve sermon. I did not succeed. Here I sat in the very place that had become for me the eye of the storm, the calm and quiet center. It was the rock, I told myself as I listened to the age-old message of joy and peace, on which I would place my footing. Again I heard the soothing melody of Michael Prätorius's "Lo, How a Rose Is Blooming," as it had sounded through St. Mary's on this night for 300 years. But I knew that when I left the church and reentered the world of war and death I would, in due time, face my moment of truth. And though I had rehearsed it many times in my mind, I was not sure whether, when the moment arrived, I would have Martin Luther's courage to say my "Here I stand, I can do no other." What made it worse for me was my strong conviction that I dare not add to my mother's worries and discuss my decision and my fears with her. I had to bear my burden in silence. As it turned out, when I returned to the school after the holidays, the school leader never returned to the subject. When my orders for Rodewald arrived and I left the school for good, I knew I had been spared the confrontation that I had envisaged and dreaded.

I took off for Rodewald with mixed feelings. I now was on my way to my eventual destination in the army, but I regarded my time with the Labor Service as an unavoidable, unpleasant interlude. The Labor Service was another Nazi organization that, by 1945, had taken over from the army its basic training function. I, like all my fellow recruits, disliked the brown uniforms with their swastikas attached to our left sleeve. But we consoled ourselves with the thought that, at least, our drill sergeants, like those in the Training School, were all decorated and severely wounded former army noncommissioned officers, and our days in Rodewald were numbered. Basic training was to last no longer than eight weeks. Then I would finally join the army and begin the life I had dreamed of all along.

The weeks at Rodewald were cold, wet, and miserable. We sixteen-year-old recruits were drilled in the basics of infantry combat. From mid-January to mid-March we were sent out day and night through swampy meadowlands that made us sink knee-deep into mud. Every ditch, hidden under snow-crusted ice, had us plunge into freezing water. We were taught how to storm make-believe enemy trenches with drawn bayonets and how to fire bazookas at haystacks. We were doused with tear gas and sent through the billowing clouds, sometimes crawling and sometimes running full speed, with our gas masks on our faces until our lungs gave out and we collapsed in the icy mud. Our barracks were cold, and we suffered from diarrhea and fevers. American bombers high above us drew their contrails across the sky. When their accompanying fighters appeared and engaged in aerial combat with German jet planes, we pressed our bodies in the water-soaked icy grass to avoid detection and being strafed. Our drill sergeants assured us that this was but child's play compared with what awaited us on the front.

By mid-March, the ordeal came to an end. We exchanged our hated brown Labor Service uniforms for our own clothes, and I was given a pass for a one-day leave home. After that I was to report to my army duty with the replacement brigade of the Division Großdeutschland north of Rendsburg, Schleswig-Holstein. My journey home took me through Hannover where I had to change trains. Just as I arrived around noon, the alarm sounded and all travelers were herded into the concrete bunker that had been buried into the ground underneath the railroad station. We had hardly found our way into the huge edifice with its steel-rod locked doors when the structure began to shake and rock as bombs exploded on and around it. The bunker's bare bulbs shed a ghostly yellow light over the motley crowd of wan-looking women and children, soldiers, and a few invalid men who huddled on the benches. Every time the ground shook and the bulbs swayed the people on the benches pulled in their shoulders; some mumbled, some groaned; little children cried softly and clung to their mothers.

But all of us stared mesmerized at the small group of youngsters, boys mainly, who sat on the floor at the center of the gray concrete hall. They were *Edelweißpiraten*—Pirates of the Edelweiss, as they called themselves—teenagers who during the last part of 1944 all over the country had begun to show openly their contempt for the Hitler Youth and the Nazi party. I had encountered them first on the Lange Herzog-straße in Wolfenbüttel while I was still with my boys of *Fähnlein* Blücher. Then I had considered them a nuisance who, in their dress and behavior, contrasted unfavorably with us boys in the *Jungvolk* and were best ignored by us. After all, I had thought, except for setting a bad example, they did no real harm.

Now as I watched them strumming their guitars and listened to them singing their sorrowful tune I could not help but be strangely moved by them. They sang of the girl who was to love her soldier at night, and who, if her lover's U-boat was not to surface anymore, if his airplane was not to return, or his parachute was not to open, was to give up waiting for him, because he, too, would return no more.[1] Who could refute the words they were singing? Would I want Ulla to wait for me if I were not to come home from the war, I thought? As we were sitting there, with the light flickering and the walls shaking, did not their song speak to us more truthfully than the Nazi slogan painted on the wall—"Wheels Roll on Toward Victory"—or our marching song in Rodewald, "Proudly do I stand on guard for Germany, always cheerful is my mind"?[2] The "wheels" outside had come to a dead standstill, and no one knew then whether they would carry us further on our road once we emerged from the bunker. In Rodewald we had not been cheerful, despite our singing. Quite the contrary. The cold, the mud, the constant pressure of air alarms and of harassment by the drill ser-

---

1. *Mädel liebst Du einen blonden Fallschirmjäger,*
    Mädel lieb ihn nur immer, wenn er abends bei dir ist.
    Und geht sein Fallschirm nicht mehr auf,
    Mädel warte nicht länger drauf,
    denn er kehrt nicht mehr zurück.
2. *Räder müssen rollen für den Sieg*

and

Stolz halt ich für Deutschland Wacht
und froh ist stets mein Sinn.

geants, the bouts of stomach flu and fevers had made us depressed and eager to leave the camp as soon as we could. The *Edelweißpiraten's* song, I thought, came closer to the truth we experienced than the slogan and the words of the marching song.

The youngsters' appearance, their song, the thudding of the bombs, and the swaying of the bunker held all of us as if bewitched. No one in that crowd on the benches seemed any longer to react to the threat of their own death, but everyone was mesmerized by the haunting melody of the song and the garish looks of the boys and girls who were singing it. Long-haired, gypsy neckerchiefs over their collars, their pants slit at the sides, the boys ostentatiously mocked the soldierly look that German youths were to show. The girls in their sweaters and skirts billowing over gray corduroy pants looked as if they had just crept out from under the bombed-out ruins outside. Their message was of death and sorrow, not of final victory, which was then the main theme of Nazi propaganda. I did not think the scene augured well for my going to war.

When the all-clear sounded and I emerged on the station's platform, repair crews were already at work. They lifted bent and torn tracks with cranes mounted on flatbed railroad cars, poured fresh gravel onto the cratered rail beds, dropped new rails on top, and, in long columns of blue-clad men rhythmically swinging their heavy hammers, fastened them in place. A locomotive slowly followed with steel bars and wheels extending from its front end grinding the new tracks to exact specifications of straightness and width. It could not have taken longer than an hour and a half after the raid that I boarded my train, which now slowly moved out of the Hannover station, taking me on my way home toward Braunschweig and Wolfenbüttel.

The day at home passed all too quickly. I went to see Ulla and talked with her at her parents' home. I promised her that I would write as often as I could, and she did the same. When we parted I took one last walk down the Lange, hoping, without really expecting it, to see a familiar face. But I did not. The street was nearly deserted; only a few housewives, shopping bags in hand, went from store to store in the hope of finding something edible for their family's dinner table. My friends were gone just as I would be gone. I went home to spend the last few hours with my mother.

The next day I was on my way to Rendsburg. When I arrived in mid-afternoon at the village to which I had been ordered to report I felt I had finally reached my goal. The reception by our company chief, First Lieutenant Preuß, and our staff-sergeant was warm and friendly. By evening I wore my new uniform with the black ribbon Großdeutschland on its sleeve. As an officer's candidate, I had been assigned my first duty as orderly. By comparison with basic training at Rodewald, my first few weeks in the army were exhilarating. Here, I felt, I was among real soldiers; soldiers as I had imagined them from all the stories Bodo Wacker and my father had told, soldiers who proudly wore the division's name. Our company chief, the sergeant-major, and our other noncommissioned officers were experienced combat soldiers who had earned their decorations and purple hearts on the Eastern front where the division had been mainly engaged. They made it a point to remind us that we were the inheritors of Prussian military tradition and honor; that our division, of which we were the replacement brigade, had grown out of the Berlin Guard Regiment. As we marched along to the training ground we sang the Guard's song:

> The name Great Germany on our sleeve,
> loyalty and honor in our hearts,
> love to our people and faith in God,
> willingness to bear arms and endure combat:
> Yes, we are soldiers and want to remain soldiers,
> loyal comrades, fighters for the fatherland.[3]

The song expressed my feelings perfectly. Loyalty and honor, love of people, faith in God, commitment to the profession of arms—these were ideals my father and Bodo Wacker had talked about to me as a youngster, these were the ideals I wanted to live by, and now I had my chance. My life as a professional soldier had begun. Yes, I was well aware now that the enemy had entered Germany, the hour was late; that the time of easy victories had long since passed; that soldiers like my father had come to doubt the righteousness of our cause. But not everything was lost, I told myself. We were being groomed to enter the fight in the war's last, decisive hour. I was among soldiers who, I was sure, thought like my father did. We would have the opportunity by our fortitude and commitment to forestall defeat, stamp out corruption, and right the injustices committed in our people's name. No matter how somber the outlook was in mid-March of 1945, we were going to live up to our oath and fight for Germany until the trumpet would call us to desist. It would be up to us to finally force the enemy to a halt and to restore our country's honor and good name.

3.   *Wir tragen den Namen Großdeutschland am Rock,*
     im Herzen die Treue und Ehre,
     die Liebe zum Volk und den Glauben an Gott,
     den Wille zur Waffe und Wehre.
     Ja, wir sind Soldaten,
     wollen Soldaten sein und bleiben,
     Treue Kameraden, Kämpfer für das Vaterland.

Here, among the soldiers of the division Großdeutschland, I no longer had to choose. I was on the side of the army whose battle was for Germany, its people, and its honor. No one here ever mentioned the party; everyone, however, was acutely conscious that we, as the army's elite division, were the army's counterforce to the Armed SS, the party's military arm. Though little was said about strained relations with the SS, our song's profession of faith in God and occasional remarks by our noncoms about the SS not living up to German military traditions and giving the German army a bad name made it clear that the division's old soldiers did not think we had any reason to admire or support the Armed SS. The depth of their contempt and hatred for the SS, however, did not show itself until a month later in combat. Then, at a village called Glinstedt, our sergeant-major, the company's most highly decorated noncommissioned officer, ordered us to our battle stations and pointed to an SS antitank battery slightly ahead to our left. Though our field of fire lay to our right, he remarked offhandedly, we could extend it to our left at will. With a smirk on his face he left us in no doubt that he meant what he said.

In Schleswig our infantry combat training lasted exactly one week. At its end, our two companies left our village quarters at night in single file, marched to a nearby railroad yard, and boarded the cars of a freight train for the journey south past Rendsburg and Flensburg. By the time we crossed the curving bridge over the North Sea–Baltic Sea Canal to Hamburg it was daylight. As we passed the anti-aircraft batteries on the bridge towers, we kept our assault rifles at the ready, on the lookout for strafing fighter planes. But the trip remained uneventful, and, toward evening, we disembarked at Sagehorn, a small railroad station east of Bremen. It was dark by the time we marched single file the six miles into Achim. There our training continued for two more days. We were issued our heavy infantry weapons, bazookas, grenade launchers, and machine guns, and were instructed in their use.

In the evening of the second day, our two companies assembled for a formal departure parade through the streets of Achim. The town's people had decorated their houses with flags, and girls stood waving on the sidewalks. I could not help but feel that now, at this late hour in the war, I experienced for myself what I had heard and read about so often, and what I had missed six years earlier when my father and his men left Braunschweig. Though there were no bands playing, I now was "marching into war." I felt a strange elation, a mixture of pride and bewilderment to be the object of adulation and pity by waving crowds made up mainly of old men and women and girls. The men looked somber, the old women had tears in their eyes, and the girls were excited, threw kisses and stuck flowers into the barrels of our assault rifles. I sensed a strangely mingled hope and anxiety, an eagerness and a fear finally to find out what it was really like to face what I had been told was the highest and truest test of myself.

As we marched west night after night toward the approaching British troops we boys of the 6th Company, 2nd Battalion, Replacement Brigade, Division Great Germany—and boys we were, I just having turned seventeen the month before—would not admit our anxiety and fear. We rather boasted of our impatience and eagerness to "meet the enemy." Lieutenant Preuß had to put a damper on our crowing more than once. He assured us that we would find out soon enough what it was like to be shot at. And so we trudged along, night after night, by moonlight and under rain-heavy clouds, over country roads and swamp paths, sometimes merrily humming and singing, at others half asleep, always in single file to minimize our exposure to strafing attacks.

On March 30, we reached Ganderkesee, a village ten miles west of Bremen, and I wrote a letter home:

Dear Mother: Today, the night of Good Friday, we rest. We have been marching every night. The night before last it was sixteen miles, last night twelve. Tomorrow night we shall march again. It's not certain where we are going; in any case, against the Tommy. But don't worry about me, mother. I know for certain that I will come home again. That's something I feel deeply inside. The only question is, when? So don't be afraid, mother, even when there won't be any mail. It will hardly be possible to send you any. I haven't gotten any at all. But I will write you as often as I can.

I meant what I said in that letter. I did know, with a certainty that I find hard to explain but which I never doubted, that I would come home again. I was sure of that. What I did not know and could not know was whether I would see my mother and Ulla again, whether Wolfenbüttel would survive the war or whether bombs and shells would wipe it off the map with all its people in it.

Rain soaked us as we marched the next two nights until the clouds cleared the day after Easter Sunday. Then we were guests of farmers in the countryside surrounding the small village of Sage south of Oldenburg. Our hosts were good to us. The war by either air or land had not touched them. Their houses and fields were well tended, and their larders and pantries were full. They fed us eggs and bacon, fried potatoes and coffee cakes. Their generosity and sideways glances, however, told us that they pitied us. One woman looked at me and asked: "Well, boy, do you still believe in victory?"

179

"Yes, of course," I said, but was struck at once by the immediacy, the automatic nature, of my response. Did I really believe in our victory? As my thoughts flashed back to my occasional doubts about the honorableness of our cause; to my father's sadness and anger about what he had seen in Poland, the Ukraine, and Russia; to my own knowledge of Nazi cruelty in Wolfenbüttel and in Poland; and to my recent encounter with the Edelweißpiraten in the Hannover railroad bunker, I wondered whether I had spoken too quickly. But if I really no longer believed in our victory, why had I looked forward so much to being a soldier and marching to war? Why did I cling to my father's words that we would, after victory, stamp out corruption and right the injustices committed in our people's name? Why? What kept me being a loyal soldier, telling the farm woman that I believed in our victory, when, deep down, I could not deny my doubts and anxieties?

One of my comrades interrupted my thoughts when he said to the woman: "We are soldiers, we don't ask many questions. We are going to meet the enemy and we are going to do our duty."

"May God protect you," said the woman.

Yes, I said to myself. That's it. We are going to do our duty as loyal soldiers. May God protect us.

From Sage we marched to Lastrup and then south to Bippen, a town sixty miles southwest of Bremen. We arrived there on April 8. Again we were drenched by rain, and the city's inhabitants invited us into their homes for a bath and dinner. My hostess, a soldier's widow, said to me and my comrades: "Do come back, every free minute you have. We like to see you. We rest our hopes on you. You, you want to fight. You are not like the others who come through here, going east and retreating. Are they really still German soldiers? You won't desert us, will you?" she pleaded.

Again we said the only thing we could say: "No, we won't retreat. We won't leave you," though we knew full well that we could not give such a promise. When the order would come for us to fall back, we would do so. What we meant to say was that we would not retreat before we received such an order, that we would not cowardly run away. We were soldiers and we were going to act like soldiers.

As it was, the order to leave Bippen reached us two days later. Even though our sergeant encouraged us to pay a last visit to our hosts, I could not bear the thought of facing them and telling them: "I, too, will now leave you. I will leave Bippen because I am ordered to do so."

And so I stayed away from my hostess's house, waiting for night-fall when our company was to march out in a northeasterly direction toward Löningen. Moving north and east, we knew, meant retreat. Our nightly westward moves to meet the advancing British troops had now been turned around. We were ordered to avoid being cut off and encircled. We reversed our course and thus did what all the other German troops had done, the ones my hostess did not want to recognize as German soldiers any more. We retreated. I felt terrible.

We reached the southern outskirts of Löningen on the morning of April 11 at about the same time that the first British units arrived at the city's western side. In *The 43rd Wessex Division at War 1944–1945* Major-General Hubert Essame writes that the British units there

> struck determined resistance, particularly in the wood to the south. They were faced in fact by a composite battalion of the Grossdeutschland Brigade, mostly boys of from 16 to 18 years of age, but including a company of potential officers . . . [who] fought with the utmost ferocity. However, before midnight they had been overwhelmed.[4]

Flattering as General Essame's description is, it does not quite match my recollections of the engagement. Our company was to take over from the 8th Parachute Division the rear-guard defense of our retreating troops. We were asked to dig in along the Hase Canal and River. The day and the night passed with frequent changes in our positions, forcing us to dig new foxholes again and again. This repeated itself on the morning of the April 12 until in the afternoon when we were dug in facing south along the river. We were unnerved by a sudden burst of machine-gun fire at our backs to the north of us where the main road led from Löningen to Lastrup. Obviously, the British were moving along the road and were about to overtake us and cut us off. We left our positions and, in single file, ran and stumbled through the swampy meadows toward the sound of the gunfire.

It was then that, for the first time, my platoon came under enemy fire. Artillery shells hurled toward us with unnerving shrieks, thunderously splashing in the ponds and watery pastures, their explosions splintering the willow trees along the ditches. Dirt, stones, tree branches, and shrapnel whirled through the air. I tasted sulphur between my teeth. Again and again the rumble, the whistling rush, and the ear-splitting crash. My stomach turned, my knees trembled. This, then, was what they called the *Feuertaufe,* the baptism by fire, I thought. I felt an unstoppable urge rising in my esophagus. Scream. Scream. I wanted to get rid of that pressure in me. I wanted to shout into the air: Stop, stop, no more, no more. But my mouth remained silent. All I could do was to stare across the flat pasture from where, in the distance, the terrible thundering, whistling, and crashing had come.

4. (London, 1952), 252.

The "lame duck," a British artillery observation plane, circled lazily above us, directing the fire. We crouched and pressed ourselves into the ditches to avoid being spotted by the plane and hit by the shell fragments that tore into the ground around us. I continued to tremble and sweat. My stomach demanded that I relieve myself. This is madness, I silently cried out, stop, for God's sake, stop. But the shells kept coming. After each burst our sergeant shouted: "Get up, get up, run." When the distant rumble announced the coming of another shell: "Take cover, take cover, hit the dirt." And so it went. We got up and raced along and we threw ourselves down. We hastened onward again, sweat running in our eyes and obscuring our vision, until finally the spotter plane flew off, the firing stopped, and our sergeant, announcing that none of us had been hurt, ordered us to resume our march.

The firing to our north had by now ceased and we followed a path through the pastures that led to a deserted farmhouse. A group of ten of my comrades was ordered to dig in a few hundred feet north of us along the wood's edge to secure us against surprise attacks from the highway. The rest of the platoon gathered in the farm yard. It had become obvious by now: We had been cut off, surrounded on all sides by British troops. Our best chance to evade detection was to keep quiet until nightfall. Then we could resume our march and break out of the pocket.

But renewed shooting broke out along the highway. Our sergeant ordered me to reconnoiter and make contact with our security guards. I grabbed a bicycle and took off for the woods. Dusk had set in. It was hard to see clearly among the trees. I put my bicycle down and crawled toward the foxholes my comrades were to have dug. There I saw shadowy figures moving around, rifles pointed downward, and pulling other, equally shadowy, figures from the ground. I had seen enough. The British had taken possession of our guard position. My comrades were being taken prisoners.

I got up and raced back to my bicycle. As I jumped on it I heard shouts and rifle shots; bullets whistled past my head. But now the darkness protected me and I escaped and arrived back at the farmhouse unharmed. As I reported to my sergeant he replied: "That's it, boys. You are on your own. You have two options: Surrender or, under the cover of darkness, make your way out of the pocket and join the battalion. I'll see you there." With that he disappeared into the farmhouse.

A debate began in the yard among the thirty or so soldiers of our company and other stragglers who had joined us. To my great horror, most of them decided to send a civilian with a white flag to the British near the highway. He was to say that here was a group of German sol-

diers ready to lay down their arms and surrender. I could not believe
it. This could not be true. If I were to join those willing to surrender without having fired a single shot, I thought to myself, how could
I ever face Etzel or Dieter again? How could I ever look in the eyes
of my boys of *Fähnlein* Blücher? It was not for such ignominious surrender that I had volunteered as an officer's candidate in the Division
Großdeutschland. Such action violated everything I had learned from
Bodo Wacker and from my father. Worst of all, it was treason: Treason
against any concept of honor and loyalty I believed in; treason against
myself. I could not possibly do that.

I decided to try to break out of the pocket. I was joined in that decision by Jochen, the closest friend I had found in my brief time with
the company. Jochen, a barber's apprentice from Silesia and, like me,
an officer's candidate, pulled me aside and pointed to a platoon of
soldiers from another division that just then marched past the farm
yard. We two attached ourselves to it. The platoon stayed well south
of the main road from Löningen to Cloppenburg, its commanding officer judging our position by the light of a half moon and by British
searchlights that plied the night sky. Despite the warmth of the spring
night, our progress was anything but pleasant. As we stumbled along
in single file, silent and full of anxious, unvoiced questions, we climbed
over innumerable barbed-wire fences separating the various cow pastures until my trouser legs hung down in shreds. We sought to stay
out of the swampy lowlands but could not avoid the drainage ditches
and creeks that filled our boots with water and mud. The British, too,
did their part to make our advance miserable. Every ten minutes or
so an artillery salvo fired at random sought us out in the darkness.
We trudged on and on until the dawn lit up the sky, the British artillery ceased its cat-and-mouse game with us, and we made our way
through the outskirts of Cloppenburg.

It was now the morning of April 13, and we went to sleep in the
hay barn of a farmhouse at the southern edge of the town. Our rest
was brief. British forces had entered Cloppenburg that very morning,
and, as General Essame writes,

> the battle raged in the streets from house to house. . . . The Gross-
> deutschland group showed little disposition to surrender and fought
> on as if they were still in Normandy.[5]

British artillery bombarded the town. As shells exploded near the barn
in which we had taken refuge, Jochen and I grabbed our rifles and

5. Essame, *The 43rd Wessex Division at War,* 253.

other gear and set out to look for our company, which we assumed to be somewhere in Cloppenburg. But we encountered no parts of it anywhere. We were, however, told by other stragglers that, while the main force of the British drive appeared to be directed east toward the military airport at Ahlhorn, our brigade had pulled out northward and was to reassemble near Oldenburg.

Thus Jochen and I decided to make our way north toward Garrel. As we raced through Cloppenburg artillery shells rained on the city. To the north, however, the way was clear. We soon walked along country roads, undisturbed by strafing planes, artillery or mortar shells. On the way we encountered other stragglers like ourselves, each of them seeking their units or, as some of them would admit, looking for a safe place where they could get rid of their uniforms, put on civilian clothes, and go on their way home. Jochen and I felt nothing but disgust for these deserters and redoubled our efforts to find our company. A few miles south of Oldenburg a military police patrol stopped us and, while checking our papers, informed us that the Großdeutschland brigade had moved east toward the Weser River and we should find them at Elsfleth.

Jochen and I asked for written orders to avoid being taken for deserters and then resumed our journey. Somewhere along our route on a country road we were halted by two unarmed army lieutenants who ordered us to hand over our assault rifles. It was immediately clear to us what these officers were about. They had left their units, thrown away their arms, and now thought better of it, evidently deadly afraid of being caught by SS patrols on the lookout for deserters.

I was enraged and fought a desperate battle with myself. On the one hand, I was furious enough to be seriously tempted to use my rifle and march these apparent deserters to the nearest military police patrol, if only I knew where to find one. On the other hand, I hesitated to disobey an officer's order. I looked at Jochen, and Jochen looked at me, and reluctantly we handed over our assault rifles.

We did not remain unarmed for long. As we came into the next village, we noticed a pile of abandoned weapons and equipment, and we helped ourselves to new infantry rifles. These were not the modern, twenty-round assault rifles we had carried, but the conventional five-round infantry rifles. But they would do, and would protect us from being suspected as deserters. When we finally reached Elsfleth, we found our old company and were reunited with our sergeant and other members of our platoon who also had managed to escape being taken prisoner. We then embarked on barges and were shipped across the Weser River to occupy new battle lines north of Bremen to stop the British advance on Bremerhaven and Cuxhaven.

13

In Battle

B Y APRIL 17, our brigade had reassembled east of the Weser River at Osterholz-Scharmbeck, not far from the famous artist colony at Worpswede. We were now to join and become part of the 15th Panzergrenadier Division, whose mission it was to hold the line against the northward British advance, first at Rotenburg on the Wümme and then at Zeven.

I remember distinctly the near-hysterical attacks of shell-fright I suffered as we were lounging in the sunshine, dozing and resting up for the battles that we knew lay ahead of us. I fell asleep and relived in my dream the distant rumble, the whistling rush, and the thundering crash of the exploding shells. As I woke up, trembling and sweat-soaked, I shrieked again silently: 'No, No, not again. I won't go. I won't go. I can't go. I cannot take this any more.' But when the order came at nightfall to get ready and march southeastward, I laced my boots, threw on my backpack, grabbed my rations, flung my rifle over my shoulder, and looked for Jochen. Then we two took our places in the slowly receding single file of gray figures moving out into the darkness.

Again we marched by night and dug our foxholes for the day. Our company commander, First Lieutenant Preuß, had appointed me to his staff as a messenger, or runner, as the position was called. During our nightly marches I joined my old platoon to be with Jochen. But when, at daybreak, we spread out in new positions or went to sleep in a farmer's barn for a day of rest, I helped establish the company command post and dug my own hole nearby. I thus became privy to most of the communications that arrived by other messengers or by field radio and knew that our company was to play leap-frog with our sister company in covering the retreat of the division to successive defensive

185

lines, first along the river Wümme and later along the Hamme-Oste canal at Gnarrenburg. Thus we could expect to be in battle for one to two days at a time, and then, after a forced nightly march, to rest the next day or two while our sister company was to stave off the British advance.

My task as runner frequently took me away on errands to other units. On one occasion, while my company had its day of rest, we received warnings that British flame-throwing tanks were to be used against our sister company. As we were notoriously short on heavy weapons support, Lieutenant Preuß ordered me to take the one bazooka we had left to our sister company, which, I was told, I would find in its position along one of the many canals criss-crossing the Wümme wetlands near Rotenburg.

I flung my rifle over one shoulder and the bazooka over the other and set out to find my way through the swamplands, looking for the other company's command post. I soon came upon a canal flowing between dikes and followed the footpath that ran along the dike's crest. In the distance I saw a farmhouse that, according to the description I had been given, was likely to be the command post I was looking for. As I approached the farm I climbed down from the dike, followed a narrow track through the heavy reeds and grasses and entered the house. It was deserted.

I found myself in a living room, and as I peered through a window in the direction of the canal I saw to my horror a British tank drawn up on the dam on the other side of the canal, its crew sitting on top and surveying my side of the canal with their binoculars. I fell to the floor, unhooked and readied my bazooka, and began to take my position behind the window curtains to fire at the tank.

My eyes then fell on a row of family pictures lined up on the dresser to my right—two twelve- or thirteen-year-old girls, a mother holding a baby. This is their home, I thought, and for all I know, the girls, the baby, and the mother may be hiding below me in the basement. If I fire through the window, I may or may not hit the tank, but the house surely will go up in flames after that. I stared once more at the tank, took another look at the pictures, dropped the bazooka and backed out of the house. I had no stomach for taking such a risk. Being at the other side of the canal from me, the tank could do me no harm, I thought, and I would not take it upon my conscience to have another farmhouse destroyed and perhaps its inhabitants incinerated in the fire. For what purpose? I wondered. I hastened away from the house, careful to keep my retreat in the shadow of the farm so the soldiers on the tank would not see me.

But I was mistaken. I had retreated no further than about 600 feet when the crew, looking over the roof of the farm, detected me and opened fire with their machine gun. The bullets whistled past my head and splashed in the swampy ground. I pressed myself into the tall reeds of the wet pasture and slowly, ever so slowly, began to crawl away. As always in these moments of dire fright my stomach and bowels revolted and I lay still to relieve myself. That proved to be my salvation because, as I ceased to move and no longer shook the reeds and thus betrayed my position, the firing stopped. I was safe for the moment. I waited for a few minutes and resumed my slow crawl until I deemed it safe to get up and look for a way back to my company.

Once I got out of sight of the tank crew I did not know what to make of the incident. I was uncertain of the correctness of my actions and angry at the turn the events had taken. What was I to say when getting back to Lieutenant Preuß? Had I acted as was expected of a German soldier? Had I deserved being shot at by the very soldiers whose lives I had spared? The sheer unpredictability of events in war and the utter arbitrariness of survival and death in battle seemed to make these questions meaningless. *C'est la guerre,* I told myself. I had survived once more, and I was not going to second-guess my own thoughts and actions. When I got back to my company's command post I reported to Lieutenant Preuß that I had not found the other company, had come under enemy fire, and had had to jettison the bazooka.

"I'm glad you're back," is all he replied.

By April 20 my company was deployed west of Zeven and, for the next ten days, resumed its game of leap-frog with our sister company, alternately retreating and defending the string of villages along the roads from Kirchtimke, Ostertimke, Ostereistedt, Rhade, Rhadeeistedt to Glinstedt. As we marched at night and sometimes also during the day we came under occasional artillery fire. We learned to listen for the rumbling in the distance announcing the quickly following arrival of another salvo. The scream of the onrushing shells had us ready to jump into the ditches along the road and immediately thereafter to get up and resume our march.

I remember the afternoon we were approaching Glinstedt, the village that was to witness our final and bloodiest skirmish of the war, which, of course, we did not then know. I was following Jochen in our usual single file along the side of the road when we caught up with and began to overtake the remnants of an anti-aircraft artillery company that no longer had any fuel to run its trucks. The soldiers had requisitioned horses and farm wagons and had hitched their guns to these sorry-looking vehicles. What woke us up from our half-sleep as we walked beside them was the shriek of an officer who, wildly gesticulating, ran toward the horses that pulled the cart next to Jochen and me and threw himself into the reins to stop them. With a grating crunch the front wheels of the farm wagon came to a halt. Only then I saw, about a foot in front of the wheel, a land mine inserted in an open wooden box and set in a small trench dug across the road. German engineers had placed the mine there provisionally, to be dug in and covered up after we had passed. Had it not been for the officer who held up the horses, Jochen and I would have caught the blast of the mine.

Shaken and dispirited, we continued on our way. We were quiet, as we were most of the time, because it was difficult to talk while we were marching single-file, leaving a distance of six to ten feet between us. But every now and then, someone would sing to break the silence and interrupt our brooding.

And so it was on this afternoon not long after the incident with the mine that I heard the "Little One"—our youngest and smallest member of the platoon—suddenly sing our company's marching song. He sounded happy and contented, at peace with himself and the world. His voice was soft yet clearly audible. I wondered as I listened to him whether he thought himself on some parade ground as he was returning with his company from an exercise or, perhaps, alone on an outing in spring when he delighted in the thought of being a soldier. He seemed oblivious to the danger we had just escaped and unmindful that, any minute, the whistle and crash of shells could chase us into the ditch again. He sang all the song's verses, and his voice then died away with the closing line, "We'll offer you our lives, beloved fatherland."

With these words still ringing in my mind, we entered the village of Glinstedt. Lieutenant Preuß ordered me, the Little One, and our medic to dig our foxholes next to the company command post in which he and our staff sergeant would stay. Jochen and his platoon moved off to a forward position. Our staff sergeant made it a special point to warn me and the Little One to be careful of a nearby SS position. SS soldiers, he said, were trigger-happy and always ready to accuse messengers running back from the forward foxholes to company headquarters of desertion and execute them on the spot. Thus, he added, if you fire at them, no one here will mind.

As I was to find out, his advice was well taken. Later, the following day, during sporadic British mortar attacks, Lieutenant Preuß had sent me out to our forward positions. As I came back, racing toward our company command post during the intervals between mortar salvos, an SS soldier jumped up before me, his assault rifle at the ready and his finger at the trigger.

"Halt," he shouted, "or I shoot. Who are you? Where are you going?"

I cursed at the guy, and told him I was under orders to report to our company chief who, he jolly well knew, had his bunker just a few dozen steps behind him. He but grunted in response, turned away, and walked back to his anti-tank gun position in a nearby grove of trees. When I told Lieutenant Preuß of the encounter he said that that was just what you had to expect from the SS.

By nightfall of the first day we had our positions well prepared and waited for the expected attack. But the night remained quiet, I slept in my foxhole, and the lieutenant found himself a warm bed in one of the houses. The next morning, too, remained relatively quiet, but soon after noon the British attack on Glinsted began in earnest with the usual artillery and mortar bombardment.

We crouched in our foxholes, cursing the "lame duck" overhead that plotted our positions and directed the mortar rounds that methodically sought us out, foxhole by foxhole. I had dug mine against a hillside, with an entrance toward the slope and a right angle extension parallel to it. Next to me, in a hole dug into the ground from above, was the Little One. As the firing commenced I huddled in fetal position, pressed to the far wall of the right-angle extension, trying to make myself as small as possible. I listened to the blop-blop-blop of the mortars being fired in the distance, and crouched even more tightly than before as the shells screamed toward me and exploded with crashing intensity outside my hole. Mother, mother, I cried wordlessly, seized by panic. Then: It's all right mother, everything's all right, nothing happened, mother.

I pushed myself out of the hole to look around. Had anyone got killed or wounded? Everything was quiet. Two or three feet away from me, between my foxhole and that of the Little One, a few, flat, bowl-like craters. Then the blop-blop-blop again. I fell back in my hole, pressed myself against the cool, moist ground. Fractions of a second went by, and then again the scream, the terrifying crash. Clumps of earth pelted me, sulphurous fumes engulfed me. I felt numbed and deaf, my eardrums shattered. One shell had landed in the entrance to my hole. A foot of earth had deflected the force of the explosion that had hit me only indirectly.

I crawled out of my hole and looked around. Our medic had emerged from his, and we both started toward the hole between our two. A shell had gone straight into it and had exploded in the body of the Little One. There was nothing we could do for him. We pulled him out of the ground and placed him in a tarpaulin and two of my comrades carried him away to bury him. In my mind I heard him sing, "We'll offer you our lives, beloved fatherland." The Little One had done just that.

"Why him?" I asked, speaking to myself. "Why not me?"

"Come," said the medic, and pointed me to my hole. "It's no use asking questions like that."

The mortar bombardment continued during the afternoon. As evening neared and the shelling subsided our company chief ordered some of my comrades to go out and reconnoiter. They came back from their brief foray with several prisoners. Evidently they had caught the British infantry by surprise. From the prisoners we learned that we could expect an attack on the village the next morning. So we hoped for a quiet night in which to get ready for the battle to come.

I went back to my foxhole to get as much sleep as I could. I did not succeed very well. My ears hurt, my stomach churned, the voice of the Little One singing continued in my head, and an undefinable sense of fear held me in its grip.

Around midnight, Lieutenant Preuß called out: "Herbst, go back to the battalion, fetch our rations and the few replacements we were promised. Ask when our artillery will begin to retaliate."

"Yes, Sir," I responded, "rations, replacements, and artillery support."

"All right," the lieutenant spit out the words, "hurry up and be careful. Don't get hurt, I need you back here."

I grabbed my rifle and took off into the darkness. I was glad I could carry out an order. It gave me no time for silly thoughts, and it made me forget the leaden weight in my stomach. I ran along a wall, through a few gardens, and hastened toward the ditch along the road when in the distance I heard the familiar thunder. I threw myself forward into the air as though there was a river I could dive into and crashed into the ditch just as the whooshing sound changed into the whistle and then burst into the crash of the explosion. I heard the shrapnel land on the road, but I was already back on my feet. There was no time to think of mother, no time to be mindful of the leaden weight. I hastened toward the battalion.

Its headquarters were located in the cellar of a farm at the other end of the village. I felt my way down the dark, winding stone steps. Moist, sweet-smelling air of half-rotten potatoes mixed with cigarette smoke engulfed me. I felt goosebumps run down my back. I searched the darkness for the commanding officer and found him sitting with other officers on crumbling potato boxes. His messengers, some half-awake, some asleep, were lying on straw bundles, awaiting orders that would send them out into the dark village streets with their broken gables and windowless shadows of buildings.

"What's going on?" the captain spoke first. I gave him my message.

"Rations and replacements are over there," he pointed into the far,

dark corner of the cellar. There I could make out five or six young soldiers, boys really, who watched me with fear-widened eyes. They had
with them three pieces of canvas full of loaves of bread and canned
beef.

"I don't know about artillery," the captain continued, "but there are
supposed to be three Tiger tanks positioned at the far end of the village. Take your replacements and look for them. When you find them,
ask them when they intend to commence firing. Then come back and
let me know."

I felt fury rise in me. You coward, I was tempted to shout. You sit
here and drink yourself senseless and want me to do the work of your
own runners, all for the special delight of the British gunners. But I
pulled myself together, saluted, and said: "Yes, captain. Will do."

Then I was outside. The six soldiers followed me, two each carrying a canvas with the rations. I turned for the shortest way back to
my company. I presumed the captain would hear for himself when the
tanks opened fire.

We hurried through the village, down the main street. Before us,
the gable of the store that had served as a landmark for me as it stood
behind our foxholes rose black into the air. Then a thunderous clap tore
through the night. The Tiger tanks, was all I could think. Everything
dissolved before me. Roof timber, tiles, the entire gable came whirling
through the air. I lost consciousness. Everything went black. Nothing.

I came to in the basement of the village store. How I got there, I do
not know. I seemed alone, I saw no one else. But I heard a trembling
voice behind me: "The war, the war, it will kill us all."

Then I knew there were other people in the basement. A woman
who, in the semi-darkness, looked more than a hundred years old,
whispered and stammered. Her wrinkled face twitched involuntarily.
Her entire body shook.

"If they will only let me keep my merchandise; if there will be no
fire," a man, hysterically running back and forth on the stone floor of
the small underground room, muttered between his teeth. "What is
that? What was this? When will it end?"

I reached into my pocket, gave him a package of cigarettes, and
rushed up the basement stairs.

Everything was quiet outside. A whitish light bathed the street. The
moon had come out from behind the clouds. A few feet from the store
I saw a canvas lying on the pavement with eight loaves of bread and a
can of meat. That was all I found of the rations and the replacements.
I searched all around, but in vain. Of the store's gable, only one beam
was left. It pointed obliquely into the sky. The clouds rushing past the
moon cast on it a play of light and shadow.

I picked up the bread and the meat, folded them into the canvas, and slung the bundle over my back. I carried my rifle in my left hand. "Private Herbst, reporting back from the battalion. With exception of eight loaves of bread, one can of meat, and one canvas, replacements and rations lost through friendly fire from Tiger tanks. Nothing new at the battalion."

"I'm glad you are back," said lieutenant Preuß. "Lie down and go to sleep."

I went back into my hole. The British artillery commenced firing again. I did not hear it anymore. I was dead to the world. When I awoke and crawled out of my hole, it was light, and the lieutenant came out of his bunker.

"Orders," he said. "Tell the soldiers in the foxholes. Withdraw behind the canal. Reassemble at Gnarrenburg."

Thus ended the war for me. On the morning of May 3, we sneaked out of Glinstedt, past the three Tiger tanks, now burnt- out shells, exploded by their own crews because of lack of fuel. To avoid drawing further artillery fire on us we made our way, one by one, across the already mined canal bridge. In Gnarrenburg we reassembled. It was here that we heard the news that Hitler had died in Berlin. There was little reaction among us. We were too numb to respond. So Hitler was dead now in the ruins of beleaguered Berlin, and an admiral had taken over command of the armed forces and the leadership of the Reich. What did it mean for us? Would the war continue? We soldiers would continue to follow our orders, but we sensed that the end was near and we were not anxious to get killed or wounded now.

That night I was sent on an errand to battalion headquarters. As I crossed the empty marketplace, the moon drenched the square in its silvery light. A lieutenant approached me from the other side. I saluted in Nazi fashion with my outstretched right arm, as the army had been forced to do after the failed assassination attempt at Hitler's life on July 20, 1944. The lieutenant looked at me, raised his right arm and touched his officer's cap in the traditional military salute. I was dumbfounded. Then it hit me like an electric charge, a jolting, joyous realization: This, indeed, was the end—the end of Hitler and the end of the Nazis. That salute said it all. The army had come back to itself.

From now on everything was anticlimactic. My company left Gnarrenburg on the morning of the fourth, marching, as always, in single file. As evening came and we had just passed a small village, Lieutenant Preuß ordered us to a halt. Our radio operator, listening in on British army transmissions, had picked up strange messages about an impending armistice. Besides, British troops who had pushed ahead of us to the east and west and were about to surround us again had opened up a veritable fireworks with rockets and searchlights. The rockets, however, were not meant for us. They exploded harmlessly above and lit up the night sky. The searchlights did not seek us out but swept erratically back and forth. The lieutenant ordered me to go back into the village we had just passed through, find battalion head-quarters, and inquire what all this meant.

I found the battalion's command in what seemed to be the village's largest building at the edge of the road. The doors and windows stood open, I could see candles flickering eerily inside, and I heard shouts and laughter. A sergeant met me at the door, an open liquor bottle in his hand. He reached back into the room for a glass, and poured me a drink.

"It's all over, soldier," he shouted. "And we are still alive!"

The battalion commander and other officers, their tunics open, their shirts unbuttoned, drinks in their hands, were crowded around a radio. One of them translated the British announcements that ordered their troops to cease firing the next morning and await further orders.

It was true. The fighting was to stop. The war was over. I stumbled out of the house to get back to my company and bring the good news. The fighting had ceased. We could relax. There was to be no more shelling, no more trembling in foxholes, no more fallen and wounded comrades. And, as the sergeant had said, we were still alive, we had survived. A feeling of immense relief overcame me. I had no desire to think about what the ceasefire might mean for me, for Germany, for my career as a soldier. The fighting was to end; the killing was to stop; I need be afraid no more.

14

Farewell to Arms

FOR THE NEXT FEW DAYS we reversed our routine. We marched during daylight and we slept at night in barns or stables. British officers appeared and ordered us to lay down our arms and ammunition in piles along the road. As we trudged along there was no longer any need to proceed in single file, and we now marched in company formation. To keep up our spirits Lieutenant Preuß ordered us to sing. We sang the song of the wind that blew through the Wester-wald, of the girl with the black-brown hazelnut eyes, and of any other girl we could think of, of Erika, of Gerda, Ursula, and Marie. We sang songs of home, of beautiful Silesia, of the Brandenburg pine forest, and, my favorite, of the boy of the Valley of the Oker, the river that flowed through and around Wolfenbüttel. We soldiers had turned into sentimentalists. There was no martial spirit left among us. We dreamt of home as we marched along; thought of girlfriends and mothers.

Thus we were all the more taken aback when a British jeep drove alongside us and a furious officer shouted at us to stop the singing. Lieutenant Preuß, his pipe in his mouth, turned around and with his hand waved at us to comply. We did. The words of the song faded away in mid-sentence. But within seconds from somewhere behind me the tune resumed, not as a song but as a whistle, and before we had really become fully aware what was happening, the entire com-pany joined in and we marched along whistling defiantly the song of the love that was hot and the snow that was white and the Red Husars who had to leave their girlfriends behind. The jeep stopped abruptly; the British officer jumped out and with a swipe of his glove sent Lieu-tenant Preuß's pipe flying into the dust of the road. For a second our column stopped dead in its track. But as Lieutenant Preuß bent down to pick up his pipe and then waved at us again with his hand to proceed, we scrambled forward, awkwardly trying to fall back into step, and marched on in silence.

There, I thought, this now was the revealing moment, the lightning flash, that brought home to me with crushing finality the realization that not only had Hitler and the Nazis come to their end, not only had the firing and the killing stopped and I had survived, but also that we lost the war and were at the mercy of the victors. The proud German army in which I had set my hopes for eventual redemption of the horrors I had dimly perceived was no more. My dreams of an honorable professional career as a soldier of Großdeutschland had tumbled into the dirt like Lieutenants Preuß's pipe. There were no longer any markers or directions for me to find my way into a future.

My thoughts went back to the night on the road when Etzel and I were walking back from Groß Denkte and the tangy smell of burnt wood soothed our nostrils. I had then wondered whether the lines I had read and that would not leave my mind—

> So we make our way, a defeated army,
> extinguished are our stars

—foretold what I would experience: defeat, desolation, death. I had wondered then whether these lines would lie at the end of my career as a professional soldier. Now I knew that, indeed, their message had come true. My stars were extinguished, and I could see nothing but a dark and meaningless void before me.

Our company marched on and in another day or two reached the small village of Westersode northwest of Hamburg. We were told that we would eventually move into permanent quarters on the Weser River somewhere south of Bremen. As we had not surrendered before the official date of the armistice on May 8, we were not considered to be prisoners of war but were now part of "The German Army under British Command." We were to resume a normal army routine, obey our officers, take part in work details, and continue a strict regimen of military drill and maneuvers.

Our life in Westersode was anything but pleasant. Jochen, myself, and several of my comrades were billetted in a farmhouse where we slept on the straw-covered cement floor of the cow barn. We were hungry all the time as our rations consisted of a plate of boiled potatoes and turnips without meat or fat. Occasionally our company cooks would ignore the nightly curfew, disappear in the darkness, and slaughter horses in the fields to feed us as stew the next day. We, too, would use whatever spare time we had to forage in the village and in the countryside for anything we could find, not hesitating to break into houses, barns, and attics in our search for food. I learned what hunger will do to a human being. I still think with shame of the night when two comrades and I climbed onto the roof of a farmhouse and broke through a dormer window into a store room to carry out buckets of flour that had been hidden there. We had lost all inhibitions to steal and plunder. Food was the focus of our waking and dreaming thoughts— food, anything that could be eaten. I remember us coming upon a barrel of salted herring with a two-inch-thick layer of salt crystals on top. We could not wait to soak the fish in a tub of water but wolfed it down, heads, bones, scales, fins, salt, and all, then ran to a pump and gulped down mess-kits full of water desperately trying to flush the salt out of our mouths. It was a miserable time.

All throughout these weeks our officers kept us under strict military discipline. We continued to salute them, and we were drilled and ordered in military exercises that, considering the drastic reductions of our daily food rations, were more exhausting than anything I had experienced either at Rodewald or during my initial week as an army soldier near Rendsburg. It was obvious that, with the war over and we soldiers anxious to go home, both British and German commanders considered their top priority to be the upholding of discipline over thousands of restless troops. They chased us up the steep walls of a gravel pit; they had us jump down from the top as though we descended on parachutes and practice landing on our shoulders on the gravelly inclines, rolling head over heels to the bottom of the pit. We stood in parade formation for an hour at a time, our stomachs hurting from lack of food, dizziness sweeping over us, and more than one of us collapsing on the ground only to be brought back to his senses by a bucket of water thrown at him by one of our noncoms. I cursed my fate and hated the British for condoning, even encouraging, our maltreatment.

But it became apparent soon that keeping us under control was not the only reason for the British insistence on the revival of Prussian drill and the continuance of German military authority after the armistice. I remember when we soldiers, distributed as we were among several farmhouses, gathered at night in defiance of a proclaimed curfew to listen to the strange noises of unending movements of large bodies of troops that we could hear but not see. The sound of trucks revving their engines, horses neighing and clip-clopping in the distance, made us wonder just when we would be ordered to join those movements and what it would mean. From all sides came rumors of the British high command having warned our officers to keep us in readiness, for the war would resume, and we were to join the British to confront any likely and expected westerly push of the Red Army.

We soldiers were ambivalent about the prospect. We were happy that the shooting had stopped and felt no desire to again take up arms, to be exposed once more to the whistle of hurtling grenades and the thunder of exploding shells. Besides, we counted ourselves lucky to be under British command and not, as so many of our fellow soldiers, in Russian captivity. Years of Nazi propaganda had painted the soldiers of the Red Army as merciless and barbarous beasts, and none of us was anxious to face them in battle. On the other hand, the thought of Russian troops conquering the remainder of our country and subjecting all Germans and all of Europe to their will did not allow us to reject out of hand the possibility of the resumption of war. And we could not discount either the thought that, once allied in battle with our former Western foes, the Wehrmacht might regain its reputation and honor as reliable and competent fighters. Perhaps, I thought, there was yet a chance for me for a life of military service.

Though today we know that preparations for a continuance of the war had indeed been undertaken,[1] it soon became clear to us that our fears and speculations concerning the resumption of hostilities were groundless. The talk of further fighting ceased, and so did the drills. We were summoned repeatedly for interviews about our knowledge and experience of various trades and finally regrouped into labor sections. Those of us whose homes were under the control of the Western powers were told that they could expect an eventual discharge. I again dismissed from my mind any thought of a soldier's life. Rather listlessly, I awaited the weekly health inspections and the daily distribution of our meager rations of stale bread, the glob of artificial honey, and the watery soup of cabbage leaves or turnip chunks. A time of waiting, hoping, and brooding had begun: waiting and hoping for an early discharge; brooding, brooding, endlessly brooding over the fate of our loved ones at home.

I often sat on a grassy knoll overlooking the village. I tried to figure how long my sweat-drenched shirt would hold together, tried to imagine how things would look at home. I wondered whether my mother knew I was still alive, where Etzel and Dieter might be and whether they had survived the war, and what Ulla was doing, and whether, when I came home, we would go to our dancing school after all, or whether that was all a senseless dream, never to become reality. I asked myself again and again whether there was any home left for me in Wolfenbüttel; whether our house was still standing, and my mother

1. For more on this, see Arthur L. Smith, Jr., *Churchill's German Army: Wartime Strategy and Cold War Politics, 1943–1947* (Beverly Hills and London: Sage Publications, 1977.)

was still alive. And what would I find if I ever got home again? How would I live? What would I do? An army career was out of the question now. There had been no victory; there would be no confrontation with the SS. Our whole world had turned upside-down. Gone were my dreams and plans. My world had collapsed.

Yet, as I sat on the knoll and looked about me, the sky was still blue, the birds were singing, the grass was green, and the wind rustled in the poplar trees as though nothing had changed. I could not fathom it all. Sun and wind, birds and grass—they had nothing to do with war and peace, victory and defeat, my hopes and my fears. It was as though I lived in a world totally removed from what I saw around me.

We received our first newspapers and I stared with disbelief at the photographs of concentration camps with mountains of corpses. Propaganda, I thought, and laid the paper aside. But I picked it up again and looked at the pictures once more. Could it be they were real? No, that could not be. Such things could not be, could never have happened, certainly not in Germany. These could not possibly be the deeds of those whom my father had had in mind when he had spoken of those who defiled our cause and besmirched our name, those who dragged us down in the dirt. But the pictures would not let me go. I thought of Etzel's aunt and Mrs. Lerner and wondered whether they had survived the war. My thoughts returned to Albert Morgenstern and the burning synagogue and to the emaciated figures I had seen in the coal mine in Cieszyn. I remembered the school leader's insistence that a National Socialist could not be a Christian and my father's outburst when I had said I thought of joining the SS, and I heard again in my mind the words of our staff sergeant at Glinstedt.

Did the photographs in the newspaper tell the truth? Could these horrors really have been committed? And if they had? If, indeed, my father and the Little One had given their lives, Etzel and I had led our boys, and I had volunteered for an army career only for us survivors to be now confronted with the realization that we had been participants in a monstrous conspiracy of evil, what then? How could we live with that? Was it possible to imagine that all this had happened in the name of Germany, in the name of the Little One's beloved fatherland, in the name of the German people, in the name of the country that, in the mind of my father's soldier friend, had been a synonym for goodness? I found no answer, only emptiness and nothingness.

When I tried to speak to my fellow soldiers about the pictures, they brushed them aside. They did not want to see them; they did not want to talk about them. They engaged instead in an unending round of self-commiseration in which I participated. We felt ourselves misunderstood, unjustly condemned to bear the guilt of others. We repeated it

198

over and over again that we had not committed such horrors; that we had not condoned them; that we had known nothing about them. Now we had to bear the accusations, and all we could do was to resign ourselves to our fate and curse it at the same time. We became experts at self-pity, and, while we nursed the pain in our stomachs and the hurt in our hearts, we waited, waited, and waited.

In my dreams and longings, the thought of home carried me through the nights of hunger, of cold, and of heat, made bearable the misery of being held against my will in an environment that seemed oblivious to my pain. The more I thought of home, the more desperately I longed to go home. Home came to be the distant pole on which all meridians converged, the pole that promised solutions to all the riddles. I told myself that there, among loved ones and friends, I would find answers to my questions. In my mother's arms I would find solace and peace. The thought of home gave me strength to persevere and it silenced, for a while, the torturing questions and the self-pity.

At the same time, however, the thought of home brought to the surface my deepest anxieties and fears. I did not know whether my mother was still alive, whether Ulla still thought of me, and whether I had a home to return to. None of my comrades knew whether they still had loved ones and a home. None of us dared face the possibility that we might not; none dared admit it. Denial was second only to our self-pity.

Deep inside me I knew that this home of mine, even if it still existed physically, was a mirage. It was no more than the fulfillment of my wants, my needs, and my will. It became one great self-deceit. All of us sensed that. There could no longer be the home that we had left, no longer the familiar rooms and faces, no longer the friends on the street, no longer the schoolrooms and teachers, and, of course, no longer the boys of *Fähnlein* Blücher. All that was gone. It belonged to a world that had vanished in the collapse of the Reich. I had no idea what my life would be like were I to return. In Westersode, as I sat in the grass and looked at the sky and the meadows, I only knew that, inexplicably, the world of clouds and sky, of grass and birds and willow trees still existed as it always had. Only the world we had thought to be ours existed no more.

What, then, was home, the place that we know did not exist and of which we dreamed with such longing? It was the place, the town of my youth where I had lived with my parents, had played with my friends, had gone to school, had fought my battles with all the other boys, had made friends with Etzel and Dieter and Ulla. Home was the small town with its narrow streets, its gaily painted, carved gables, its dark woods at the edge. Home was a spring day, light blue and mild; a foggy October afternoon with the drizzly rain stroking my face. Home was our apartment with its high-ceilinged rooms, bookshelves along the walls, a vase of flowers on the table. On winter evenings when outside the snow fell silently and inside the soft orange light of the reading lamp cast its glow across our faces and I sat with my parents before the white tile stove, a book in hand, a bowl of apples on the tea cart— that was home. It was the black framed painting of the heather moor above the piano, the quick steps of my mother in the hall. It was the creaking of the garden gate, the rumbling of the trains at the nearby station, and the tolling bell of St. Mary's.

Home was the past, the sum of things gone by. Home was everything that once had been and whose memory comforted me. But I knew it existed no more; it would never return. Clinging to such a phantom only postponed the confrontation with the truth, a confrontation that, I sensed, was my only way of overcoming the torment and that, at the same time, I feared and sought to avoid. I knew, though I did not want to admit it, I could not go home again.

In June the discharge of a comrade finally brought an opportunity for me to send a message to my mother. I had not heard from her since I had left her in March and I could not know whether my words would reach her and whether I would hear from her in return. This is what I wrote:

My dear, dear Mother!
Now, after a long and difficult time, you finally receive news again from your boy. Know that he is well and that he survived unhurt the thunderstorms of battle. I hope this letter will reach you. . . . Of course it is my greatest worry to know how you survived this war and whether you still live in Wolfenbüttel. I hope to come home within the next three months. So, dear mother, no more unnecessary fear because of me. I am very well, indeed. . . .

A month after I had written the letter we left our quarters in Westersode and were trucked to the Weser south of Bremen to begin the restoration of the river dikes. Under the circumstances it was highly unlikely that, even if there was to be any mail arriving at all, it would follow me to my new quarters.

In my new occupation on the Weser dikes I had to accept the probability that I would not hear from my mother at all. Besides, the assignment there also had made an early discharge for me less likely than it had been before. As my uncertainty over my mother's fate became more and more unbearable, I decided to take matters into my own hands. Early in September I forged for myself civilian identity papers, borrowed civilian clothes from my host family, and arranged with my sergeant to count me present for the next three days. If I did not return thereafter, he would report me as absent from duty. In German military parlance, I took leave on my word of honor.

My journey home began early in the morning before the sun was up and the curfew had been lifted. I left the farmhouse in which I had been quartered, hurried along the village street to the brook that flowed down to the Weser River, and followed it, well hidden from the view of British patrols by the willow trees along its banks. At the river I hurried along its steep escarpment until I reached the railroad bed that led to the heavily damaged bridge. Once at the bridge I gingerly stepped on the first tie of the single rail strand that stretched precariously across the slow-moving water. The track hung loosely between the metal bridge work to my left and right and was bent slightly downward and tilted toward the left until it curved upward again and reached the shell-pocked stone pillar in the middle of the Weser. I carefully jumped from tie to tie until I reached the lowest point and then used both hands and feet to crawl upward to the pillar. I breathed a sigh of relief as I reached it and saw that the bridge before me was in better shape than the part I had just crossed. Two rows of track, straight and undamaged, led to the far bank, and I easily ran across one of them. On the other side I was in American territory in the enclave of Bremen.

I climbed down from the railroad tracks and followed a footpath toward the nearby highway. As I walked along it a mile or so further I came upon a checkpoint where American GIs inspected a long line of trucks that were headed in southerly direction. I joined a forlorn-looking group of other foot travelers, men and women of all ages, most of them loaded down with dilapidated boxes and scarred and roped suitcases. The GIs on duty, obviously eager to get rid of the many refugees and wanderers, ordered the truck drivers to take along as many hitchhikers as they had room for. Thus I ended up with several other travelers under the canvas of an empty truck that was headed for Hannover. We sat in silence as the truck made its way south and, four or five hours later, stopped and let me off at the Autobahn entry north of Hannover. There, after another wait of an hour or so, I was picked up by a truck on its way to Braunschweig.

This was an open vehicle with low side boards, carrying a group of men and women about my age. They were a more cheerful lot than the people I rode with in the other truck. They sang songs, passed a bottle of schnapps, and exchanged tips and information on how to survive on the road. It was now approaching toward evening and curfew time, and I was becoming worried about where to spend the night.

It was clear that I would not make it to Wolfenbüttel. As I asked the others what to do, one of the young women on the truck gave me a slip of paper on which she had written a Braunschweig address and her signed request that the bearer be given shelter. She told me to give that slip of paper to whoever opened the door.

The truck let me off in the city center and I set out to find my shelter. I recognized the address as on the highway leading from Braunschweig to Wolfenbüttel, and I was more than glad to seek out the house and ring the doorbell. When, after half an hour's walk, I got there, darkness had fallen, and the electricity had been cut off at curfew time. Thus I could not see whoever opened the door. I stated my request for shelter and handed over the slip of paper. The person—I couldn't tell whether it was a man or a woman—motioned me inside, went through a long dark hallway, and opened a door to a room whose outlines I could barely make out in the dim light that came through the two windows. "There are a few people sleeping here," the person said, "but over in the right corner is a straw sack on the floor that is empty. You can take that." With that the door closed.

I made my way to the sack and lay down. I could hear whispered conversations among my room mates. Gradually it dawned on me who they were and what they were doing here: I had been taken into a rest stop on the underground railroad of ex-Nazi dignitaries. I heard them discuss their plans and how they hoped to reach Spain and South America. I listened for a while but soon fell asleep. When I woke up in the morning I was the only one left in the room.

Now that I was so close to home I could not bear any delay or any distraction. I dressed, raced out of the house, and climbed on the next truck that was willing to take me to Wolfenbüttel. The driver took the old highway through the villages, dropping off bundles of papers and cartons of mail. Once we reached Wolfenbüttel he took me to the entrance of the Harztorwall and I, once my feet hit the pavement, began running toward my home. "Thank God," I kept thinking, "thank God, all the houses are there, none has been destroyed. Thank God." I reached our garden gate, rushed up the front steps, pushed open the house door and rang the doorbell at our apartment. My mother opened the door. "Jürgen," she shrieked.

"Mother," I sobbed. We fell into each other's arms—I was home.

I stayed most of that morning with my mother. We talked and we talked. I told her of my friendship with Jochen and how, in Westersode, he had taught me the tricks of his barber's trade. I spoke of my appreciation and respect for Lieutenant Preuß and of my sergeant, a tailor by trade, who, in Westersode, had taken a piece of canvas and turned it into a waterproof jacket for me. But I did not mention Glinstedt and I said nothing of my encounter with the SS guard. I gave her a glowing report of my Easter celebration in the farm homes of Sage, but I remained silent on the questions the farm woman had asked us. I described to her the Little One and his singing on the march, but I said nothing of his death, of the mortar shells, of my fear and dread. In turn, my mother spoke of her encounters with the first American troops entering our house, searching for weapons and demanding she lead them into all the basement rooms, and, on their departure, leaving her with a jar of powdered coffee. She showed me the first postwar letter she had received from my grandparents in Chemnitz and she told me how much she hoped they would join us in Wolfenbüttel. We both were so intent on sharing our joy of being able again to look into each other's eyes that we remained silent on anything that might bring back from our memory the horrors we had experienced. I did not mention the questions that still tormented me and she did not speak of the loneliness that had haunted her and still weighed her down. It was enough that we could hear each other's voices and hold each other's hands.

In the afternoon I visited Ulla in the apartment over the jeweler's shop and spent a happy hour talking with her and her family. Here, too, I did not dwell on the horrors of war and the questions that pursued me now but tried to present myself as the proud warrior who had escaped all danger and had come home to claim his prize. We all realized there was no time for Ulla and me to be alone with each other, but we were happy that we were both alive and content in the knowledge that our day of love and kisses now would surely come. I then went to the Büchers' house to find out about Etzel. Elli Bücher embraced me, tears glistening in her eyes. She told me that they had heard nothing from him ever since the war had ended. She also said there had been no word from Dieter. I left the Büchers' somber and worried. Back at home I shared my mother's meager rations of turnips and potatoes, and went to sleep in my own bed. When I said goodbye to my mother in the morning, I assured her that it could not last very long now and then I would be home for good. Once on the road I hitched rides going north toward Hamburg and then angling over toward Bremen. I arrived in my village in the evening and reported back to my sergeant. I had kept my word of honor.

Work on the dikes ended late in September, and my company moved back to Westersode. My hopes for a quick discharge were dashed as we regrouped and formally became a labor company of the Disarmed German Army under British Command. Though my worldly fortunes brightened—I was billeted in a butcher master's shop, ate at his table, and received British military rations to boot—my impatience and longing to be discharged mounted daily. Time passed slowly as there was little for us to do. Most of the time we removed tree stumps from clear-cut hillsides or trucked left-over shells, bombs, and mines to Cuxhaven where they were loaded unto ships and dumped into the sea. Thus passed the remainder of September, and then the month of October. In November, finally, my orders came. I was to go home.

Standing with others on the bed of a truck, swaying with its movements as it lumbered south toward Camp Munster in the Lüneburger Heath, only one thought, only one word, was on our minds: Home. Patiently we stood in line, silently we ate the slice of bread or the bowl of cabbage soup handed to us. Home, home, that was the refrain that accompanied us. The formalities in the camp were blessedly brief. British officers interrogated us for the last time, checked our armpits for the telltale SS tattoo, and a German military physician certified that we were deloused and free of infectious diseases. Then we boarded the train that was to take us out of the camp.

I changed trains a couple of times and finally stepped onto the platform of the Wolfenbüttel station. As I made my way through it, unrecognized and unnoticed by anybody, and walked out into the street I knew that I was back home but that this was not the home I had left. The world I had left, the world I had grown up in, the world of the boy soldier with its codes of honor and values of loyalty and comradeship had faded away and disappeared. The future that I had then anticipated, the life and career of the soldier, had vanished. I now had to come to terms with a world that I could neither see nor imagine, of whose contours, risks, and potentialities I did not and could not have the faintest idea. It was as though I stared into a featureless, meaningless void, a nothing. I neither feared it nor loathed it, because, as there was nothing there, I had nothing to fear and nothing to loathe. I looked into that void with neither dread nor anticipation. I was still numb of any recognizable sensation. I knew I was about to begin life anew, but I had no idea what that newness might be like. Now that I already knew that my mother and Ulla were alive and I would be with them, the only hope I still harbored was for Dieter's and Etzel's return. Perhaps, together with them I would be able to find my way into a new future.

15

Home

M Y FIRST FEW MONTHS in Wolfenbüttel told me that I was home, but that home was not the one I had remembered. People spoke the same language as before, but they did not understand me. They all had their own misery to relate and the injustices they had suffered. They paid no heed to my questions. I did not know whether home had remained the same and I had changed, or whether home had changed while I had remained in the past. How could I find my way back to the home I had longed for so desperately? Was there such a way, or was I condemned to remain a stranger in my own home? I, who had hoped to find here the answers to all my questions, only found more questions awaiting me, and nobody willing or able to answer mine. Now that I had reached the pole of all my longing it had vanished.

Unbeknownst to me, even before my return, my mother had signed me up in the first available make-up course offered by the city's school system for veterans like me whose schooling had been terminated prematurely during the war. Many, though not all, of my old classmates—not Etzel, not Dieter—were back in the city now, and on November 16 we returnees, together with a motley assemblage of refugees from all parts of Germany, commenced our studies for the *Abitur*, the final comprehensive high school examination that would give us the right to enroll in any German university. My assignments in English and German literature and Latin—the three fields I chose for the examination—diverted my attention from the questions that had haunted me the preceding months and for which I had not found any answers.

Food was scarce in those days and of little nourishment, and was to remain so for the next two years. Our meals consisted of one or two slices of crumbling dark bread for breakfast with jam or syrup made of turnips or beets and a cup of ersatz coffee; for lunch turnips and potatoes boiled in water with at most half a teaspoonful of margarine or some gristly meat scraped from a soup bone, and the same once more for supper. The few slices of sausage and the few grams of cheese we received on our ration cards every month we saved for Sundays, as we did also with the quarter-pound of oatmeal that we boiled in watered-down skim milk with our sugar rations sprinkled on top. An occasional package from abroad was a godsend that would brighten our spirits and fill our stomachs with luxuries. I still remember the heavenly taste of thick, sweet condensed milk spread over a hard roll or a cupful of uncooked oatmeal. I thought to myself that if I ever was to live through this misery and see better times again I would never be without a kitchen cabinet full of cans of sweet, condensed milk.

Heavenly though these gifts of manna were, I also recall the bitter disappointment that overcame me when, early in December, before we ever had received our first package from abroad, I answered our doorbell and faced what I thought was a British officer. My immediate thought was that he had come to requisition our apartment and evict my mother and me, and as a result I was fearful and suspicious. But he introduced himself as Captain Holloway of the U.S. army and a friend of an American librarian who had been a colleague and correspondent of my father before the war. He brought us greetings and a small package that he carried under his arm. He asked whether he could talk to me for a while to learn about my father and what our lives had been like during the war.

As my mother happened to be out I ushered him into our living room and we commenced our conversation. It lasted, it seemed to me, for an eternity. His curiosity appeared insatiable, while my eyes and thoughts were trained on that little package wrapped in brown paper, lying now on our living room table and making me dream of unimaginable delicacies. When Captain Hollaway finally rose and took his leave, I tore into the wrapping paper to see what I might find. As it came off it revealed a roll of corrugated cardboard tightly taped, and it was followed by tissue-paper padding at least half an inch thick. From it, finally, a small brown bottle of vitamin pills slipped into my hand.

I felt cheated. I was hungry and here I was given stones for a meal. My mother, when she came back that afternoon, asked me not to be ungrateful. The pills, she said, were harbingers of better things—real food, that is—to come. And she was right. Not long after, when Captain Holloway had notified our American friends of our survival, we received our first food package from them.

As winter approached—and it was to be a winter with long weeks of below-freezing temperatures—we were cold as well as hungry. Getting up hungry in the mornings in unheated rooms when the temperatures outside stood at ten below was torture, especially when I tried to shave with the trickle of ice-cold water that would come out of our half-frozen pipe in the kitchen. Often we had no water at all when the pipes were frozen solid. As electricity and gas were rationed, we had to wait for the city to turn them on for the two-hour daily allotment. Only then could we unfreeze the pails of water we had set aside the day before. And many an evening I sat in our kitchen by flickering candlelight, dressed in my heavy winter coat with mittens on my hands, trying to write my school assignments.

As Christmas drew near, word began to circulate that the British military government was systematically rounding up former party and Hitler Youth leaders for internment. I was not certain whether my past position as *Fähnleinführer* would qualify me for that fate, but I had to assume that and prepare for the worst. I packed my bag and stored it near the apartment door. On the days before Christmas and on Christmas Eve itself my mother and I anxiously listened to every footstep approaching our house, fearing that it heralded my being picked up. It turned out that, as so often in the past, my birth year—and the additional fact that I had not become a member of the party—exempted me from arrest. But we did not know that then, and our anxiety cast its shadow over the holidays.

It also became progressively more apparent that my mother's health was failing. Years later, when my relatives gave me copies of her correspondence, I learned just how terrible a toll the loss of my father and the worry about my fate and that of her family in Chemnitz had taken. I read the letters that she had written when she knew nothing of my fate and that of her parents. "It would be so much easier to write this letter," she told her parents in one of them,

> if I knew that these lines will find you in the old beloved home, and all of you being together with one another. I sit here alone in this dreadful time. For me the worst is not to be able to share my pain with anyone. Loneliness is beginning to devour me. But I still don't give up hope that one day we shall again be united.

When the holidays had passed, severe winter weather set in in earnest. We had no central heating and only one iron stove in our living room, which we could heat for a few hours only. Thus the room was cold or moderately warm at best for most of the time. As, in addition, my mother denied herself the best of the food that we could scrounge up in order to keep me fed, the cold and the insufficient nourishment made her shiver and run a persistent low fever. Soon she began to lose color and weight, but she kept on ignoring her own condition and my and our friends' pleading to take better care of herself.

I was worried and distraught. I did not know what I could do —what anyone could do—to bring her relief and restore her health. I could count myself lucky, I told myself, if she would stay on her feet throughout the winter, and I hoped and prayed that when spring finally came, she would recover. To cheer her up I wrote her a note on her birthday in January. I told her that I had searched far and wide in the shops to find something for her birthday, but I had been unsuccessful. There was nothing suitable to be had. So, instead of bringing her a gift, I composed a letter. I wrote:

Tomorrow you will be one year older. This has happened to you each year on this day but—you always remained the same. I don't know you in any other way than as my mother.

Do you know what I do not like? When, as happened so often in our recent past, the love of mothers and the veneration of motherhood was shown and lauded in so public and official a manner. I think that belongs solely to the family and not before the eyes of the whole world. When done publicly, this love becomes shallow and is drawn into a morass. It becomes a meaningless matter-of-course. Yes, it should be a matter-of-course, but not when it no longer stands at the center of the quiet, dear life of the family.

So, I don't like that, and that's why I never have shown it that way, dear mother, but, nonetheless, I love you so much just because you are my mother, and on your birthday, you should hear that from me.

I then told her of the circumstances under which I had written this letter and ended by saying:

Mother, sometimes you are so sad. I am too, sometimes, and then I am helped by some words that fit and that happen to come into my mind. How do you like these: "There is only one heroism in this world: To see the world as it is, and to love it." That's right, isn't it?

But now, dear mother, let me wish you everything good for your birthday; above all, stay well in your new year and remain as before, my dear mother!

During these winter months my meetings and walks with Ulla, too, had come to a halt, and I saw less and less of her. When I watched her walking one cold and blustery day with another school friend of mine I sensed that our relationship had come to an end without either of us having been aware of it. There had been no confrontation, no ill words, no tears. The music to which we both had listened had faded away, had grown softer and softer until we both realized that it had ceased.

Throughout all this time, from November into April, I had attended the make-up course for veterans. The conditions under which we studied were not ideal. The *Große Schule* at that time still served as an emergency hospital, and we make-up scholars received our lessons in the city's old *Schloß*, the stately moat-surrounded castle.

In school a source of inspiration was my German literature teacher, Friedrich Kammerer. Dr. Kammerer had been a Quaker all his life, and he represented to me the best of German culture. It did not decrease my esteem for him that, late in the spring when my relationship with Ulla had come to an end, I had struck up a deep friendship with Christa, Dr. Kammerer's daughter. Soon I fell head over heels in love with Christa. I joined both her and her father on Sunday mornings at Quaker worship meetings in Braunschweig. I could not but listen with fascination to the stories I learned about Dr. Kammerer, who, like my father, had been a reserve officer.

During the war he had served in Norway. Being a Quaker and a pacifist in a nation where, during war time, resistance to serving in the military was punished by death, Dr. Kammerer obeyed the orders to military duty. But, as Christa told me, all throughout the war he carried on his belt a carved wooden revolver in which had been burned the words: "Thou shalt not kill." It had been Dr. Kammerer's way of serving his country and his God at the same time.

In Dr. Kammerer's class I took my first step to unburden myself from the trauma of war and death. Dr. Kammerer had us read Rainer Maria Rilke's *The Manner of Loving and Dying of the Cornet Christoph Rilke*.[1] For me that reading came as a shock of recognition. I saw myself in every phase of my soldier's life as a companion to the Cornet Christoph Rilke. It seemed to me that every episode that unfolded in Rilke's story paralleled events I had lived through.

So, as homework assignment, I rewrote the *Cornet* and, by fusing Rilke's narration with my own experience, freed myself from my memories' oppressive burden. I wrote of the experience of soldiering, of the marching, the longing for mother and girlfriend, the parting of comrades, the riding into battle, the receiving of mementoes and commendations. I wrote of the losing of oneself in wildness and beauty, of being engulfed in tenderness and being carried away by love, of

---

1. Rainer Maria Rilke, *Die Weise von Liebe und Tod des Cornets Christoph Rilke* (Leipzig: Insel Verlag, 1906.) An English-language edition, translated by Constantine Fitz Gibbon, was published in 1958 by Allan Wingate, London.

the writing of letters that would never be read, of being thrown into hate, ugliness, terror, and of the meeting of death in the flash of sabers and the screaming of shells. The *Cornet* was my coming to terms with my life as a soldier, a life that, unlike the cornet's, continued to go on searching and that, as I then prayed, would cease only when the search was finished and the cornet and I should be united again.

We had fun, too, in Dr. Kammerer's class. Once he gave us the assignment to write a composition on a quotation from Nietzsche: "Two things the real man desires: Danger and play." He did not reckon with our ingenuity to find the source of the quotation, which went on: "Therefore he chose woman as his most dangerous toy." Our compositions, even Dr. Kammerer admitted, were memorable, even though, he added, they did not do us much credit. Did we not know that men and women both were made in the image of God and neither was a toy of the other?

When school finished and I received my *Abitur* at the end of April 1946, I desperately searched for employment. No longer a student, I now faced the British occupying authorities' draft of all able-bodied young men into the coal mines of the Ruhr. Unpleasant as that prospect would have been for me, it also meant that I would have to leave my mother alone again and without help. I could not possibly let that happen.

So I was overjoyed when through coincidence I was introduced to Dr. Stöcker, a geography lecturer at the Teacher Training College in Braunschweig. Dr. Stöcker offered me an unpaid position as his assistant. Not only did this solve the immediate problems my mother and I would have faced if I were to leave; it also appeared to be my first step on the road to university study and my apprenticeship to a prosional career. I could look toward the future with some degree of confidence.

Spring had finally come to Wolfenbüttel. The beeches and oak trees in the park added their darker hues to the tender green of the birch trees that stretched their branches toward the white-speckled blue sky. Birds were singing, and, as I commenced my daily walks along the Harztorwall to catch the streetcar to Dr. Stöcker's office on the road to Braunschweig, a light breeze wafted the delicate fragrance of lilac blossoms toward me. I could only think of Paul Gerhard's hymn of the golden sun that brought us heart-warming loveliness after our long illness. And when I came home one evening and rang our apartment's doorbell for my mother to let me in, there, as the door opened, stood my grandmother Alma, tears in her eyes, my mother close behind her, a radiant smile on her face. My grandmother took me in her arms, and we could only stammer our words of jubilant surprise and love.

Grandmother Alma, at age seventy-two, had taken the arduous trip from Chemnitz to the eastern edge of the Harz Mountains in a succession of slow, short-haul train rides. Then, to avoid Russian and British military patrols, she had made her way on foot trails across the Harz Mountains at night; had slept, as she told us, on the floor of a deserted hunter's cabin in the woods; and, the next morning, once she had made it into Bad Harzburg, had taken the train to Wolfenbüttel. Grandmother Alma told us of the terrible bombing raids on Chemnitz in the last days of the war, and of the Russian occupation and the starvation rations they received. She told us that Uncle Heini, Aunt Mausi's husband, had not returned from the war and was believed to be dead. But Grandfather Felix, my uncle Gerhard, and my aunt Mausi and her three small children had survived, though they suffered much from hunger, and Gerhard had contracted a severe case of tuberculosis.

My mother begged and implored my grandmother to stay with us in Wolfenbüttel and urge the others to come as well. Life was easier under British occupation, she argued, and if all of the family crowded into our rooms we would no longer have to fear to have our apartment requisitioned and occupied by strangers. But it was to no avail. Grandmother Alma did not want Aunt Mausi's children to leave their home. She feared that in their weakened condition neither Grandfather Felix nor Uncle Gerhard would survive the trip she had just undertaken. So we shared our meager supplies with my grandmother for a few days, and then she left us with many hugs and tears to go back to Chemnitz the same way she had come. Several weeks later, in July, we heard from her again through the mail. She had arrived safely back in Chemnitz only to find that Uncle Gerhard had been taken to a sanatorium in the Ore Mountains and that Grandfather Felix no longer could leave his bed. As we learned later, he passed away near the end of the month of exhaustion and malnutrition.

By that time, as the freshness of spring had given way to a wet and rainy summer, my mood had darkened again as, soon after my grandmother left, Dr. Duisberg and the county health authorities recommended urgently that my mother leave home and undergo treatment at the Tuberculosis Sanatorium in nearby Grasleben. I was very fortunate that the British Quaker Relief Team stationed in Braunschweig, whose members I had come to know through attending the Braunschweig Quaker Meeting, visited the Grasleben Sanatorium on a regular basis and invited me to come along. Thus I had the chance to see my mother every two weeks until she was allowed to come home again shortly before Christmas.

Much as I had hoped and longed for her return I was also much concerned how we would live through the coming winter. I was painfully aware how strongly my mother's health depended on a reliable supply of nourishing meals and sustaining warmth. Freezing temperatures and snow again had arrived early, and I was worried by the shortages of food and fuel that were daily more apparent.

Thus, during late September and early October, immediately after the potato harvest, a friend of mine and I set out on a number of expeditions to scour the fields of neighboring villages for discarded or leftover potatoes. We would leave home before dawn, a wooden handcart in tow, and join the throng of like-minded searchers. Most of the time we were the only young people among a group of dispirited elderly men and women who, silent and apathetic, set out listlessly across the railroad tracks, their eyes staring ahead, their feet slowly carrying them into the white, silent landscape of an early winter, empty fields stretching toward the horizon on either side of the road.

With one hand a woman would clutch her cart's handlebar, with the other she would pull closer the rough and torn shawl around her neck. Men would pull their carts in just the same way, though the fingers of their other hand would grab the broken, cold tobacco pipes in their coat pockets. Shabby coats, which long ago had lost their buttons and belts, were held together by safety pins. Pieces of string and old leather straps had taken the place of shoe laces.

So we walked for miles until, one by one, we would drop off from the column to the right and to the left and begin our search for the frozen remnants of potatoes under the thin cover of snow. Our backs strained as our feet stumbled and our fingers, barely protected by torn mittens or gloves, groped through the icy tangle of weeds and grasses. Slowly, agonizingly slowly, our treasures began to fill our sacks and they, in turn, would pile up in our carts. When the task was nearly done, we would straighten up, wipe away the tears from our eyes, tears with which the icy blast from the East had painted our faces, only to bend down once more, to stumble on and grope to complete the job. At mid-afternoon, when the winter's early dark descended over the fields, we would turn back to town, cross the rails once more, and disappear in our homes, tired and hungry but glad in the knowledge that, at least, there would be something to eat in the months ahead.

Just as we searched for food, so we also battled for fuel. Coal had become a rarity, and in our stoves and ovens we burned the wood we could find, having chopped down the trees on our streets, swept clean the ground of the Lechlum Woods, and broken to pieces every bit of furniture we could do without. From the nearby station I heard every night the cling-clang of the barrier bell and the whistles of trains that roared by without stopping. The barriers would descend, and the heavy, black worm of steel would thunder past, the cars loaded high with black, shiny coal, and then disappear, trailing a lazy plume of smoke underneath the low hanging sky. Red dots gradually dimmed in the gray-white desert of the cold country until they were extinguished by the black of the night. The barriers would rise again, without the cling-clang of the bell, until the red-white fingers pointed into the sky, silently accusing, as it seemed, the equally silent bank of clouds. The trains rolled all winter long, the hooting of their whistles sounding to us like bitter mockery.

People would steal out of their houses late at night and line up at the tracks to catch the chunks of coal that might spill from the rushing trains. A piece here, another there, a whole little pile further along the dam—they were like promises of a warm stove and warm food, for a night or two, perhaps for a little longer.

As November turned into December, a friend of mine and I joined the nightly furtive crowds, hid in bushes and culverts along the track, ready to pounce once a train thundered past and had spilled its black gold from above. As the weeks passed, the game became more dangerous. Men we did not know joined us. They came with long poles, hooks at their top, and lay in waiting to tear coal from the cars or, if they could manage, to rip apart the train's brake hose.

But the trains now carried searchlights and guards. The lights would pierce through the night and the bushes; the guards would use their guns. Shouts and shots would ring out; sirens and whistles would go off; and angry commands would sound in a foreign language. Soldiers would appear from behind the tracks, herding people, men and women, crying and begging for mercy, into the waiting trucks to carry them off to jail. On my mother's pleading my friend and I gave up our nightly forays. My mother wanted me home, even if that meant that our room was going to be cold.

The winter of 1947 became a winter of despair. The months that had preceded it since my arrival home had brought me no further in my quest for answers. In fact, they had aborted that quest because the immediate tasks of survival, of fighting hunger, cold, and illness, left scarcely any time for sustained thought. Whatever direction my schooling, and particularly Dr. Kammerer's teaching, could give, led me and Christa into poetry, literature, and music. But this was, as I dimly sensed even then, partly an escape from our misery and partly a search for a new footing; partly an evading of the questions that pressed on our conscience—questions of our collective past and our individual responsibility for the immensity of evil that our nation had loosed on the world—and partly a search for a platform from which we could, with some hope of success, deal with and answer these questions. We felt like the outcasts we had become in the eyes of the world. If Dr. Kammerer's teaching addressed our fate, it helped us seek escape from the treadmill of never-ending self-pity and, mired though we were in need and despair, started us, though we did not recognize it then, on our path to recovery.

16

The Search

WHEN SPRING FINALLY ARRIVED my spirits were buoyed by the return of Etzel from Soviet captivity and the news that, beginning in June, I was permitted to enroll in a veterans' preparatory course at the University of Göttingen. Though Etzel's return was by far the most joyous event, it was darkened by the message we received a few weeks later that Dieter, "the General," would never be with us again. His body had been found in the Harz Mountains where his unit had been caught in one of the final engagements of the war. We now knew that of us thirty-one *Große Schule* classmates six had lost their lives in the war.

Etzel and I now lived through a few wonderful months until I left for Göttingen to begin my studies. We met almost every afternoon in his room and, over a black market cigarette and a cookie or two from his aunt, shared our everyday woes and our hopes for the future. His aunt and his uncle often joined us for a few minutes and encouraged us to raid their library and invited us to share with them their supper table—in those days of hunger and deprivation no small matter. I especially appreciated the wonderful dishes Etzel's aunt Elli prepared with the wondrous delicacies she received through the Jewish Relief Fund.

It was during one of these meals, too, that I listened with rapt and horrified attention to the story of Etzel's aunt's survival. A local policeman and two Gestapo agents had knocked at the Büchers' apartment door at two o'clock on a cold February morning in 1945. When Otto Bücher opened, these men said to him they were there for his wife and would he, please, ask her to get dressed and come out. Etzel's uncle stared at the men and broke out in a desperate cry: "You beasts, you inhuman beasts. Your fellow henchmen came here last night and took her away, and now you are back to mock me and pour salt in my wounds. Get out of my sight."

The men allowed that there must have been some mistake and that they would check at headquarters. They turned around and went down the stairs. By the time they came back, Mrs. Bücher had been spirited away to a hide-out prepared long before in an attic in a business house on the Lange Herzogstraße. There she survived the last few months of the war.

"No," Etzel's uncle added, "it was not a miracle. Wolfenbüttel is a small town, and though I had never before seen the Gestapo agents, I had known the local policeman for years. He was the one who did the talking and who suggested to his colleagues that they better check at headquarters."

During our afternoons and evenings in Etzel's room we spent many an hour trying to make sense of our lives as *Jungvolk* leaders and soldiers. We asked ourselves whether the love for our boys and our willingness to fight for our country had all been ghastly mistakes, whether there had been anything true and noble in our past at all, and whether there was anything left in which we could still believe and by which we could live.

While we, as everyone else in those days, were hungry all the time, we learned that our spiritual hunger was at least as pressing or more so than the pain in our stomachs. Absence of food was no obstacle to talk, and the pain of physical hunger gave urgency to our conversations. We had seen for ourselves how hunger of any kind roused hate, greed, and envy and led to despair, betrayal, and violence. We now found that hunger also was a fount of love, friendship, and confidence. We recognized that it severely tested our bodies and souls, that it pronounced the harshest verdicts, that it lightened as well as darkened our lives but also brought the richest rewards. We learned that we did not stand alone in our search; that our friendship was a gift of inestimable value; that as we probed and explored we could detect glimpses of possibilities for a new world and a new life.

Our spiritual pilgrimage extended over vast territories. In our quest for purpose and meaning we felt freer in our thoughts than ever before. We no longer had to consider tradition and stated norms. We became individualists, and we cut ourselves loose from those who did not understand us and whose clinging to conventions we abhorred. I remember the contempt we felt for one of our neighbors who, as he inspected the list of candidates in one of the earliest democratic local elections, carefully marked as acceptable those whom he knew attended church regularly. Was not this pure hypocrisy and the unthinking acceptance of bourgeois middle-class standards that we had begun to detest? Had the Lutheran church spoken out and condemned ⟵ the evils of Nazism, evils that, we now were told, they had been aware of all along? How many Propst Rosenkranzs and "Parson" Willes had we known, men who by their own example had kept us from unthinkingly accepting the party's directives? All too few, we told ourselves. Church membership alone, we felt, meant nothing. My grandfather Felix had been right when he had warned me of the hypocrites who loved to pray in the synagogues and on the street corners. The church as institution, along with everything else of the past, had lost its meaning and authority. As we thus rejected and discarded old ways and conventions, Etzel and I felt liberated rather than alienated. We appreciated the new freedom that, although it made us rudderless and bereft of guidance, called on us to accept the responsibility of building a new world for ourselves. Slowly we felt ourselves growing to accept that challenge.

The search led us inward at first, away from the reality of the misery outside. For a time we became romantic idealists. We read and embraced Friedrich Meinecke's *Die deutsche Katastrophe* with its fervent wish for a rebirth of the spirit of Goethe. In Etzel's room we sought to realize for ourselves Meinecke's dream of creating small reading circles throughout the land in which, through the sound of the human voice, we could touch the hearts of listeners with "the most lively testimonials of the German spirit . . . the noblest German music and poetry."[1] We gathered other friends around us and read the German idealist poets and tried to lose ourselves in their world of friendship and love. We wrote and read to each other our own poems, short stories, and essays. With Christa and Etzel's girlfriend Hannelore we went to concerts, the theater, and the opera. We played recorders and violins and joined choirs to sing motets and cantatas. We believed that finally we had found a world of goodness, beauty, and truth.

What we did not realize then was that, by immersing ourselves in poetry and music and shutting our eyes to the world that surrounded us and turning our backs on the past we had lived through, we could not come to terms with either our past or our present. We comforted each other and ourselves with the soothing aspects of an idealized, prettified past as we might have relished the perfumed drawers of an old family wardrobe but kept closely shut all others for fear of finding out what they might contain. So the wardrobe stood there, beckoning and threatening us at the same time. Perhaps it was impossible for us to open all its drawers. Perhaps it was a necessity of our need to sur-

---

1. Friedrich Meinecke, *Die deutsche Katastrophe: Betrachtungen und Erinnerungen* (Wiesbaden: Eberhard Brockhaus Verlag, 1946), 175.

vive that, after so much horror and death, we so desperately searched for the beautiful, the pure, and the true. Perhaps it was the only way we could move on.

In June I left Wolfenbüttel and my mother to begin my studies in Göttingen. I owed much of my good fortune in being admitted to the university to my apprenticeship with Dr. Stöcker. The training he had given me in geography, its methods and approaches, had enabled me to pass the qualifying examination with flying colors. Encouraged by my success I now determined that I would follow my father's course as a scholar and prepare myself for a career as a high school teacher. I signed up as a student of geography.

In the months before my move I had gotten to know a British major, like Otto Bücher an artist by profession, in a British–German discussion group in Wolfenbüttel. Just as my studies began in Göttingen the major had been transferred to Kassel. On weekends he continued to visit his German fiancée in Wolfenbüttel, and he offered me rides so I could return home occasionally to help my mother and do chores for her. On these journeys we became good friends, he pumping me dry about my life during the war and the conditions under which we students now lived in Göttingen, and I vastly improving my facility in English conversation and increasing my store of English folksongs. We merrily sang as we drove along, skipping from

> Oh, dear, what can the matter be,
> Two old ladies locked in the lavatory,

to

> My bonny lies over the ocean,

and

> You are my sunshine, my only sunshine,

the latter being the major's favorite. While at home I would meet with Etzel and Christa and my other friends but there was little time to continue our conversations. Etzel had found a position as a merchant apprentice in Braunschweig and Christa had begun her studies at the Braunschweig Teacher Training College. We each were preoccupied with our different problems and projects and began to go our separate ways.

In Göttingen daily life was grim. The town was overrun with refugees and discharged soldiers who could not go back to their former homes in areas then occupied by Poland. Ghostlike figures of former prisoners of war returned from the Soviet Union. They were living skeletons clad in rags, some without a leg on crutches, others without an arm, their only possession an aluminum spoon sticking out of their breast pocket. They staggered and limped up the street from the railroad station past the university library, where I watched them from a side street. They were searching for a Red Cross shelter or a hostel where they might find a bite to eat and a bed on which to lie down.

Under those overcrowded conditions housing for students was scarce and virtually nonexistent. We freshmen slept in gymnasia at first, on straw mattresses on the floor, with a thin, worn blanket or our overcoat as a cover. Pretty soon I was plagued again with body lice and fleas, pests I thought I had left behind for good when I was discharged from the army. When winter came the lack of fuel made matters worse. I had been moved from the gymnasium to the attic of a former fraternity house, and woke up one morning with half an inch of snow covering my blanket and my head. The attic roof had lost its tiles in a wartime air raid, and it had never been repaired. Eventually, after roaming widely through Göttingen's suburbs and ringing doorbells, I found a bed and room for myself alone, though even then I discovered that I had exchanged the lice and fleas of the straw mattresses for the company of bedbugs in my room.

Food was even more scarce in Göttingen than it had been at home. My fellow students and I took our noon meals in the *Mensa*, the university's student mess hall where we could spend our ration cards to best advantage, though the *Mensa*'s watery soups and slices of meat-substitute sausage never fully stilled our hunger. In the evenings we sought out the city's restaurants, studied the menus posted outside, and tried to decide where we might get the most nourishing meal for our money. When the restaurants closed early in the evening to save on fuel and electricity, we roamed the streets looking for the shadowy figures who lurked in doorways and alleys and offered their wares on the black market for survival. The price of a cigarette—six otherwise worthless *Reichsmark*, worthless because, without ration cards, there was nothing to be had for them—was the same as for a slice of bread, and confronted with that choice we took the cigarette rather than the bread. A cigarette would numb our hunger for longer than a slice of bread could. The worthless money thus became our last resort. And thanks to it being worthless, we had plenty of it. There had been little that we could have bought with it during the war, and thus it had accumulated in our hands literally for years. Now it helped us to survive on the black market.

During those winter months the lack of writing paper, fuel, and electricity turned attendance at lectures into a trial for both professors and students. I sat in cold and dark classrooms, thick socks on my feet, an old army overcoat wrapped around me, and mittens on my fingers, and tried awkwardly to grasp a pencil stub with which I took notes on long strips of the torn-off white margins of the daily newspaper. A Hindenburg candle—as the shallow brown bowls of wax were called— stood between me and my neighbor and cast a flickering light on what we wrote. I don't believe our teachers—men such as the world-famous philosopher Nicolai Hartmann and the historian Hermann Heimpel— ever had more attentive students than us. We were starved for what they had to say, and neither cold nor bodily hunger could keep us away. They, too, knew what service they were performing for us, and they, despite their hunger and infirmities, never let us down.

If, during daytime, we were not in the lectures and seminars, we haunted the library and reading rooms. I read as though my life depended on it. I seemed instinctively to recognize how much I had missed during my school years. Still aglow with my enthusiasm for literature I signed up in my first semester for a seminar in German poetry. I was appalled and bewildered by what I found. There was no empathetic understanding of the poets' souls, no participating in the miracle of lyrical creation. The study of poetry, I learned, was a technical matter, an analysis of language, rhyme, and meter. Our teacher never spoke of poetry's beauty and the inspiration it could provide to human beings in love and the consolation it held out for those in despair. I decided that this was not what I wanted, and I immersed myself in the study of geography and my readings in philosophy, history, political science, and sociology. There, I thought, we at least dealt with reality and looked for ways to sound its meaning.

With friends I made among my fellow students we sat up late into the night and debated the various contending political philosophies and systems. For a few pennies we could buy from a Communist press the collected works of Marx, Lenin, and Stalin. In the library I turned to Max Weber, Ernst Troeltsch, and Ferdinand Toennies. I devoured books on the British parliamentary system, the French Revolution, and the history of Quakerism. Somewhere, my friends and I hoped, light would shine and give us guidance.

While even then we realized that such hope, expressed in such naive fashion, was farfetched, each one of us had his or her favorite authors whom each was willing to try as a guide to see how far they might lead. For me they were Reinhold Niebuhr and Albert Camus. Niebuhr's epigram that man's capacity for justice made democracy possible and that man's inclination to injustice made it necessary gave me a foothold in the real world around me.[2] It seemed to hold in balance my experience of human frailties and misery and a faith in mankind's latent potential for overcoming the obstacles in its way. Niebuhr's realism, I thought, was far more persuasive than the so-called scientific socialism with its doctrinaire manifestos and calls to arms. Of those, I thought, we had had enough. Camus's *Myth of Sisyphus* told me that man could be superior to his fate, stronger than the rock that he will have to push up the mountain, again and again.[3]

Above all, it was the existential philosophy that underlay Camus's resolution to struggle that appealed to me and my fellow students. It was a philosophy that placed reliance on the individual as he or she existed, not on some program that was supposed to provide direction and support. Social life with all its organizations, clubs, and rituals as we had known them had ceased to function. The ideals for which we had been ready to offer our lives in battle had all become questionable. Except for the few friends that each of us had come to cherish and rely on, we had lost all confidence in collective action. What was still left to us and on what we could still rely, we felt, was ourselves, our individual selves. And we were determined to struggle against all odds, like Camus's Sisyphus, to turn back and push our rock up the hill, over and over again, if that was what fate would demand of us.

So it was Reinhold Niebuhr who, at least in abstract terms, made democracy plausible as perhaps the least bad among all social forms of life. And it was Albert Camus who, challenging me to make myself the creator and arbiter of my life, took away all excuses behind which I might have hid and made me, and me alone, responsible for what I achieved and suffered. Niebuhr and Camus allowed me to see myself beginning to function again in the world as it was. With them at the starting point, I could define myself anew, could answer the question of who I really was, could face the future, and could begin to think of my place in it.

2. Reinhold Niebuhr, *The Children of Light and the Children of Darkness: A Vindication of Democracy and a Critique of Its Traditional Defense* (New York: Charles Scribner's Sons, 1944), xiii.

3. Albert Camus, *The Myth of Sisyphus and Other Essays*, trans. Justin O'Brien (New York: Vintage Books, 1959), 89.

17

Requiem

URING THE WINTER RECESS OF 1947 I was back in Wolfenbüttel
to spend Christmas with my mother. I was sad and hopeful at
the same time. My mother's health, while not having taken a
turn for the worse, was nonetheless precarious. Another cold winter
with little food did not promise improvement. Yet a ray of hope had
fallen into our lives with an invitation to my mother to visit her two
cousins, who owned a home for physically and mentally handicapped
children on Lake Zürich in Switzerland. My mother's cousins asked
her to join them and stay there to regain her health. So Christmas for
us was a time of both sadness and hopeful anticipation.

Again, I faced the dilemma of not being able to find much in the
stores, and so, for a Christmas and farewell gift, I turned once more to
the written word. I put together a small selection of my favorite poems
and Bible passages. I chose Psalm 34: 18:

> The Lord is near to the broken-hearted,
> and saves the crushed in spirit,

and I selected Rilke's poem *Autumn,* as it seemed to me to express so
perfectly the mood of sadness and decline, and, at the same time, the
comfort of hope and love that surrounded us:

> The leaves are falling, falling as from far,
> as though in skies in gardens far they faded;
> they're falling with denial in their gestures.
>
> And in the nights the heavy earth is falling
> from all the stars into deep loneliness.

> We all are falling. This hand also falls.
> And look to others, too: It's in them all.
>
> And yet there is One who supports this falling
> so gently soft and strong in both His hands.[1]

In the middle of January I accompanied my mother to Hannover where she took the night train to Switzerland. I returned to Wolfenbüttel and, a day later, went back to my studies in Göttingen.

In the months that followed letters from my mother and her two Swiss cousins, my aunts Annelies and Ruth, gradually but inexorably made it clear that, despite the best and most loving care, my mother's health was not improving. Repeated attacks of bronchitis and pleurisy eventually caused a renewed outbreak of tuberculosis. By Easter she had to be moved to a hospital.

In her letters my mother always reassured me that, though the course of her illness was a constant up and down of fever sweeping over her body, her prospects were good and her spirits were high. She took part, as much as she could, in my discoveries of poetry and philosophy and encouraged me in my reading of the French existentialists Camus and Sartre, although she confessed that she did not find much originality in the latter's philosophy. She followed world events, expressed great unease over the Soviet activities in Finland and Czechoslovakia, and inquired anxiously what I planned to do in case the Red Army would indeed start to move westward. "You cannot stay," she wrote, and added that when the day came that I should be forced to make a final decision, I would find that which was right. "I trust in that," she wrote.

Just when I heard the news that my mother had been moved to the hospital I received a telephone message that I was being considered for participation in a seven-week International Student Seminar in the United States. The seminars were organized by the American Friends Service Committee, and I had been nominated by members of the English Quaker Relief Team in Braunschweig. I was told that, if a fellowship could be found, I might subsequently stay for one academic year as a student in an American university.

This unexpected news threw me into inner turmoil. There was no question in my mind that such an invitation was the greatest gift that I could possibly have received. I wanted to go. But could I? How could I leave my mother when she was so desperately ill and there existed the very real possibility that I might never see her again?

1. Author's translation.

The author's mother in Switzerland, 1948

My mother answered my question before I ever asked it. In response to my letter telling her of the telephone call she wrote back immediately that, should such an invitation really arrive, I must accept it. She was not going to hold me in Europe, though, she added, "it is bitter, indeed, that we shall have to part without a farewell. I don't think I will be back in Germany before you leave. . . . Come, rush over to Switzerland and say goodbye."

That, it seemed to me at the time, was an impossibility, given the restrictions imposed on the citizens of occupied Germany. My mother, too, scarcely meant her plaintive cry to be taken seriously. But unbeknownst to her, the British Quakers in Braunschweig, together with my aunts, had already begun to get for me a travel permit to Switzerland.

At the beginning of May the definitive invitation to the United States arrived. I spent the next few days racing back and forth between my home in Wolfenbüttel and offices in Braunschweig and Hannover to obtain travel permits and visas to Switzerland and the United States. By the tenth of the month I had succeeded, and by the evening of the next day I was on my way to Switzerland.

In my pocket I carried the most recent letter I had received from my mother. In the train I read it over and over again. It became clear from my mother's words that she did not expect to see me before I left for the United States, and that, without ever saying so directly, she now wanted to prepare herself and me for a final farewell. She reflected on the relationships between us and between us and my father. "The *three* of us," she wrote, "will always be united; as long as you make your way here on earth with a pure heart and good will you can always be joyful in the thought of your father and mother—our being united then will not be ended in death either. It is only a passage to a higher world."

My eyes were blurry with tears. I, too, knew that we were approaching the final farewell.

We had three days together in my mother's hospital room. I could be with her at most for only two hours at a time. Then the nurse would remind us that it was time for her to rest. We spoke of our lives together and of my father. But, again and again, she would revert to her wishes and dreams for me. She made me promise, regardless of what would happen to her, to leave for the United States. There was nothing, she said, that she could do for me in Europe, and if I wanted her to be happy then I should leave for a better world.

When, on the third day, we said goodbye, neither of us had spoken directly of her approaching death. As I later learned from my aunts, in his funeral sermon the Swiss pastor referred to our last conversations and said that we both had wanted to spare each other the pain of that final recognition.

But my mother had left me a last message in which she quoted from Walter Flex's little book about World War I, *Der Wanderer zwischen beiden Welten.* The book itself is a poetic requiem for the thousands of young Germans who, like the Little One at Glinstedt, in youthful idealism and love for their country, had given their lives. Near the end of the book Flex meditates on the meaning of the requiem. It was these lines that my mother wanted me to take with me as a testament from both her and my father:

> Mourning your dead, fellow, is no good service for them. Do you want to turn your dead into ghosts or do you want to let them enter your homes? There is no third way for hearts struck down by God. Don't turn us into ghosts; allow us entrance. We would like to be allowed to step into your circle without disturbing your laughter. Don't turn us into senile somber shadows; let us keep the fecund smell of gaiety that lay over our youth, bright and shimmering. You who live, allow us entrance that we may dwell and stay among you in dark and in joyful hours. Don't cry for us so friends shrink away from talking about us. Help your friends to have courage to talk about us and laugh. Let us enter as we did when we were alive.[2]

With these words on my mind I set out on the journey home, sad and yet comforted, conscious in my own mind that I, too, was now a wanderer between two worlds, one world forever closing behind me, another strange, threatening, and promising opening before me.

The journey home, however, was a descent into disaster and despair. It was as though the world that lay behind me was slamming its door with a curse and mocking derision.

It began when early in the morning I stepped out of the international express train in the Hannover station and asked a railroad employee for my connecting train to Braunschweig. The man, a grimy figure in torn and oily work clothes, looked me up and down, cast his glance at the express train that was then steaming out of the station, and, with a grimace on his face, said to me: "Where you come from, they should have told you." He then turned and walked away. These were the first words addressed to me in my own country, and they hit me like a slap in the face.

The second scornful rejection came at noon in Wolfenbüttel at the People's Kitchen where I wanted to exchange my daily meal ticket for a pail of soup. After having grumpily taken my ticket the attendant ignored me. When I remonstrated and said I wanted my meal, she bel-

2. Walter Flex, *Der Wanderer zwischen beiden Welten: Ein Kriegserlebnis* (München: C. H. Beck, n.d.), 94–95. Author's translation.

lowed that I was lying when I said she had already taken my ticket. I wanted to cheat her, she shouted, and threatened to call the police.

The third rejection broke my spirit and killed the last spark of feeling I had for my country and my people. I had walked home after the incident at the People's Kitchen to unburden my heart to a good friend and neighbor. She listened sympathetically and filled my empty pail with soup of her own. Then she mentioned, parenthetically, that she had just heard another neighborhood woman say that I did not seem to be affected very much by the illness and the coming death of my mother.

It was then that I broke down. My friend sought to console me, but I ran out of her house and collapsed on the couch in my home. I lay there, trembling, wrecked by spasms of sobs and cries, shouting soundlessly, "Mother, Mother," just as I had done when the artillery and mortar shells exploded around me. I felt a tearing sensation inside my chest, and now I knew what it meant to have a broken heart. I was convinced I had at that moment lost the power to care and to love.

Something, I knew, had been sundered forever for me, something that was irretrievably lost. The people I had loved most were dead or dying. As for the others, my countrymen, they had rejected me and I now rejected them. I had passed an invisible boundary.

The next four weeks until I boarded the ship in Bremerhaven were made tolerable for me by the preparations for my coming departure. Etzel and Otto and Elli Bücher stood by me in my despair. They helped me to focus my thoughts on what lay before me rather than on what I was leaving behind.

It was more difficult with my grandmother in Chemnitz. She had lost her husband, my grandfather Felix, the Lutheran pastor and *Gymnasium* professor who had married my parents and given me, through them, my life's guiding Bible verse. Now she was about to lose her daughter, my mother. Her son, my uncle Gerhard, was also hospitalized with tuberculosis. Every day, after school was out, my grandmother watched her three small fatherless grandchildren in Chemnitz search the ruins of the bombed-out city and the neighboring fields and gardens for food and firewood; the childrens' mother, my aunt Mausi, earned a few marks as a saleswoman in a store.

I knew all this, and yet I felt pressed that I had to unburden myself, that I had to tell her how I felt, though I also knew that I would hurt her deeply. So I wrote her that I wished "nothing more ardently than to turn my back on my country for ever. . . . When I traveled to Germany from Switzerland I found out," I wrote, "what human beings really are like and how vile they can be. I am so very glad that I shall be able to leave this land that once was my home."

My words must have pained her even more deeply when I rejected her and my grandfather's religion as a source of comfort and consolation. I confessed my belief in God as my father but I rejected the need for a church and for human mediators between father and child. With my expected departure from Germany on my mind, I wanted to cut myself off from all things German, including the Lutheran religion. "I do not need a Luther," I wrote, "a Bodelschwing, a minister, [and] . . . I shall send them away if they want to come between me and my God." To drive home my point, I added: "As long as the reformer Luther is at the same time a clamoring ruffian with no regard for proportion and limits, as long as ministers preach holy war and bless the arms of murder, you will not ask me that I revere and honor them. . . ." My despair had made me destroy even the last bridge that might still have held me to my past.

And so only the requiem in Walter Flex's *Wanderer between Both Worlds* traveled with me across time and space and remained my link to my German past. It has become the requiem for my growing up as boy soldier, for the life of soldiering I had anticipated, for the friendships and loves of my youth, for the trauma and death of war that accompanied my growing up. It is the requiem for my parents, for Etzel and Dieter, for Etzel's aunt and uncle, for Mrs. Lerner and Albert Morgenstern, and for all whom I have loved and still love and in whose memory I shall always celebrate this requiem of love and overcoming.

The knowledge that there was friendship and love in that German past will never and can never excuse or make me forget or even overcome the vileness and unspeakable evil that surrounded that past. It does, however, remind me that even in the midst of darkness there shone and will always shine a light of hope, faith, and love, even though it may but flicker at times. It is that light that lets me celebrate my requiem and consecrate my loves and friendships.

Appendix

The author in front of the *Große Schule,* Commencement 1996

Commencement Address, June 15, 1996

Delivered to the Graduating Class of the *Große Schule* in Wolfenbüttel in the Presence of the Graduating Class of 1946

Principal Selle,
Dear Classmates of yesterday and dear Graduates of today,
Colleagues on the teaching staff,
Dear Parents and dear Guests:

My fellow classmates have asked me as their youngest member, who has been away from this school for the greatest distance and longest time, to say a few words to our graduates, words which are to convey to them what this school has given us on our way through life, what it has meant to us and still means today.

This magnificent *Aula*, dear graduates, which in our days was decorated with the busts of Homer and Sophocles, of Virgil and Tacitus, Dante and Shakespeare, Schiller and Goethe, Lessing, Luther, and Melanchthon, and with paintings illustrating their works, reminded us of the heritage of the Graeco–Roman world, Christianity, and the German classics, a heritage which through this school and this city of Gotthold Ephraim Lessing, Wilhelm Raabe, and Wilhelm Busch became for us a lifelong commitment. And this, too, is your heritage which you, as

231

proud graduates of this school and as young people who grew up in this city, will take with you on your way.

It is, I think, no exaggeration to tell you that we grew up in this school at the worst of all possible times. During our first year, when Hermann Lampe was still allowed to serve as our principal, our teachers were able to place before us the heritage of humanity in our classes in religion and German. Exemplary educators such as Ernst-August Wille and our first homeroom teacher, Bodo Wacker, remain unforgettable in our memories.

As ten-year-olds we knew little of the courageous opposition of "Parson" Wille—that's what we called him—to the antireligious policies of the school administration in Braunschweig. But we learned our hymnal and trusted his assurance that, even if we couldn't understand it then, soon there would come times in which we would derive comfort and strength from the hymns we had memorized. How right he was!

Bodo Wacker, our first homeroom teacher, had his own way of teaching us to distinguish between deceit and truth. When he entered our classroom in the morning, he approached the mapholder in the corner, raised its wooden arm toward the ceiling, saluted it silently, turned to us, smiled and said: "Good Morning, boys, sit down."

There was no German salute, no "Heil Hitler," in his classroom, and we knew exactly what risks he took. When I told my parents about this, my father looked me in the eye and said: "You will never tell this story to anybody." He didn't have to tell me why not.

And it was in the yard of this school where, on the morning of November 10, 1938, still out of breath from having run over to see the smouldering ruin of the synagogue on the Lessingstrasse, I heard from a classmate his story of how he watched when, in the middle of the night, his friend and his parents had been dragged out of the house. When I at noon excitedly told my mother about all these events, she interrupted me and said: "Jurgen, if your father and I had been Jewish, you too would have been dragged out of your bed last night." I was then ten years old, but I have never forgotten what I saw and heard that day.

And when the war began, Hermann Lampe and many of our best teachers had disappeared; others, less gifted, took their places. We didn't learn much any more, because other, war-important tasks, called us. We marched through the streets singing; we gathered rags, bones, old iron and paper; helped bring in the harvest in the fields and canning factories. We slept in the basement of this school to be there when incendiary bombs needed to be put out. Fortunately, this never became necessary in this building, though we had our share of putting out fires and digging out neighbors from underneath their bombed houses in and around this town.

And here, too, memories bring us back to this *Aula* when we here as guardsmen, at four o'clock in the morning, in the darkened room, gathered around the grand piano, with the moon shining its bright light through the great windows, and gave our "concerts," until slowly the great doors would open and Mr. Manselmann, our custodian, would appear in his dressing gown, a flashlight in his hand, shaking his head and saying: "Boys, it's enough. The neighbors would like to sleep."

Yes, even in those days we experienced the usual high-jinks of school life: The last outing to the *Asse* in our traditional school uniforms of white trousers and blue jackets; the absentminded Latin teacher who would stare at me and ask: "Herbst, what is your name?"

But all of this disappeared in May 1943 when most of us were called to man the anti-aircraft batteries around the Salzgitter Industrial Complex and later at the Soese Dam. Then came labor service, combat at the front, prison and internment camps, and, for some of us, adventurous escapes to find our way back home. Of the thirty-one of us, only twenty-five returned, and it is only right that we think silently of our six who fell in battle: Dieter Dosse, Gerhard Even, Helmut Haase, Gerhard Hanne, Walter Meyer, and Dieter Streck.

And then, for those of us who survived, came the years of hunger and the return to school to prepare for our *Abitur.* Then, our ways parted. Some stayed home, some went to college; some took part in development projects or laid pipelines overseas. Others returned to Wolfenbüttel or are still living far from this dear, little town. And today, half a century later, you see us here as farmers, managers and builders, as chemists and watchmakers, as businessmen and engineers, as ministers and professors, as civil servants and lawyers, as husbands, fathers, uncles, and grandfathers. We raised our children, tilled our fields, served our customers, designed our projects, wrote our books, and gave our lectures and sermons.

But in all this variety, one thing has kept us together and today joins us with you: the heritage of this school of which I spoke at the beginning. And if our class may add its special contribution, then, I think, it is the renewal of the recognition—centuries old—that it is less the specific knowledge that this school could give you or, in our case, was hardly able to give us, than the strength of conviction and character which it did bestow on us and thus enabled us to find our way through one of the darkest times of German history. From its roots in the era of humanism and the Reformation, with the inheritance of the ancient world, Christianity, and the German classics, this Great School gave us and you also a precious gift on our way. It has been for us a lifelong source of strength, and, if you will accept it and know how to treasure it, it will be the same for you.

The best I can wish for you today is that, *deo volente,* in fifty years you will gather again and pass on to the graduates then assembled here the blessings of this gift.

PhD Harvard — Hal how-old?
nuclear?
how come USA?

Hanover–Okn 1928 → 1948 → USA

SS / German regular army
Prussian
unstated, jew of Moral awakening
how easy not grounded end
up ↑ Nazi

few in English — Jewish German

billeted provides home — dinner table
expressed anger, disillusion

age 12 Hal WW II started   father died
Married 1913   Flavus Rice → Germany worse
1930
Diana

Uncle Hanover Frankfurt worked AZ (like GE)
Aunt brother of mother, Lisa & Ann
wife Idaletta Hilde (for Spain)

Kristn   every 2 yrs. → Germany
Nacht Synagog   burning
firemen standing / not do anything